Austerity and Law in Europe

T0375001

Edited by

Marija Bartl and Markos Karavias

WILEY Blackwell

This edition first published 2017
Editorial organization © 2017 Cardiff University Law School
Chapters © 2017 by the chapter author

Blackwell Publishing was acquired by John Wiley & Sons in February 2007. Blackwell's publishing programme has been merged with Wiley's global Scientific, Technical, and Medical business to form Wiley-Blackwell.

Editorial Offices
350 Main Street, Malden, MA 02148-5020, USA
9600 Garsington Road, Oxford OX4 2DQ, UK

For details of our global editorial offices, for customer services, and for information about how to apply for permission to reuse the copyright material in this book please see our website at www.wiley.com/wiley-blackwell

Registered Office
John Wiley & Sons Ltd, The Atrium, Southern Gate, Chichester, West Sussex PO19 8SQ.

The right of Marija Bartl and Markos Karavias to be identified as the author of the Editorial Material in this work has been asserted in accordance with the Copyright, Designs and Patents Act 1988.

Designations used by companies to distinguish their products are often claimed as trademarks. All brand names and product names used in this book are trade names, service marks, trademarks or registered trademarks of their respective owners. The publisher is not associated with any product or vendor mentioned in this book. This publication is designed to provide accurate and authoritative information in regard to the subject matter covered. It is sold on the understanding that the publisher is not engaged in rendering professional services. If professional advice or other expert assistance is required, the services of a competent professional should be sought.

Library of Congress Cataloging-in-Publication Data
Library of Congress Cataloging-in-Publication data is available for this book

A catalogue record for this title is available from the British Library.

ISBN: 978-1-119-38001-6

Set in the United Kingdom by Godiva Publishing Services Ltd
Printed in Singapore by C.O.S. Printers Pte Ltd

Contents

Contents

JOURNAL OF LAW AND SOCIETY
VOLUME 44, NUMBER 1, MARCH 2017
ISSN: 0263-323X, pp. 1–9

Austerity and Law in Europe: An Introduction

Marija Bartl* and Markos Karavias*

I.

It is close to a decade since the peak of the global financial crisis in 2008, which heralded a recession unlike anything the world had witnessed since the Great Depression of the 1930s. The impact of the 2008 crisis is still being felt across the world, as even today a number of states, predominantly in Europe, are struggling to recover. Nonetheless, the policy responses to these two seismic events could not have been more markedly different. Whereas the post-Depression era ushered in Keynesian thinking and 'New Deal' approaches, the European response to the 2008 crisis has been dominated by the politics of austerity.

Austerity has been defined as:

> a form of voluntary deflation in which the economy adjusts through the reduction of wages, prices and public spending to restore competitiveness, which is (supposedly) best achieved by cutting the state's budget, debts, and deficits.[1]

Austerity is a commonsensical cure of, and minimizes the risk of, contagion associated with a 'sovereign debt crisis'. States cannot make their way out of public debt by piling up more debt. Thus, they need to tighten their belts and balance sheets, in order to send signals to private investors which boost the latter's confidence in the state's commitment to pursue economic development. The abandonment of fiscal stimulus strategies and the move towards 'fiscal consolidation' was aptly summarized by Jean-Claude Trichet who, in his capacity as the President of the European Central Bank, opined in 2010:

* University of Amsterdam, Oudemanhuispoort 4–6, 1012 CN, Amsterdam, The Netherlands
M.Bartl@uva.nl   M.Karavias@uva.nl

1 M. Blyth, *Austerity: The History of a Dangerous Idea* (2013) 2.

1

Sound public finances are a decisive component of economic stability and sustainable global growth. With hindsight, we see how unfortunate was the oversimplified message of fiscal stimulus given to all industrial economies under the motto: 'stimulate', 'activate', 'spend'![2]

The turn towards austerity as the preferred policy response first and foremost consolidated the view that the crisis in Europe has, if anything, been a 'public' or 'sovereign debt' crisis associated with the profligacy of states that needed to be reined in. According to this narrative, certain states in Europe had bridged the widening gap between public expenditure and public revenue through sovereign borrowing, resulting in an explosion of public debt. Public debt was seen as crippling any efforts to end the recession cycle and spur growth. Indeed, a well-publicized but also controversial academic paper suggested that external debt in excess of 90 per cent of GDP resulted in growth being 'roughly cut in half'.[3] If debt was the obstacle to growth, then the solution was obvious: reduce spending, cut down on the debt, and growth will follow.

As so happens, common-sense, natural remedies do not always work. The case of Greece is emblematic as far as the nefarious consequences of austerity go. Greece, the poster-state of the 'sovereign debt crisis', has had to implement a series of painful austerity measures as a prerequisite for a series of EU/International Monetary Fund (IMF)-sponsored bail-outs. Such austerity measures include significant cuts in wages and pensions, tax increases, the privatization of public services, a lowering in the number of civil servants, and the deregulation of the labour market. The catastrophic results of this austerity package have all too often been documented.[4] The size of the Greek economy has shrunk by a quarter, whilst unemployment in 2015 spiked at around 25 per cent.[5] What is more, the debt-to-GDP ratio has continued to rise as GDP has collapsed: in sum, Greece's debt load is getting more marked by the year, thus making it harder for any government to actually pay off its debts. It should come as no surprise, then, that in 2013 the IMF, in an evaluation report on the measures taken vis-à-vis Greece, admitted that there were 'notable failures':

> Market confidence was not restored, the banking system lost 30 per cent of its deposits, and the economy encountered a much-deeper-than-expected

---

2 J.-C. Trichet, 'Stimulate no more – it is now time for all to tighten' *Financial Times*, 22 July 2010, at <https://www.ft.com/content/1b3ae97e-95c6-11df-b5ad-00144feab49a>.

3 C. Reinhart and K. Rogoff, 'Growth in a Time of Debt' (2010) 100 *Am. Economic Rev.* 573–8.

4 On the impact of austerity measures on human rights in Greece, see FIDH/HLDR, *Downgrading rights: the cost of austerity in Greece* (2014), at <https://www.fidh.org/IMG/pdf/downgrading_rights_the_cost_of_austerity_in_greece.pdf>.

5 On the latest unemployment rates, see EU Commission, *European Economic Forecast Autumn 2016: Greece*, at <http://ec.europa.eu/economy_finance/eu/forecasts/2016_autumn/el_en.pdf>.

2

recession with exceptionally high unemployment. Public debt remained too high and eventually had to be restructured, with collateral damage for bank balance sheets that were also weakened by the recession.[6]

There are several reasons why austerity does not work. One of them has been identified by Blyth as the 'fallacy of composition' problem.[7] Put simply, we cannot all be austere at once. It would make sense for a state to try to reduce its debts, yet if all its trading partners are doing exactly the same at exactly the same time, then austerity is self-defeating. In the case of Eurozone members embracing – willingly or unwillingly – an austerity agenda, the problem is further exacerbated by participation in a single monetary union, where the option of currency devaluation is lacking. Not only is austerity not effective, it also raises issues of distributive justice. It has been documented that, in the case of Greece, the effects of austerity were not distributed evenly, with those at the lower end of the economic scale being hit comparatively harder by the measures than those at the upper end.[8]

The downsides of austerity are not only economic and social in nature, even though these are the more pronounced and tragic from the perspective of poverty-stricken individuals plunged into precarity. For once, the portrayal of austerity as the 'logical' response to the 'sovereign debt crisis' brought about by the profligacy of states has obscured the burden placed on states by the need to bail out and refinance the global banking system. Indeed, the astronomical sums of money pumped into the banking sector by states resulted in these states' public debt ballooning. Austerity, nonetheless, is mainly aimed at states, not at banks. And it serves to perpetuate the myth of the 'profligate state', whilst saying little, if anything at all, about banking practices. Furthermore, austerity serves as an ideological device in the core-periphery debates within Europe. Austerity measures are reserved for serial offenders at the periphery, those branded as the PIIGS.[9] This is nothing but a smokescreen though. It is hard not to admit that one state's deficits are the mirror-image of another state's surpluses. Jabko noted in this vein that:

> Germany's export surplus, in conjunction with German banks' lax lending and investment practices could have easily been held responsible for the piling of public and private debts in peripheral countries . . . [German politicians'] advocacy of austerity served to deflect attention from Germany's share of responsibility in the debt crisis.[10]

6 IMF, *Greece: Ex Post Evaluation of Exceptional Access under the 2010 Stand-By Arrangement* (2013), at <http://www.imf.org/external/pubs/ft/scr/2013/cr13156.pdf>.
7 Blyth, op. cit., n. 1, pp. 8–9.
8 See D. Vaughan-Whitehead, *Work Inequalities in the Crisis: Evidence from Europe* (2012).
9 The five Eurozone nations considered weaker economically following the financial crisis, namely, Portugal, Italy, Ireland, Greece, and Spain.
10 N. Jabko, 'The Political Appeal of Austerity' (2013) 11 *Comparative European Politics* 705, at 708.

Finally, and more significantly, it is hard to avoid the moral, almost theological, overtones of the concept. Austerity is a form of chastisement, of atonement for past sins, the way to financial salvation. Tellingly, the then French Minister of Finance Moscovici spoke in 2013 of the 'dogma of austerity'.[11]

Austerity politics have not gone uncontested. On the contrary, anti-austerity pledges have found their way into national political parties' programmes, manifestos, and declarations. National elections have proven a fruitful political terrain, most notably in the cases of Greece, Spain, and Portugal where left-wing parties have fought for power (and in the case of Greece, succeeded) on the basis of an anti-austerity political agenda. What is more, a 'turn to law' has manifested itself, in the sense that trade unions and civil society groups have commenced efforts to make use of available legal avenues – most notably in the human rights field – in order to challenge austerity measures.[12] '[T]he legal discourse of social rights has been put to work to fill the normative void that lies at the heart of the political discourse of a "social Europe".'[13]

The charge against austerity has ultimately not been enough to overturn the agenda, but it has made significant dents in its façade. As of late, austerity discourses have started receding into the background of European politics, overshadowed by the increase in refugee flows, the Brexit referendum vote, and the TTIP/CETA negotiations. The desensationalization of austerity debates should serve as food for thought. This may suggest that the concept has managed to enter the language of European law and politics, and become accepted as an orthodox policy fiat.

It is then timely, and crucial, to refocus on the concept, its historical pedigree, its contemporary manifestations, its consequences. The ambition behind this volume is to unpack the concept of austerity and its relationship with law in the context of the European Union, and beyond. This relationship has been empirically assessed in a piecemeal fashion, in the sense that it has been tackled with respect to constitutional or human rights law. Still, it is submitted that we need a holistic approach to the intricate synergies between law and austerity. What is more, there is a normative claim undergirding the contributions, namely, that it is imperative to unpack the discourses developed in the context of these synergies.

The starting point behind the analyses is that the relationship between law and austerity is not unidirectional or unambiguous. On the contrary, it is

---

11 See J. Hertling, 'France Ends [*sic*] Austerity Over as Germany Shows Flexibility' *Bloomberg*, 6 May 2013, at <http://www.bloomberg.com/news/articles/2013-05-05/france-declares-austerity-over-after-germany-offers-wiggle-room>.

12 For a comprehensive analysis, see M. Salomon, 'Of Austerity, Human Rights and International Institutions' (2015) 21 *European Law J.* 521.

13 C. O'Cinnaide, 'Austerity and the Faded Dream of a "Social Europe"' in *Economic and Social Rights After the Global Financial Crisis*, ed. A. Nolan (2014) 169, at 189.

4

dynamic, reciprocal, and – at times – fraught with complexity. This collection of articles aims at shedding light on the dual role played by the law in Europe, *both as a sword*, in the sense of a tool enabling austerity, and *as a shield*, as a means of battling against austerity. By bringing together a range of contributions, from a wide array of epistemological backgrounds, the present work seeks to highlight the mutations sustained by EU law in order to accommodate austerity politics. Finally, the work aims to highlight alternative strategies to fight against the encroachment of austerity politics into the legal field, and towards reclaiming political and social spaces.

II.

The collection opens with a novel take on the historical pedigree of austerity by **Clara Mattei**. Mattei revisits the two International Financial Conferences convened by the League of Nations in Brussels and Genoa in 1920 and 1922 respectively. These two Conferences, comprising predominantly economics experts, aimed at reconstructing the capitalist economy, which had been shattered by the First World War, and which was increasingly coming under the threat of the spread of socialist ideas across Europe. Essentially, the Conferences sought to reconsolidate social and economic order. Mattei scrutinizes the documents produced by the Conferences as precursors to modern conceptualizations of austerity, understood as a full blown *rationality,* which is intrinsically theory and practice, policy and pedagogy. Such a conception of austerity was implemented, following the Conferences, in fascist Italy, which serves as an intriguing case study. Whilst plagued with social upheavals, the fascist regime in Italy pressed on with a far-reaching set of austerity measures, including budget cuts, regressive taxation, public layoffs, and privatization. Reading through the description of the austerity programme implemented in Italy in the 1920s, it is hard not to draw parallels with the measures implemented in Europe today. Mattei reaches beyond austerity as an economic programme and delves into its interlocking with technocracy. Indeed, the programme, mirroring the rationality of the economic and political elite of the time, was designed and implemented by a number of prominent Italian academics-turned-politicians. It was a programme with overt moral undertones, ultimately aimed at *disciplining* and *taming* men. So much can be gleaned from Mussolini's statement with respect to the austerity measures implemented, when he suggested that they can be epitomized as follows: 'thrift, labour, discipline'. Frugality, then, is not simply the end result of austerity measures, but also a moral duty on citizens who, for the benefit of the nation, accept that they must sacrifice.

The key points on technocracy and the role of law, whether international or domestic, in the implementation of austerity programmes are picked up by the next three contributions, which focus on European law, and the manner in which it has been transformed to accommodate austerity measures. A

5

focus on Europe is only natural considering that the continent emerged as a key laboratory for the furtherance of austerity politics post-2010. **Clemens Kaupa** opens this trilogy by unpacking the various claims made regarding the relationship between EU law and austerity. According to Kaupa, one needs to distinguish between two strands of argumentataion. On the one hand, on a normative level, it has been argued that the imposition of austerity measures constitutes a *legal obligation* established by the European Treaties. On the other hand, on a causal level, it has been suggested that the institutional structures of the European Union *contribute* to the imposition of austerity measures. Kaupa goes on to debunk both strands. The normative strand, which speaks to existing legal obligations upon states to enact austerity measures, does not withstand scrutiny, considering the ambiguous or indeterminate nature of the relevant provisions in the European Treaties, such as Article 125 of the Treaty on the Functioning of the European Union (TFEU). Equally, the causal strand raises a host of epistemological problems, associated predominantly with the problematic translation and transposition of economic concepts into the legal vernacular. At the end of the day, the work of Kaupa goes to show that portraying the imposition of austerity measures as legally necessary and politically coherent essentially obscures the fact that the turn to austerity signifies a *strategic, political choice* within the framework of a pluralist European economic constitution and, as such, a choice that can be contested.

Following this trail of argumentation, **Agustín Menéndez** traces the impact made upon European law by the turn to austerity as a means of addressing the downsides of the financial, as well as fiscal crisis. In other words, Menéndez exposes the paradoxical and pernicious policy choices made in Europe from the perspective of legal theory. Arguably, the reaction to the financial and fiscal crisis has resulted in the erosion of the rule of law in Europe. The issue, then, is not solely one of constitutional ordering, but a far deeper, ontological one: what is the function of the law per se and how is it insulated from politics? Menéndez couples the review of the governance of the financial crisis (through 'non-conventional' economic measures and public aid programmes to financial institutions) and the fiscal crisis (through the transformation of private debt into public debt and the absorption of such debt by the periphery exchequers) with insights into the structural limits of the European constitutional order. The latter has been perforated by ad hoc decisions and the adoption of constitutional conventions which, in turn, have been locked in through the adoption of 'quasi-constitutional' Treaties, such as the Fiscal Compact, and the case law of the Court of Justice, most notably in *Pringle*.[14] Perhaps the most significant mutation identified by Menéndez is the move from the *social and democratic Rechsstaat* to the *consolidating state*. Such a move is highlighted by the elevation of the objectives of public

---

14 C-370/12, *Pringle*, ECLI:EU:C:2012:756, s. 135.

6

action, such as financial stability, full faith and credit of public debt, and economic growth to *free-standing ends* and *meta-principles of European law*. Economic growth no longer serves the realization of substantive policies. On the contrary, the provision of substantive policies has to fit the Procrustean bed of economic growth. The role of the law in all of this, always depicted in its immaculate 'pure legal' form, remains painfully under-theorized. But the autonomy of European law from politics is a sleight of hand. Menéndez closes his contribution exposing the mutation of European law into a cloak of arbitrariness disguised as technocratic governance. The stories narrated by Mattei and Menéndez are spaced almost a century apart, yet the insistence on technocracy as a means of legitimizing and ultimately realizing austerity politics undergirds both narratives.

The final contribution in the trilogy by **Harm Schepel** shines a light on the legal construction of 'market discipline' and the distortions it produces in European law as a result of bending it to fit the contours of an austerity agenda. Schepel takes his cue from the formulation of the *Pringle* judgment on the purpose of the 'no bail-out' clause, which – according to the Court – is to ensure that member states 'remain subject to the logic of the market when they enter into debt, since that ought to prompt them to maintain market discipline'. The election of the 'logic of the market' as the standard of legality vis-à-vis financial assistance to member states in debt, and as a justification for the imposition of austerity, is in itself controversial as it presupposes the existence, and – what is more – the prudence of such logic. The reading of *Pringle* in Schepel's contribution highlights the pitfalls of the law being pegged to the 'logic of the market'. In order for such logic to work, 'it is vital that creditors live in fear of losing money, and that debtors live in fear of full-blown disaster'. In other words, states within the Eurozone will only work towards achieving financial stability if a credible threat exists, namely, that of financial instability. Taking this train of thought to its logical conclusion, Schepel notes that there is an obligation on the ESM to be 'as ineffective as possible, and to inflict as much pain and misery on the populations of debtor states as feasible'. The misery of a state becomes an incentive to the rest to keep within the tight fiscal rules of the Eurozone, if they are to escape the harrowing effects of austerity.

The contributions by Kaupa, Menéndez, and Schepel raise a host of fundamental issues regarding the European project in the last decade. First and foremost, they highlight the willingness on the part of European institutions to embrace the concept of austerity. Austerity emerges as a prudent policy response to the crisis, a response for which no alternative exists. Austerity has gradually assumed a quasi-constitutional status mutating the substance and structure of the European constitutional order. Seen from the angle of political economy, these contributions lay to rest any pretence of solidarity among EU member states, whilst underscoring the tensions between creditor and debtor nations, core and periphery, prudence and profligacy.

7

Yet, austerity is not an exclusively European phenomenon. Long before the world's attention shifted to the strife of the Greek people, Argentina had been there first, as it were. **Pablo López and Cecilia Nahón**'s contribution thus serves as an essential counterpoint to the European experience. The decade up until Argentina's 2001 sovereign default was a period of austerity. With the hope of regaining access to international capital markets, the government enacted a set of measures, including capital deregulation, market liberalization, and the privatization of public utilities and the pension system. The debt restructuring and the pegging of the Argentine peso to the US dollar only set the stage for a new phase of over-indebtedness that peaked in 2001. Following the Argentinian default on its sovereign debt, the country sought to restructure its debt, charting a new path not involving the IMF or the World Bank, thus avoiding any conditionality on economic policy. One of the key aspects of this restructuring was that it had to be deep enough to provide for sustainable economic growth with social inclusion. In sum, Argentina had to grow as a precondition of honouring its debt. As documented by López and Nahón, restructured bondholders benefited from Argentina's high growth rates until 2011, as GDP every year surpassed the threshold value. Such growth was due to the policies enacted by Argentina to promote production and reactivate the domestic market. But the effort made by the state was essentially sabotaged by a segment of creditors, most prominently hold-out 'vulture funds' that initiated litigation against Argentina before United States courts. López and Nahón trace the origins, conclusion, and consequences of this litigation, which arguably plunged the country into a renewed austerity cycle. The Argentinian case testifies to an effort to think outside the box in terms of debt restructuring aimed at debt sustainability. Yet, when similar ideas were floated in Europe, especially by the Greek SYRIZA government, they did not find fertile ground.

The contributions restate and vindicate one key premise: austerity politics is unsustainable economically and socially. Nonetheless, government officials and policy makers have time and time again passed the poisoned chalice from one indebted state to the next. Lawyers have, at best, sought to mount challenges against austerity before domestic and international courts and tribunals with limited chances of success and, at worst, played second fiddle to market rationalities. Still, austerity is neither divinely ordained nor inevitable. It is therefore imperative to devise strategies in order to reclaim the political space occupied by austerians. This collection of essays closes with two contributions, which aspire to re-engineer the relationship between austerity and the law, opening up avenues of contestation.

Emilios Christodoulidis turns to *social constitutionalism*, a vital approach considering that the field of social rights protection has borne the brunt of austerity measures. As he notes, 'the spectre of sovereign debt has come to displace social constitutionalism as such', in the sense that social rights claims against a state beholden to the market through sovereign debt have lost any sting. Social rights are reconfigured as debts. The question

8

then emerges as to whether social rights in this truncated, emaciated guise can serve as a means of contestation. To Christodoulidis, such an instrumental use of social rights necessitates laying to rest the theories of those rights' accommodation within advanced capitalist democracies. Indeed, over the last decades, many theories have been advanced which portray political and social rights as standing on a continuum. Such a take on social rights makes paper tigers of them, watering down their normativity to the point of apology. Christodoulidis proposes a novel strategy of contesting austerity by relying on social rights institutionalized on the basis of *solidarity*. There is thus a contradiction between social constitutionalism and capitalist democracy, and Christodoulidis invites us to act on such contradiction, realizing the antinomic significance of social rights.

This collection closes with a contribution by **Marija Bartl**, which focuses squarely on the contestation of knowledge as a strategy. Indeed, a key aspect in the relationship between austerity and the law has been the presentation of austerity as necessity. To Bartl, Europe's democratic deficit is not solely a problem for its democratic legitimacy but also for the epistemic validity of the knowledge through which it governs. The *input* and *output* perspectives merge in this case. Dissociated from democratic institutions, it is argued, the EU governing knowledge is prone to bias on the level of articulating both goals and means. Bartl selects three case studies, in order to exhibit the modalities of knowledge production. Tellingly, these studies are austerity, the TTIP/CETA negotiations, and the BREXIT vote. All three centre on the problem of the disembeddedness of European institutions, which has admittedly justified their lack of legitimacy in the eyes of the European polity. At the same time, these three studies provide us with insights as to the options available (or not) to the people of Europe, spanning from *exit* to *voice*. Indeed, the BREXIT referendum might be seen as a manifestation of *exit*, whilst the protests against the TTIP/CETA as the echo of *voice*. Beyond these two options, austerity emerges as a field in which neither *exit* nor *voice* are possible, reaffirming the need to contest the very basic knowledge on which the austerity edifice rests.

JOURNAL OF LAW AND SOCIETY
VOLUME 44, NUMBER 1, MARCH 2017
ISSN: 0263-323X, pp. 10–31

The Guardians of Capitalism: International Consensus and the Technocratic Implementation of Austerity

Clara E. Mattei*

Current debates on austerity often forget that these policies are almost a hundred years old. This article explores how the combination of austerity and technocracy acted as a powerful tool to secure the compliance of European countries with socio-economic stabilization after the First World War. Austerity emerged as an economic, moral, and technocratic message as economic experts sought to educate restless post-war civil society. The article analyses primary austerity documents from the international economic conferences of Brussels (1920) and Genoa (1922). In addition, I use a case study of Italy (1922–1925) to show how austerity succeeded under the first years of Fascism, when the government authorized prominent economics professors to implement the international financial codes devised at Brussels and Genoa. I also consider the scientific writings of De Stefani, Ricci, and Pantaleoni in order to examine the theoretical roots of the technocratic nature of austerity.

INTRODUCTION

After the First World War, social and economic turmoil brought an unprecedented challenge to capitalism that was crushed by a strong and conservative commitment to uphold the socio-economic status quo.[1] I demonstrate that the combination of economic technocracy and austerity acted as a powerful tool for securing the plausibility of, and especially compliance with, post-war stabilization. This twofold tool evolved at the international economic conferences of Brussels (1920) and Genoa (1922), the first worldwide inter-

* Economics Department, New School for Social Research, 6 E 16th St, New York, NY 10003, United States of America
matteic@newschool.edu

1 C. Maier, *Recasting Bourgeois Europe* (1975); A. Tooze, *The Deluge: The Great War and the Remaking of Global Order 1916–1931* (2014).

10

national financial conferences in history. These conferences are largely overlooked by scholarship, yet they were of major ideological significance. Genoa and Brussels formally articulated austerity as a technocratic solution in a major capitalist crisis. For a contemporary reader, the striking similarity with the present remedies for the European debt crisis immediately emerges. I will show how the 'financial code' drafted at Brussels and Genoa was *successfully* implemented: Italy, a country noted for its post-war social upheavals and progressive claims, became one of the best 'students' of austerity, thanks to the direct intervention of economic experts in Mussolini's cabinet.

Tooze and Maier identify the economic deflationary wave of the 1920s as the main driver for the restoration of order on the continent, both domestically and internationally. I supplement their masterful analysis with a thorough discussion of the austerity rationale and the role of economic experts as novel and decisive legitimizing tools. In this article, 'austerity' does not merely refer to the economic policy of budget cuts and price deflation[2] but, rather, to a full-blown *rationality*,[3] which is intrinsically theory and practice, policy and pedagogy. Austerity was an economic, moral, and technocratic message with which the economic experts sought to educate and civilize a restless post-war civil society. I will show that Fascist Italy achieved this objective in a particularly efficient way; in a country of extraordinary upheavals, austerity measures were rigorously applied. Social

---

2 Austerity as an economic policy comes in both fiscal and monetary forms. Most scholars consider austerity's fiscal form, which may be defined as deliberate government budget cuts and deficit curtailment for the purpose of increasing investors' confidence in the government's ability to manage its finances (S.J. Konzelmann, *The Economics of Austerity* (2014) xiv). The purpose implies that austerity is usually a response to actual or anticipated economic crisis. Austerity measures include tax increases (mostly regressive taxation), privatizations, and public payroll cuts. Austerity's monetary form is considered by fewer scholars but goes hand in hand with the fiscal form. Mark Blyth defines it as a 'form of voluntary deflation': M. Blyth, *Austerity: The History of a Dangerous Idea* (2013) 2. More precisely, monetary austerity may be defined as deliberate monetary contraction by the central bank for the purpose of deflating prices in general or increasing interest rates, thereby increasing confidence in the value of money or the central bank's ability to maintain a fixed exchange rate. The fiscal and monetary forms of austerity are not only similar in aim, but are interconnected: by constraining the government's ability to finance its spending with money creation, monetary austerity tends to impel fiscal austerity. Yet it may be possible to practice one form but not the other. After the First World War, both forms were put into practice in most European countries and in the United States. After the 2008 crisis, fiscal austerity predominated in Europe. Austerity becomes a valid response to capitalist crisis once one separates what is good for profit from what is good for people. Privatizing state activities, increasing unemployment, and even contracting the economy to weaken labour and to cause smaller companies to fail – all of this can serve the interests of bigger companies and international capital. What is called 'market friendly' is actually 'profit friendly'. In any case, neither need be 'people friendly'.

3 The term austerity 'rationality', rather than rationale, has been chosen to stress the relationship between austerity policies and standard economic rationality, an all-encompassing view that weds practical policies and economic theory.

11

order, accompanied by a balanced budget, were achieved in just a couple of years of Mussolini's regime. While Italian trains were famously running on time, the needs of civil society were disregarded in the name of financial orthodoxy.[4]

The first section of this article reconstructs the explosive socio-economic context that the conferences were called to normalize. The second illustrates the technocratic features of the international conferences, that are fully appreciated through an analysis of the austere content of their resolution (third section). The last sections tackle the case study of Fascist Italy. I focus on the thought of the *engagé* Italian professors, in particular on their mission as economists, in order to explain the foundations of the technocratic nature of austerity.

THE STRUGGLES OF CAPITALISM AND THE TECHNOCRATIC INTERNATIONAL CONFERENCES

In the aftermath of the First World War capitalism was under attack. The pre-war social and economic order was shattered. Contemporaries indeed felt it:

> A sense of a world coming apart, fantasies of conspiratorial communist influence, a pressing state of economic crisis, a wave of strikes and industrial conflict, fuelling drastic rhetorics of class conflict and violence on both sides. The nineteenth century had been haunted by revolution. Now was the moment, it seemed, that revolution had arrived.[5]

In the same tone, Maier comments that: 'Late 1918 and early 1919 brought a wave of apocalyptic militancy punctuated by general strikes. Attackers and defenders alike shared moments of belief that the bourgeois order was near collapse.'[6] The words of the famous liberal economist Luigi Einaudi in the *Corriere della Sera*[7] epitomize the feelings of the upper classes of the time:

> The victory of socialism seemed too close and too easy. It was the time in which one would speak of the Bourgeoisie as a corrupt social class; in which it seemed that a shoulder shove would suffice to knock the so-called capitalism regime to the ground. The communistic millennium seemed near; the reign of equality close to ensuing.[8]

The extraordinary escalation of class conflict was felt everywhere. Workers demanded greater economic democracy. The intensification of the struggle was marked by political demands for democratic rights and freedoms, and

---

4 On the contemporary antagonistic relation between austerity and social rights, see Christodoulidis in this volume.
5 Tooze, op. cit., n. 1, p. 354.
6 Maier, op. cit., n. 1, p. 136.
7 Milan's major daily, reflecting the editor Luigi Albertini's elitist liberalism until his removal in 1925.
8 In L. Einaudi, *Cronache Economiche e Politiche di un Trentennio, Vol. 7* (1966) 905.

12

socio-economic appeals in the sphere of wages, length of the working day, working conditions, social insurance, and so on.[9] In France, strikes reached an all-time high in 1919–1920. The Paris engineering strike of June 1919 was followed by the February railway strike and culminated in a great general strike on 25 May 1920. In Italy the Biennio Rosso was fierce. Around four thousand strikes occurred with the participation of almost four million workers; industry occupations in the North were widespread.[10] From 1919 to 1920, a wave of agricultural strikes swept through not only the Po Valley, but also the previously quieter regions of Veneto, Umbria, and Tuscany. By 1920, the socialist-affiliated 'red-leagues' of Federterra (National Federation of Agrarian Workers) counted almost one million workers. Between 1919 and 1921 more working days were lost in Great Britain than in revolutionary Germany and Italy. Especially notable, the battle of George Square in Glasgow (1 January 1919) was fought in the name of shorter working hours and reduced unemployment. It was halted with the intervention of tanks sent by the British government. Nonetheless, workers were granted the right to a seven-hour working day.

This explosion of labour struggles and protests was primarily due to the growth in the organization and strength of the working class. From 1916 onward, union membership increased steeply in the United Kingdom, Germany, France, and Italy.[11] The urgent necessity to raise war production induced governments to recognize unions and allow concessions in their favour. The post-war labour market was characterized by diminished labour flexibility since the processes of collective bargaining increased. What is more, the state widely expanded its economic domain. It gained an active role as producer and regulator,[12] but also became a social resource: during the war and in the post-war years, there were consistent social reforms as compensation for the enormous war sacrifice of soldiers and civilians.[13] It

---

9   For studies of conflict and strikes, in Europe, see: L. Hamison and G. Sapelli, *Strikes, Social Conflict and the First World War: An International Perspective* (1992); C. Wrigley (ed.), *Challenges of Labour: Central and Western Europe, 1917–1920* (1993); C. Bertrand (ed.), *Revolutionary Situations in Europe 1917–1922* (1977). Concerning Italy, see A. Lyttelton, *The Seizure of Power: Fascism in Italy, 1919–1929* (1973); A. Tasca, *Nascita e Avvento del Fascismo* (1965); R. Vivarelli, *Storia delle Origini del Fascismo* (1991). For England, see J.E. Cronin, 'Strikes and power in Britain, 1870–1920' (1987) xxxii *International Rev. of Social History* 164.

10 The Communist Party was founded in 1921, seceding from the Italian Socialist Party (PSI). With almost 43,000 members, the Communists obtained 4.6 per cent of the votes at the 1921 national elections, while the PSI got 24 per cent of the votes. Both parties were outlawed by the Fascist regime in 1926.

11 In the British election on 14 December 1918, the Trade Unions were strong enough to pay for half of Labour's candidates. See M. Cowling, *The Impact of Labour 1920–1924: The Beginning of Modern British Politics* (1971).

12 See texts listed in n. 9, above.

13 In France, Clemenceau granted the eight-hour work day in April 1919. In Italy, it was obtained in the same year. In Germany, the eight-hour work day had already been

was expansive fiscal policies that fulfilled the new demands for social security and public benefits advanced by the trade unions, with post-war economic difficulties giving rise to greater social claims. In particular, inflation mounted during the war but reached a legendary high in 1919–1920. Rising prices threatened real wages, hence even more workers were driven into the ranks of the trade unions.[14]

Inflation proved that the capitalist crisis was not merely an exogenous political shock, but had deep economic motivations. Demand structurally exceeded supply, and one of the persistent causes of inflation was certainly the dire straits of public finances, made worse by the ending of inter-allied war credit and financial cooperation.[15] Enormous amounts of savings and capital were lost; there was also a shift in income distribution.[16] The words of John Maynard Keynes demonstrate that contemporaries were well aware of the structural revolutionary effects of hyperinflation: 'a continuance of inflationism and high prices will not only depress the exchanges but by their effect on prices will strike at the whole basis of contract, of security, and of the capitalist system generally.'[17] The fragility of the capitalist system was once again epitomized by the unprecedented fluctuation in the business cycle: the boom of 1919–1920 was followed by the slump that began in the spring of 1920.

It was in this explosive socio-economic context that the Council of the League of Nations called for the economic conference of Brussels (24 September–4 October 1920). It was the world's first 'International Financial Conference'.[18] Less than two years later, at Cannes, the Supreme Council of the Allies announced the Genoa economic financial conference (10 April–19 May 1922). Both winning and losing countries participated.[19] In Brussels, thirty-nine nations, comprising three-quarters of the world's population, were represented. In Genoa, thirty-four nations participated. The sense of

---

achieved in 1918. In Italy, a legislative decree of October 1919 introduced official mandatory insurance against unemployment. In April 1919, insurance for disability and old age became mandatory and covered all private sector workers, which accounted for more than 10 million people.

14 Tooze, op. cit., n. 1, p. 356. In Italy, during 1919 the membership of the CGIL rose from 350,000 to 800,000 adherents. Federterra, by 1919, had almost doubled its wartime complement to reach 457,000 militant members and doubled it again to almost 900,000 (Maier, op. cit., n. 1, pp. 47–53).

15 On the inter-allied debt problem, see H.G. Moulton and L. Pavlovsky, *War Debt and World Prosperity* (1971).

16 Maier, op. cit., n. 1, pp. 43–4.

17 Tooze, op. cit., n. 1, p. 356.

18 P. Clavin, *Securing the World Economy: The Reinvention of the League of Nations, 1920–1946* (2013) 17.

19 For a good reconstruction of the conferences, see C. Fink, *The Genoa Conference: European Diplomacy, 1921–1922* (1984); D.E. Traynor, *International Monetary and Financial Conferences in the Interwar Period* (1949); J.S. Mills, *The Genoa Conference* (1948).

urgency in dealing with the social-economic post-war problems is clear from the language used by the Council of the League of Nations to announce the conferences. It spoke not of economic problems, but of a financial crisis.

The aim of the conferences was to formulate a programme for international economic stabilization and normalcy. The capitalist economy had to be reconstructed on solid foundations; the compliance of each single country was crucial. The urge to reconsolidate the social and economic order transcended immediate political affiliation for both governing conservatives and progressive liberals. In fact, with the war, politics had lost prestige and was willingly disqualified. A new source of legitimacy was sought in the *super partes* truth of economic science and of the experts who spoke that language of truth. It was the reuniting of the European establishment under the flag of technocracy

The few economic historians who have studied the conferences speak of a failure: economic and monetary international cooperation was not achieved.[20] Nonetheless, if one reads the testimonies of several contemporary economists, the perspective changes: a real enthusiasm for the high scientific level of the conferences is expressed. The common view was that the success of the conference lay in sanctioning the vital role of technocracy.[21]

The technical imprint of the conferences is visible in three different aspects. First, the social composition of the national delegations was officially without political affiliation. Of the delegates of each country, 'very few of the representatives were either politicians or diplomats, but fewer still were representatives of Labour.'[22] The majority were business and financial experts. As Davis wrote, 'The representatives were in the main leading bankers and treasury officials, "who attended as experts and not as spokesmen of [existing] official policy".'[23] Most of the same experts also sat at Genoa.

Secondly, technical documentation was unprecedentedly abundant. The secretariat of the League of Nations requested that states and their banks submit information on currency, public finance, international trade, retail prices, and coal production. About Brussels, Siepmann said: 'No conference was ever so well provided with documents as this one.'[24] Preparing for the event, the secretariat of the economic and financial section of the League of Nations compiled fifteen documents. The *Times* described them as being four inches thick. As Davis, the British delegate said: 'The volumes of

20 B. Eichengreen, *Golden Fetters: The Gold Standard and the Great Depression, 1919–1939* (1992) 153–62; C. Fink, A. Frohn, and J. Heidenking (eds.), *Genoa, Rapallo, and European Reconstruction in 1922* (1991) 1–9.
21 J.S. Davis, 'World currency and banking: the first Brussels financial conference' (1920) 2(12) *Rev. of Economics and Statistics* 349, at 349.
22 H.A. Siepmann, 'The International financial conference at Brussels' (1920) 30 *Economic J.* 437, at 443.
23 Davis, op. cit, n. 21, p. 349.
24 Siepmann, op. cit., n. 22, p. 441.

statistics are not merely collections of crude figures. On the contrary, the data are selected, worked up, and carefully presented as a basis for interpretation.'[25] In preparation for Brussels, a preliminary conference was held on the standardization of national statistics for international use.

Significantly, it was economics professors who drafted the most influential body of memoranda. It was a novelty to consistently deploy academic expertise. Professor Maffeo Pantaleoni (Italy), Professor Charles Gide (France), Professor Gijsbert Weijer Jan Bruins (Holland), Professor Arthur Cécile Pigou (England), and Professor Gustav Cassel (Sweden) submitted papers to instruct conference participants. Subsequently, upon request, the five economists met and prepared a joint statement that set out the agenda for the conference.[26]

The Genoa conference displayed the same technical characteristics, and was similarly guided by reports drafted by economic scholars, financiers, businessmen and bankers Basil Blackett, Joseph Luis Avenol, Robert Brand, Gustav Cassel, Luis Dubois, Rudolf Havenstein, Sir Henry Strakosch, and Gerard Vissering, among others.[27]

The theoretical and practical weight of the experts' wisdom is unmistakable if one compares their statements with the official resolutions of the conference. Their advice was fully represented in the resolutions. A common rationality was expressed and agreed upon: austerity. As will be explained below, austerity is inherently technocratic, since it encompasses both theory and practice. Thus, economic orthodoxy calls for the *technical*, *political*, and *moral* compliance of each national government. Both the Brussels and Genoa resolutions, and their concrete implementation under Mussolini show that the three dimensions were closely intertwined. The nature of austerity itself calls for its enforcement. The next section will expand upon this crucial point.

AUSTERITY AND THE FINANCIAL CONFERENCES

At Brussels and Genoa, delegates and experts discussed many issues, and exposed contrasts between the theoretical and the political. A particular point of contention concerned commercial tariffs and the workings of the gold standard.[28] Interestingly, there was outright consensus on the urgency for

25 Davis, op. cit., n. 21, p. 350.
26 League of Nations, *International Financial Conference, Monetary Problems XIII: Introduction and Joint Financial Statement of the Economic Experts* (1920).
27 League of Nations, *Reports of the Committee of Experts Appointed by the Currency and Exchange sub-commission of the Financial Commission* (1922).
28 Concerning the conferences and the main points of controversy, see Siepmann, op. cit., n. 22; Eichengreen, op. cit., n. 20, pp. 153–67; Fink, op. cit., n. 19; L. Einaudi, *Cronache Economiche e Politiche di un Trentennio, Vol. VI* (1963) 703–9; G. Cassel, 'The Economic and Financial Decisions of the Genoa Conference' *Manchester Guardian Commercial*, 15 June 1922, 139–42.

financial orthodoxy and budgetary rigour. The resolutions of the international commissions show a fully-fledged austerity rationality emerging as the common guiding principle.

The first ten days of the Brussels conference were devoted to the hearings of the financial statements of the different countries. The resolutions of the Commission of Public Finance manifest a clear sense of alarm for the 'extreme gravity' of their financial prospects. Resolution I states:

> The examination of these statements brings out the extreme gravity of the general situation of public finance throughout the world, and particularly in Europe ... *Public opinion is largely responsible for this situation* ... The first step is to bring public opinion in every country to realize the essential facts of the situation and particularly the need for re-establishing public finances on a sound basis as a preliminary to the execution of those social reforms which the world demands.[29]

After giving empirical evidence of the 'disastrous' financial situation, the cause of such 'evil' is not found in structural economic contradictions or in the decision to wage war but, rather, in the individual faults of the nations' citizens: this desire to live above their means. The solution is immediate economic reform. However, public opinion must first be cultivated; the sense of alarm must be spread, the right economic priorities must be understood:

> In order to enlist public interest it is essential to give the greatest publicity possible to the situation of the public finances of each State ... countries should be urged to supply as complete information as is possible on the existing system of taxation, and any suggestions which may appear to each State to be useful for *the financial education of the public opinion of the world* [...] (Resolution IX, 15).

In their words, people have to be made to understand that excess in government spending, and particularly public deficit, is the primary obstacle to economic recovery, causing both inflation and currency instability (Resolution II). Thus, Resolution II ends with telling austere rhetoric: 'The country which accepts the policy of budget deficits is treading the slippery path which leads to general ruin; to escape from that path no sacrifice is too great.'[30] Consequently, the most urgent social and financial reform 'on which all others depend' is a broad cut, both in ordinary and extraordinary public expenditure (Resolution III). Resolution IV emphasizes that the first cut should be in armaments and war expenditures. The following resolution declares that the policy revisions should also include welfare and social expenses, the demise of price controls over primary goods, the restriction of unemployment benefits, and a redefinition of the excessively low utility charges of postal and transport services. These policies were all condemned as wasteful public expenditures and interferences with markets. It reads:

29 League of Nations, op. cit., n. 26, p. 13.
30 id.

17

> The Conference considers that every Government should abandon at the earliest practicable date all uneconomical and artificial measures which conceal from the people the true economic situation; such measures include: (a) The artificial cheapening of bread and other foodstuffs, and of coal and other materials by selling them below cost price to the public, and the provision of unemployment doles of such a character as to demoralize instead of encouraging industry. (b) The maintenance of railway fares, postal rates and charges for other government services on a basis which is insufficient to cover the cost of the services given, including annual charges on capital account (Resolution V, 14).

Universal taxation was also proposed as a means of financial diligence (Resolution VI, 14). The declarations of the other commissions mirrored the austere position of the Financial Commission. The Commission on Currency and Exchange focused on inflation (Resolution I, 17), citing artificial expansion of national currency as its principal cause. Inflation is an 'unscientific and ill adjusted mode of taxation' that produces higher living costs and consequent 'labour unrest'. The Commission proposed possible remedies. First, governments should limit their expenditure to their revenues. All superfluous expenditure should be avoided. Secondly, banks, in particular banks of issue, should be technocratic bodies, independent of political pressures, in order to guarantee that they act solely 'on the lines of prudent finance' (Resolution III, 18). More specifically, interest rates should rise in order to restrict the volume of credit available. Indeed, 'if the wise control of credit brings dear money, this result will in itself help to promote economy' (Resolution VII, 19).

Resolutions V and VI pinpoint the relationship between inflation and real wealth: inflation can be reduced through a decrease in consumption 'both on public and private account and not only in impoverished countries, but in every part of the world' and an increase in production (Resolution VI, 19). The latter objective should be attained thorough a decrease in 'those frequent strikes' which 'aggravate instead of help to cure the present shortage and dearness of commodities' (Resolution VI, 13). Moreover, the privatization of industry is invoked: business should be put in the hands of private traders 'whose enterprise and experience are a far more potent instrument for the recuperation of the country' (Resolution VI, 19).

While the Commission of International Trade focused on the necessity of abolishing any form of protectionism and economic barriers in order to restore global laissez-faire, the Commission of International Credit openly promoted austerity. An orthodox economic policy was considered a pre-requisite for any further step towards receiving international credit:

> The Conference is, moreover, of opinion that the revival of credit requires as primary conditions the restoration of order in public finance, the cessation of inflation, the purging of currencies, and the freedom of commercial transactions. The resolutions of the Commission on International Credits are therefore based on the resolutions of the other Commissions (Resolution II, 24).

18

The same prerequisite for access to credit appears, more rigorously stated, two years later in the report of the Resolutions of the Financial Commission of Genoa:

> Proof of serious efforts to improve the condition of its public finances will be the best guarantee which the borrowing country can offer to prospective lenders ... In arriving at a balanced budget attention should be concentrated on the following points: a) Ordinary revenue and expenditure should be equalized by reducing expenditure and in so far as this is not possible, by increasing revenue. b) All expenditure of an extraordinary character should be progressively reduced until it is entirely abolished [...][31]

The Financial Commission of the Genoa conference fully endorsed the principles established in Brussels: most of the resolutions merely reiterated the recommendations made two years before.

Notwithstanding its entanglement with monetary stability, on which Genoa mostly focused through the main tool of the Gold Standard, in both conferences financial orthodoxy had an important independent value. The underlying reason for fiscal austerity lay in the belief that budgetary reforms were the only way to resurrect the market economy. Economic progress could only occur with financial rigour, as it produces the right incentives for the vital economic agents in society, that is, savers. Whenever capital loans are necessary, they 'must be met out of the real savings of the people' (Brussels, Resolution VIII, 15). Thus only through private savings is capital accumulation secured. Clearly, thrift is virtuous economic behaviour not only for the state, but for each individual economic agent. In order for savings to increase, there must be confidence in the state's financial stability. Indeed, revaluation itself favours savers by preventing monetary uncertainty and increasing the nominal value of their savings.

The concluding resolution of the Commission of Public Finance of the Brussels Conference encapsulates the severity of the austerity rationality: no other solution to the economic crisis is deemed possible; whoever does not comply will be ruined. Furthermore, it explicitly states upon whom the burden of economic sacrifice should fall, namely, 'patriotic' citizens and, accordingly, calls for ever more frugality in lifestyle and discipline in labour.

> The Conference is of opinion that the strict application of the principles outlined above is the necessary condition for the re-establishment of public finances on a sound basis. A country which does not contrive as soon as possible to attain the execution of these principles is doomed beyond hope of recovery. To enable Governments, however, to give effect to these principles, all classes of the community must contribute their share ... Above all, to fill up the gap between the supply of and the demand for commodities, it is the duty of every patriotic citizen to practice the strictest possible economy and so to contribute his maximum effort to the common weal. Such private action is

---

31 *International Economic Conference Genoa: Resolutions of the Financial Commission Recommending Certain Resolutions for Adoption by the Conference* (Cmd. 1650; 1922) 7.

the indispensable basis for the fiscal measures required to restore public finances (Resolution X, 15–16).

These words declare that Austerity must be enforced. The main aim of the Conference conforms to its economic message: technical expertise in favour of austerity recommendations pressures national governments to put austerity measures into operation, taming the wasteful desires of citizens. One of the main convictions was that 'the problems, though common to many nations, must in the main be attacked nationally. Although international action must supplement, it cannot supplant vigorous efforts in individual countries.'[32]

The conferences' proceedings reveal what is not observable in the formal resolutions. The technocratic message of the resolutions is now strengthened by normative weight: not only is austerity deemed scientifically true, it is also considered morally virtuous. In fact, the speeches of the Italian and French delegates (which follow the presentation of the resolutions of the Financial Commission at Genoa's second plenary session) draw attention to a peculiar trait of austerity: it encompasses both the economic and the moral. Indeed, compliance with austerity principles had moral importance. Both M. Picard (French delegate) and Mr. Shanzer (Italian delegate) open their speeches by emphasizing the normative value of the austerity rationale. Picard declares: 'The foundations of all monetary and financial construction are moral.'[33] In a similar tone, Mr. Shanzer asserts:

> But is not the reduction of expenditure a moral problem? The reduction of expenditure means the abandonment of all the selfish and excessive claims and pretensions of the individuals, groups and classes which are all eager for improved conditions.[34]

The sins of luxury, pleasure, irresponsibility, and dissipation are in opposition to the virtues of thrift, frugality, sacrifice, and prudence. The search for improved welfare and labour conditions is viewed as a selfish claim, which governments should resist. Shanzer's speech continues: 'The balancing of our budgets, which is essential if we are to avoid inflation and depreciation of the currency, depends upon the general and political attitude of each country.'[35] Just a couple of months later, the 'political attitude' of Italy certainly became very favorable to a technocratic government. The next section explores how, once the Fascists came to power (October 1922), the austerity agenda found fertile political grounds for enforcement in Italy. The excessive social claims of the Italian people were thus quickly silenced.

---

32 Davis, op. cit., n. 21, p. 357.
33 W.N. Medlicott and D. Douglas (eds.), *Documents in British Foreign Policy 1919–1939, First Series, vol. XIX* (1974) 710.
34 id., p. 712
35 id.

A key message that stemmed from both conferences was the aspiration that austerity rationality should make a *real* impact on European national policy. The sanctioning power that the technical resolutions should have on domestic economic measures appears once more in this hyperbolic statement by the President of the Genoa Financial Commission, Larning Worthington-Evans:

> The resolutions come to by the commission, which this conference is asked to adopt, constitute a financial code not less important to the world today than was the civil code of Justinian. The institutes of Justinian have been the basis of the jurisprudence of not merely a large part of Europe, but of the world itself. Here at Genoa there have been assembled experts in finance and economics [...] and their combined wisdom [...] has resulted in agreement upon a series of resolutions which will be a guide, and I hope a code, to be followed and observed in the same way as the laws due to the learning of Justinian.[36]

Was this just empty rhetoric or was the 'new Justinian code' of austerity actually adopted? The case study of Fascist Italy in the twenties demonstrates that austerity rationality was rigorously implemented there. The practical success of the international economic 'wisdom' was due to the extremely favourable political state of affairs conducive to this end: the Fascist government endowed the economic profession with unprecedented top-down power. During the 1920s, Italian economists implemented the austerity rationale, not just in theory but also in practice; indeed, they overtly directed Fascist economic reforms. Hence, Italian economic policies, undeniably austere in nature, were not accidental or merely due to external pressures. Economic orthodoxy had solid domestic roots in the rationality of the economic-political elite of the time.

Alberto De Stefani had the leading role in formulating the first Fascist economic agenda. A distinguished Professor of Economics,[37] he led the Ministry of Treasury and Finance from 1922 to 1925. On 3 December 1922, a royal decree sanctioned the delegation of full powers to the government for the reform of the tax system and public administration.[38] The Act marked the beginning of the 'period of full-powers' (*periodo dei pieni poteri*), securing legal authority to implement drastic austerity measures. Never in the history of Italy was such absolute power entrusted by a parliament to the executive, in particular to a Finance Minister.

De Stefani's recipe was twofold, comprising tax reforms and spending cuts, and was well summarized by the motto: 'nothing for nothing: for every

---

36 id., pp. 705–6.
37 De Stefani (1879–1969) was Professor of Political Economy at the Venice Scuola Superiore di Commercio.
38 Legal Decree for the Delegation of Full Powers to His Majesty's Government for the Rearrangement of the Taxation System and of Public Administration (Law 1601/ 1922) *Official Gazette*, 15 December 1922.

hundred billion of greater State income, a hundred billion less expenditure.'[39] To carry out his austerity agenda, the Minister called other reputable economists into the cabinet. Maffeo Pantaleoni[40] and Umberto Ricci[41] became De Stefani's closest technical advisers. An Italian Senator at the time, Pantaleoni was arguably the most internationally renowned scholar. A founding father of the school of pure economics, in 1920 he was amongst the select band of economists to be called to Brussels to issue practical advice. On that occasion, his primary contribution was a vigorous denunciation of government interference in the market economy as the root of all post-war evil. In particular, Pantaleoni complained of its distributive and welfare functions, which he denounced as 'state socialism' or paternalism. For Pantaleoni, government's proper functions ought to be limited to the maintenance of law and order and the sanctity of contracts, particularly private property.

The liberal Professor Umberto Ricci undertook extensive political activity within the Fascist government. To serve in this capacity, he was relieved from many of his professorial duties until the abrupt end of his collaboration in February 1925, when he distanced himself from Mussolini's regime. Pantaleoni and Ricci participated in many governmental committees. In particular, they led the commission of technical experts for the Revision of Balances and the Reduction of Public Expenditures (*Commissione per la revisione delle tariffe dei bilanci e delle spese*). Pantaleoni chaired the commission.

Surrounding these key governmental experts was a plethora of other moderate and liberal economists who publicly supported Mussolini's austerity policies.[42] Among these, the most influential was Luigi Einaudi. At the time a Senator and prolific journalist, Einaudi would become the leading representative of the Italian Liberal party in the Constitutional Assembly (1946), and Italy's first elected President of the Republic (1948). Throughout the 1920s, his articles in the national press and especially in *The Economist* supporting Fascist economic policy had enormous influence on public opinion.

Italy presented its *Report on the Application in Italy of the Resolutions of the International Financial Conference held in Brussels in 1920* to the provisional Economic and Financial Committee of the League of Nations in July 1922.[43] This document attests that Liberal governments attempted to

---

39 A. De Stefani, *La Restaurazione Finanziaria 1922–1925* (1926) 8.
40 Pantaleoni (1857–1924) had been Professor of Political Economy at the University of Rome, La Sapienza, since 1901.
41 Ricci (1879–1946) held the chairs of political economy in Pisa (1919–1921) and Bologna (1922–1924) and succeeded Pantaleoni at La Sapienza University (1924–1928).
42 R. De Felice, *Mussolini il Fascista: La conquista del potere, 1921–1925* (1966) 390.
43 League of Nations, *The Application of the Resolutions of the International Financial Conference at Brussels (1920) Vol. II: Italy* (1922).

22

conform to the international prescriptions, making efforts to reduce the deficit in 1921–1922, but it was only during the Fascist years that the country's economic agenda embodied austerity. In particular, fiscal austerity peaked between 1922 and 1925. These years, in which De Stefani led the Ministry of Treasury and Finance, are known as the normalizing phase of the Fascist government. Monetary austerity, which demands fiscal rigour and wage deflation, characterized the second half of the decade. This trend represented a drastic change of direction with respect to the social and distributive reforms of the war and immediate post-war years.[44] After the March on Rome in October 1922, Mussolini's first cabinet brought the democratizing trend to an abrupt halt. Austerity became the guiding principle, supplanting hard-won social reforms.

With his first speech in Parliament (16 November 1922), Mussolini made it clear that his primary economic objective was to balance the budget:

> The directives of domestic policies are epitomized by these words: thrift, labour, discipline. The financial problem is crucial: the budget has to be balanced as soon as possible. Austerity regime:[45] spending intelligently, helping national productive forces, ending all war controls and State interferences.[46]

Mussolini's words represented the common ground for moderate and liberal public opinion; the majority of the national press depicted Mussolini as the only individual capable of rebalancing the economy. Many influential liberal economists and politicians were ready to test Mussolini's ability to normalize the financial situation. He delivered: thanks to Minister De Stefani's reforms, the budget was balanced by the end of the 1926 fiscal year (30 June 1926).

Tax reform was highly regressive: the government sought larger tax revenue at the expense of workers and peasants, while medium-high income groups benefited from tax reliefs. As to the budget deficit, the Fascist government reduced it mostly through striking cuts in public expenditures: between 1922 and 1926, public spending fell from 27.6 per cent to 16.5 per cent as a share of GDP.[47] Investments were reduced in all social sectors. Ricci and Pantaleoni worked day and night to revise all items in the state budget.[48] The results were impressive. Drastic cuts followed, in particular from the budget entry 'War expenses and war employees'. In three years, the

---

44 For the progressive trend in the economic policies of the immediate post-war years, see Vivarelli, op. cit., n. 9; G. Toniolo, *L'Economia dell'Italia Fascista* (1980) ch. II; and P. Ciocca, *Ricchi per sempre? Una storia economica dell'Italia 1796–2005* (2007) ch. VII.
45 Literally '*regime della lesina*' where '*lesinare*' is an Italian synonym for 'to economize'.
46 B. Mussolini, *Discorsi* (1933) 22.
47 V. Zamagni, *Dalla periferia al centro. La seconda rinascita economica dell'Italia 1861–1990* (1990).
48 U. Ricci, *Dal Protezionismo al Sindacalismo* (1926) 612.

23

budget went down from 20.3 billion to 3.1 billion lire. This decrease meant a dramatic reduction in subsidies for war veterans and their families. Public investments also suffered severe cuts:

> During the whole period in which Italian public finances were directed by De Stefani, the expenditures for public works continued to decrease, until, in the years 1924–1925 and 1925–1926, they reached numbers that were inferior to the pre-war financial years.[49]

Budgetary rigour also drove the 1923 reform of the bureaucracy.[50] The public administration pursued efficiency through drastic public layoffs: more than 65,000 people were fired. Of all sectors, public services experienced the strictest 'spending review'. Following a press campaign that had exposed their deficits, postal and railway services fell under De Stefani's axe. The railway administration was forced to lay off 15 per cent of its employees: between 1923 and 1924, 27,000 workers were idle. Regressive increases of fares secured greater income. Prices of third-class tickets increased by 15 per cent, second-class by 6 per cent, while first-class tickets remained unchanged.[51] Diminishing investments in track maintenance also helped improve the budget.

A large privatization of public services and state monopolies took place. Bel calls it 'the earliest case of large-scale privatization in a capitalist economy'.[52] The analysis of a few cases shows the drastic change with respect to economic policy at the start of the century. For example, in 1907 the state had become the main provider of telephone services, which were previously owned by private firms. In February 1923, however, a Royal Decree[53] established the conditions to grant the franchises to private providers. By 1925, the telephone sector was fully privatized. Another example concerns the insurance industry. In 1912, the Istituto Nazionale delle Assicurazioni was created. Life insurance, previously controlled by foreign firms, would now rest in the public domain. However, on 29 April 1923, a Royal Decree abolished the state monopoly: a de facto duopoly by private companies (Assicurazioni Generali and Adriatica di Sicurt) began. That same year, the state even gave up the control of match sales, which it had gained in 1916. In 1923, private firms took over the building and management of motorways. Users funded the enterprise by paying a toll. In addition to the contribution made by local government, the state provided private businesses with annual subsidies.[54]

---

49 S. Cecini, 'Il Finanziamento dei Lavori Pubblici in Italia. Un confronto tra Età liberale ed epoca Fascista' (2011) 27 *Rivista di Storia Economica* 325, at 333.
50 Royal Decree no. 2395, 11 November 1923.
51 Toniolo, op. cit., n. 44, p. 50.
52 G. Bel, 'The First Privatization: Selling SOEs and Privatization of Public Monopolies in Fascist Italy (1922–1925)' (2011) 35 *Cambridge J. of Economics* 937.
53 Royal Decree 399/1923, 8 February 1923.
54 L. Bortolotti, 'Origini e Primordi della Rete autostradale in Italia, 1922–1923' (1992) 16 *Storia Urbana* 35; G. De Luca, 'La costruzione della rete autostradale italiana: L'autostrada Firenze-mare, 1927–1940' (1992) 16 *Storia Urbana* 71.

Budget cuts, regressive taxation, public layoffs, and privatizations represent the measures of fiscal austerity pursued by De Stefani. In the second half of the 1920s, monetary austerity became the government's prevailing goal. Mussolini's famous speech in Pesaro on 18 August 1926 began the 'battle of the lira'. After one year, the lira had re-achieved full convertibility against gold through the Decree of 21 December 1927 and, under the *Quota Novanta*, the exchange rate was fixed against the British pound.

Revaluation policy further ignited fiscal austerity measures: financial rigour was essential to make up for the increased deficit in the balance of payments. In addition to savings, wage deflation constituted a crucial variable of an economic policy coherent with currency revaluation. A stronger lira required lower labour costs, leading to lower prices and thus greater international competitiveness, which in turn had the potential to improve the balance of payments. The revaluation policy promoted a solid and permanent intervention to lower nominal wages. By the 1930s, 'the overall nation-wide reduction of real wages, could be calculated as 15–40% with respect to 1920–1921'.[55] Finally, in 1927 the Labour Charter was signed. Any possibility of class conflict or workers' bargaining power was definitively suppressed.

In sum, Fascism performed thoroughly all the recommendations of the international financial conferences. A contemporary observer would find it difficult to identify the difference between these measures and the structural readjustment reforms that the European Central Bank or the International Monetary Find urge on Italy or other European countries today.

THE ITALIAN ECONOMISTS AND TECHNOCRACY

The first Fascist government proudly promoted austerity. It was primarily thanks to such economic policies that Italy achieved social and economic normalization. The revolutionary years of the Biennio Rosso, the fear of the collapse of the market economy in the name of socialization of resources and class claims, seemed to be distant ghosts. The establishment and its institutions were again secured. Undoubtedly, austerity had served to give Mussolini's government national and international legitimacy.

In those years, Einaudi's articles in *The Economist* reported the austerity achievements in a very satisfied tone.[56] In 1922, he states:

> The first financial acts of the Fascist Government are promising [...] the most important act of the new Cabinet [...] authorizes [...] to reform the civil and

---

55 B. Buozzi, *Le condizioni della classe lavoratrice in Italia* (1972).
56 Einaudi's enthusiasm for Fascist austerity policies is well documented by his articles in the *Economist*. See, in particular, L. Einaudi, *From our Italian Correspondent, Luigi Einaudi's articles in the Economist, 1908–1946*, ed. R. Marchionatti (2000) 266 (27 November 1922) and 269 (31 December 1923).

military services; to suppress this or that public service; to transfer railways and the other industrial State concerns to private hands; to reduce, simplify, or increase existing taxes, and to introduce new ones; to act as they will in the domain of public administration and finance.[57]

One year later:

The Mussolini Government is working in earnest [...] the Minister for Public Education reduced the total number of employees in his department from 1898 to 1159. An experiment which will be watched with the utmost interest is the appointment of Mr. Edward Torre, M.P., to the newly created post of Extraordinary Commissioner for State Railways [...] It is said that Mr. Torre is determined to dismiss 50,000 railwaymen, and truly nothing short of such a drastic measure can save the railway budget.[58]

An anonymous article in the *Times* entitled 'Mussolini and his Lieutenants' reveals the international awareness of the reason why the Italian financial and political stabilization was successful: in those years, Italy had put technocracy into power. The glorifying tone for Italian compliance with the international call for austerity is clear:

Materially Fascismo is merely an anti-waste government which has secured more than bourgeois backing, and as such its task is measurable by time. But morally it is 'discipline, order, work', and these things call for permanence.

Indeed, permanence is secured thanks to technical expertise:

The most interesting of all Mussolini's lieutenants is the forty-four year old ex-university professor who is in sole charge of Italian finance. De Stefani [...] reminds one strongly of an Oxford Don – of which type, indeed, he is the Italian parallel. His virtues are well-known – a charming courtesy, a dogmatic certainty of opinion, perfect honesty of mind, and an undeviating conscientiousness. These essential qualities produce a simplicity of policy too often lacking in the professional politician. [...] One or two [...] other men are around him [...] and all are soaked in the English economists. Their unconcealed ideal is to 'apprehend and copy' the British system of public finance.[59]

The executors of austerity, De Stefani, Pantaleoni, and Ricci were all very prolific scholars. They participated in academic debates, where they exalted 'pure economics' as well as regularly contributing to national newspapers.[60] Through the analysis of this complex body of literature, the austerity rationality of the three economists comes to light.

De Stefani, Pantaleoni, and Ricci do not perceive their governmental action as historically contingent, but the authentic realization of their mission

---

57 id., p. 266.
58 id., p. 269
59 Anon, 'Mussolini and his Lieutenants' *Times*, 2 July 1923, 13.
60 Pantaleoni made frequent contributions in the press (especially *Il Mezzogiorno, Il Popolo d'Italia,* and *La Politica*). Editori Laterza collected and published many of his articles as books. The same was true in Ricci's case, and De Stefani's public speeches and press articles were published by the publisher Treves.

as economists. The practical vocation of the 'pure economist' is a clear trait of this group of economists; it helps explain their function as exemplary executors of the international 'Justinian code' drafted at Genoa and Brussels.

While Umberto Ricci covered the topic most extensively, the writings of De Stefani and Pantaleoni reveal that Ricci expressed an outlook common to all three. According to Ricci, the economist has the tough but vital task of being the *super partes* guide for the redemption of austerity. He must educate humanity to embrace correct economic behaviour in order to bring forward economic equilibrium and progress. Ricci gave two important speeches on the matter: one in Pisa, for the opening of the academic year 1921–1922, entitled 'The alleged decline of political economy', and the other at the University of Bologna in January 1922, 'The unpopularity of political economy'. On both occasions he conceded that ignorant and opportunistic masses hated economists and viewed them as public enemies.[61] His rhetoric properly conveyed the idea of the economist under siege by brutal and irrational citizens, much like the economic system was under siege by class claims. Austerity policy was especially loathed:

> By proclaiming the principle of universal taxation, promoting the shutdown of useless public offices, the dismissal of redundant employees, the abandonment of public works, the economist surely doesn't make new friends.[62]

The economist should never be discouraged, however, because in his purity he is spiritually gratified. In the conclusion of the Bologna speech we read:

> Not always are [the economist's] words listened to, not always is the consciousness of accomplishing his duty accompanied by the joy of the result. But if sometimes he is affected by the sorrow of having spoken in vain, a reward awaits him, one that no human force may take away from him. As he progressively climbs the ivory tower, and abandons at each floor his prejudices and interests, his vision gets ever more refined, his horizon is enlarged; eventually, when the high summit is reached, he discovers the unity in truth, the order in disorder [. . .] one is capable of distilling rigorous and elegant laws, worthy of competing with the laws of celestial mechanics. This vision of beauty is the economist's sovereign reward.[63]

PURE ECONOMICS AND THE ROOTS OF AUSTERITY

The three authors shared a positivist view of economic knowledge: economics was a rigorous and universal science, with the same epistemic legitimacy of other hard sciences: 'The socialist and the protectionist are to the economist like the astrologist to the astronomer, the alchemist to the chemist, the sorcerer the doctor', Ricci wrote in 1926.[64]

61 Ricci, op. cit., n. 48, p. 72.
62 id., p. 102
63 id., pp. 104–5
64 id., p. 25.

27

De Stefani and Ricci considered themselves direct disciples of Pantaleoni, who was internationally recognized among the founding fathers of 'pure economics':[65]

> Pantaleoni saw something that today is more than obvious, that is, that there must be a theoretical part of economic science, a nucleus of doctrines, independent of opinions, as well as of ethical, political and religious predilections. Something similar to physics and mathematics ... Pantaleoni appeared as the archangel with the flaming sword, to do justice against all false schools and proclaim pure economics sovereign.[66]

'Pure economics' reaches truth status by using mathematical tools and an analytically deductive method to investigate the phenomenon of economic equilibrium. It is based on logic. The outcomes of these mental experiments lead to rigorous laws: given certain premises, the fundamental economic theorems follow. The universality of economic theorems allows disregard for the institutional and historical-relative character of economic phenomena. It follows that pure economics is endowed with *normative neutrality*, confirming its universality and analytical power. Pure economics aspires to the excellence of Platonic form. Yet, austerity rationality occupies the space between theory and practice. How can pure economics be relevant to its analysis? The three economists were *engagés* precisely because, despite its 'purity', economics has an undeniable practical aim. Thus, we can reconcile the economists' frequent interventions in public conversation or in policy making with their self-portraits as champions of universal economic truths. Such economic truths have no partisan and political implications but, rather, are in the interest of all. Ricci and De Stefani agreed with a famous passage of Pantaleoni's magisterial book, which emphasized economic theory as a prerequisite for policymaking:

> First of all, one must be well-read in pure economics, then trained in applied economics, that is, pure theory; finally, one can embark on the resolution of concrete economic problems, that is, the peculiar and contingent issues that everyday reality puts under our eyes and whose core is economic.[67]

In short, the models and theorems must dispense practical economic knowledge. During a controversy in the *Giornale degli economisti* against W.J. Ashley, a leading figure of the British historical school, Ricci wrote: 'It is the honest desire of any good theorist of political economy that theoretical constructions be deemed not merely a luxury of the intellect, but necessary to

65 Pantaleoni's *Principii di Economia Pura* (published in English as *Pure Economics* in 1898) had vast scientific impact. Apart from its contribution to international scholarship, the book was a theoretical and methodological turning point for economic studies in Italy, paving the way for the Marginalist School. On the point, see P. Barucci, 'La diffusione del Marginalismo 1870–1890' in *Il Pensiero Economico Italiano 1850–1950*, ed. M. Finoia (1980).
66 U. Ricci, *Tre Economisti Italiani: Pantaleoni, Pareto, Loria* (1939) 44.
67 M. Pantaleoni, *Erotemi di Economia* (1963) 45–6 [my emphasis].

explain and forecast events, and *essential to tame men*.'[68] Even if economics as a science is pure and abstract, at its core it has an epistemological right of way over individual behaviour and thus over economic political reality (seen as an aggregate of individual behaviours). As economic historian Piero Bini put it, an 'idealisation' of the relationship between theory and policy emerged, in the form of 'a continuation of scientific knowledge into practical action'.[69]

A scrutiny of their works reveals that the pre-eminence of economic principles over the concrete practice of human beings is due to a sturdy ontological foundation: pure economics' epistemological priority over reality descends from its reference to real-life facts. Abstraction brings formal exactness, yet correspondence with the real world is not lost. Ontological realism and ontological universalism give legitimacy to pure economics, and thus to the policies stemming from it.

The hedonistic principle is the peculiar characteristic of the *homo economicus* and the founding element of pure economics. It is identified as a real-life phenomenon that economists understand in a formal manner. Pantaleoni's second chapter of *Pure Economics* extensively discusses how the hedonistic principle is the sole realistic guide for human behaviour.[70] His disciple De Stefani taught the same to his students:

> The fundamental law of conduct, which is revealed through observation, is the law of minimum sacrifice and maximum self-interest: economic progress is the historical explication of this universal norm of economic conduct.[71]

The maximizing conduct of the *homo economicus* brings about individual equilibrium and, through aggregation, the general equilibrium of the economy. Hence, even general equilibrium – that quintessential theoretical construction – is a fact of the real world:

> The recent theoretical progress of economic studies precisely consists of an ever more general formulation of the concept of economic equilibrium [...] This equilibrium is a *fact*, just like the equilibrium of our organism, or of any other organism or system one may think about.[72] [my emphasis]

In sum, the absolute epistemic and ontological authority of economic science over human lives is the basis of the austerity rationality. Hence, the techno-cratic vocation of our authors is fully explained. The practical upshot is that economic categories achieve absolute pre-eminence in shaping the policies that affect individuals' material lives. This is due primarily to a methodo-logical reason: economic categories are not perceived as theoretical con-

---

68 U. Ricci, 'Rassegna del movimento scientifico: economia' (1908) 36 *Giornale degli Economisti* 385, at 388–9.
69 P. Bini and A.M. Fusco, *Umberto Ricci (1879–1946): Economista Militante e Uomo Combattivo* (2004) 306.
70 Pantaleoni, op. cit., n. 65, p. 11.
71 A. De Stefani, *Economia Politica Appunti* (1920) 4.
72 id., p. 8.

structions; on the contrary, they represent direct counterparts in the real world. Ricci, Pantaleoni, and Einaudi seem to be trapped into what Marx calls 'negative' ideology,[73] and thus lose the awareness that the true genealogy of the 'economic' lies in the subjective and material life of human beings. Hence, a structural conflict between human life and economic theory and policy ensues.

In a famous speech at La Scala theatre in Milano De Stefani explicitly used the term austerity. We may now understand the meaning of this term. He employed it to encourage individual sacrifice and, in particular, the giving up of social protections in the name of the state's superior financial needs:

> Today, as yesterday, I need to place on the national agenda the conscious renunciation of the rights gained by the crippled, the invalids, the soldiers. *These renunciations constitute for our soul a sacred sacrifice: austerity.*[74] ['*austerità*' in the original text, my emphasis]

Through Fascism, De Stefani, Ricci, and Pantaleoni were able to carry out their task of *super partes* guides for the redemption of austerity. Hence, the post-war progressive political trend was silenced. Through austerity not only was order imposed: Fascism gained domestic and worldwide admiration.

CONCLUSION

Austerity has a long history. Its historical and intellectual roots date much prior to the so-called neoliberal movement that started after 1945 (say, the Mont Pelerin Society and the like) and triumphed with the Thatcher and Reagan administrations in the 1980s. Indeed it was during the critical historical moment of post-First World War socio-economic turmoil that austerity emerged as the consensus of the international economic establishment in order to legitimize post-war stabilization and normalcy. I have analysed the two international economics conferences of the time, Brussels and Genoa, to illustrate how they called for economic expertise to prevail over political affiliation. I have shown how their resolutions fundamentally prescribed austerity. The prospect was of a disastrous financial situation of inflation and deficit, due primarily to the individual fault of citizens: they had lived beyond their means. In this view, citizens must be educated to true

---

73 The Marxian meaning of ideology is twofold: (i) ideology in the positive sense, that is, the collection of conceptual representations at whatever level of sophistication: no conceptualization is independent from the subjective and historical reality which creates it; (ii) ideology in the negative sense, that is, the non-recognition of the real and historical foundation of a conceptualization: hence the tendency to universalize. See R. Geuss, *Philosophy and Real Politics* (2008); M. Henry, *Marx: Une philosophie de l'économie* (1976/1991).
74 De Stefani, op. cit, n. 39, p. 34.

economic science in order to be aware of the inescapable personal sacrifice necessary for economic recovery. In a nutshell, the path towards redemption was defined by drastic cuts in public expenditure, especially social expenditure, 'fresh taxation', privatization, and labour flexibility, but also political independence of central banks, restriction of currency issue, and restriction of credit. Furthermore, international credit had to be conditional to the restoration of order in the public finances of states. It speaks for itself that this economic recipe concretely foreshadowed the reforms imposed upon European countries after the 2008 sovereign debt crisis. My study proves how austerity and technocracy were complementary and intrinsically inter-related: the very scientific message of austerity called for practical enforcement. Citizens had to abide by economic orthodoxy, thereby renouncing distributive claims.

The early years of Fascist Italy exemplify the practical success of austerity. Fascism gave the austere economics professors the power of putting the international financial code into practice. Italian society could finally be normalized and moralized in the name of economic orthodoxy. The outside world applauded.

31

JOURNAL OF LAW AND SOCIETY
VOLUME 44, NUMBER 1, MARCH 2017
ISSN: 0263-323X, pp. 32–55

Has (Downturn-)Austerity Really Been 'Constitutionalized' in Europe? On the Ideological Dimension of Such a Claim

Clemens Kaupa*

In current debate, it is frequently argued that EU law requires or facilitates the implementation of 'downturn-austerity', that is, spending cuts, wage deflation, and tax increases during an economic downturn. More specifically, this 'thesis of the constitutionalization of downturn-austerity in Europe' has two dimensions: a (narrow) normative and a (broader) causal one. The former holds that downturn-austerity is a legal obligation under EU law; the latter assumes that the European constitutional framework effects downturn-austerity without necessarily claiming a legal obligation. I will argue that the former is incorrect, and yet shapes the hegemonic understanding of EU law. I will maintain that the normative constitutionalization thesis should be understood as an ideological communication, which aims to cloak the significant distributive effects of the crisis measures with an unwarranted aura of legal necessity, political coherence, and academic legitimacy.

INTRODUCTION

In current debate, it is not uncommon to read that the European Treaties require or facilitate the implementation of spending cuts, wage deflation, and tax increases during an economic downturn, measures which are commonly termed 'austerity' policies. For reasons explained later, I will describe these policies as 'downturn-austerity' and distinguish them from 'upturn-austerity' (spending cuts and tax increases during an upturn). As the European Treaties are frequently conceptualized as 'constitutional' law, this assumption can be described as the thesis of the 'constitutionalization of downturn-austerity' in the EU.

* *VU University Amsterdam, Faculty of Law, De Boelelaan 1105, 1081 HV Amsterdam, The Netherlands*
c.kaupa@vu.nl

In this text, I will distinguish between a (narrow) legal and a (broader) social-science dimension of this constitutionalization thesis: the former implies a *normative* claim, namely, that European primary law *prescribes* the implementation of downturn-austerity policies. The latter is a *causal* claim, holding that the legal and institutional setup of the EU facilitates or contributes to downturn-austerity-oriented outcomes in some form. Drawing this distinction is important, as otherwise the hegemonic interpretation of law might be mistaken for the law as such. This could lead to the unwarranted conclusion that the Union's current downturn-austerity enforcing *practice* would indicate that this practice is also *legally required*. However, this is not the case: it will be argued that the constitutionalization thesis in its *normative* dimension is incorrect. European law does not in fact prescribe downturn-austerity; it is simply too open or underdetermined, and thus cannot be interpreted as requiring the implementation of downturn-austerity, or as precluding the implementation of alternative socio-economic programmes. This claim as to the 'pluralist character' of the European economic constitution has been extensively developed elsewhere, but will briefly be reiterated here and illustrated with a few examples.[1] From a more practical perspective, it is in fact quite obvious that the crisis measures enacted since 2008 – which range from the bank and industry rescues to the unconventional central bank measures – hardly conform to any coherent understanding of downturn-austerity as a socio-economic programme.[2] This further undermines the *normative* constitutionalization thesis.

In the light of the incorrect nature of the *normative* constitutionalization thesis and the conflicting practice just described, its *causal* dimension requires renewed scrutiny as well. It will be suggested that the causal constitutionalization thesis should be sharpened as holding that the European legal and institutional framework causes or facilitates downturn-austerity- oriented policies, *despite the fact that it does not prescribe them in a (narrow) legal sense.* This formulation emphasizes the tension between the pluralist character of European law on the one hand, and the Union's current political practice on the other, and seeks to avoid the potential misconception of European law as defined by the current political practice sketched above.[3] This, in turn, suggests a new look at the *normative*

---

1 C. Kaupa, *The Pluralist Character of the European Economic Constitution* (2016).
2 See A. Menéndez, 'The Existential Crisis of the European Union' (2013) 14 *German Law J.* 453, as well as Menéndez's contribution in this volume.
3 The existing 'tensions' or 'contradictions' within the European constitutional framework are emphasized by many of the authors cited in this article. Some of them suggest, as I do, that these contradictions may allow a renewed understanding of European law as a potential resource for resistance against downturn-austerity: see, for example, G. Anderson, 'Beyond "Constitutionalism Beyond the State"' (2012) 39 *J. of Law and Society* 359, at 375–6; S. Gill and C. Cutler, 'New constitutionalism and world order: general introduction' in *New Constitutionalism and World Order*, eds. S. Gill and C. Cutler (2014) 9.

constitutionalization thesis as well, which – despite being incorrect – has been and continues to be of considerable influence in both legal and non-legal discourse. In other words, we encounter a claim that is wrong in legal terms, and which yet seems to shape the hegemonic understanding of European law. To make sense of this apparent contradiction, it will be proposed that the (incorrect) normative constitutionalization thesis could be understood as a communication that serves an ideological purpose. As such, it has two aspects: first, it suggests that the Treaties should be interpreted *as if* they prescribed downturn-austerity, even though they do not. It thereby seeks to limit the discretion subjectively available to those applying European law, or to provide (false) legitimacy for what are in fact *discretionary* choices. Second, the normative constitutionalization thesis suggests or at least does not refute the impression that the measures enacted during the economic crisis conformed to a coherent understanding of downturn-austerity, which is assumed to be supported by economic theory. The legitimacy deriving from this alleged intellectual coherence and academic support could, in turn, be unduly mobilized in defence of the enacted measures. In other words, the normative constitutionalization thesis suggests that the enacted measures should be understood *as if* they conformed to downturn-austerity as a coherent socio-economic policy, and *as if* they were supported by relevant academic scholarship, even though neither claim is correct.

The measures enacted in the wake of the crisis have been found to have significant distributive effects: the costs of the banking crisis were shifted from the bank shareholders to the general public and from high-income to low-income individuals (functional redistribution), particularly in the peripheral member states (regional redistribution). The normative constitutionalization thesis obscures this important distributive dimension of the crisis, cloaking the enacted policies in an unwarranted aura of legal necessity, political coherence, and academic support. The normative constitutionalization thesis thereby plays a problematic ideological role, obscuring what are essentially *political choices* by the European institutions and national governments in favour of a specific distributive outcome, and thereby shielding them from political challenges. Thus, the answer to the question posed in the title of this text is that downturn-austerity has *not* been constitutionalized in Europe, at least not in a narrow legal sense. However, the claim that it has, while incorrect, plays an important ideological role in obscuring the political nature of regulatory choices that have significant distributive effects, and thereby constitutes an important resource in political debate.

34

'UPTURN-' AND 'DOWNTURN-' AUSTERITY AND THEIR IDEOLOGICAL ROOTS

In this section I will argue that the concept of 'austerity' in current discourse is liable to ideological misuse, and that it is therefore preferable to use a more precise vocabulary. I propose to speak of 'downturn-' and 'upturn-' austerity. In the broadest sense, the term 'austerity' in socio-economic discourse describes policies in which individuals or the government abstain from something in order to achieve certain socio-economic objectives. In principle, such policies are not tied to any specific worldview: over the past decades, they have been put forward in communist and capitalist countries alike, and in the West by both right- and left-wing parties.[4] Within the existing global capitalist structure, spending cuts, tax increases or wage deflation *may* serve left- as well as right-wing political objectives, depending on their configuration and the context of their enactment. In this regard, it is important to recognize that the concept of austerity is commonly understood to be related to notions such as frugality and even personal sacrifice, which are ethical reference points across the political spectrum.[5] However, it would of course be incorrect to claim that the concept of austerity, in common and current usage, did not also carry an ideological bias. This bias becomes manifest, for example, in the distributive effects of the measures commonly pursued under this headline: budget cuts commonly target public services and social expenditure rather than, for example, corporate or fossil-fuel subsidies; austerity tax increases usually include regressive consumption taxes rather than progressive income or wealth taxes, or the closure of tax loopholes; and austerity income cuts are usually demanded in the form of wage deflation rather than profit moderation.[6] Consequently, the policies pursued under the headline of austerity have a distributive bias, placing the costs on labour rather than capital, on small rather than large businesses, and on low-income rather than high-income individuals. It is therefore necessary to employ a terminology that acknowledges both the fact that the concept of austerity is as such not tied to a specific worldview and relates to widely shared ethical views, as well as its association with a specific socio-economic paradigm in common discourse.

4 See, for example, A. Meyer, 'The Comparative Study of Communist Political Systems' (1967) 26 *Slavic Rev.* 3, who argues that 'strict consumer austerity' was a characteristic aspect of the Communist industrialization strategy (p. 6); see, also, how the Italian Communist party (PCI) came to embrace austerity in the late 1970s, as described by M. Sodaro, 'The Italian Communists and the Politics of Austerity' (1980) 13 *Studies in Comparative Communism* 220. Interesting also in that regard is the PCI's self-perception, as expressed by G. Napolitano, 'The Italian Crisis: a Communist Perspective' (1978) 56 *Foreign Affairs* 790.

5 On this, see Mattei's contribution in this volume.

6 M. Blyth, Preface to *Austerity: The History of a Dangerous Idea* (2013); see, also, E. Stockhammer, 'The Euro Crisis and Contradictions of Neoliberalism in Europe' (2013) Kingston University London Economics discussion papers, no. 2.

Because in current debate the term austerity appears mostly in relation to public debt, it makes sense to sharpen the terminology in that context. There, austerity describes public spending cuts (and, to a lesser extent, tax increases) aimed at reducing public debt and fostering growth. Understood in such general terms, austerity has, again in principle, no ideological bent: most economists or policymakers probably agree that it is preferable to reduce high (in relative terms) public debt over the medium or long term.[7] It is from this perspective that Keynes, for example, stated that '[t]he boom, not the slump, is the right time for austerity [...].'[8] However, in current debate, the concept of austerity is usually not employed in such a way. Rather, it is commonly used to describe a specific socio-economic strategy, namely, the implementation of spending cuts (and, to a lesser extent, tax increases) as well as wage deflation during an economic downturn.[9] This strategy is deeply contested, as many experts, most notably Keynesian economists, believe that it stymies growth, and therefore ultimately increases, not reduces public debt.[10] Consequently, describing this specific, contested strategy with the general term 'austerity' is a misnomer that is liable to ideological misuse, as the non-desirability of high public debt, and the consequent need to engage in debt-reducing policies, is not as such contested.[11] Rather, the key conflict between the different economic schools is about which strategy is successful in restoring growth, how and when austerity is to be implemented, and who should bear its costs, as well as what the macroeconomic mechanisms are that are supposedly at work. The Keynesian view essentially holds that a growth-oriented policy during an economic downturn is the only functional way to reduce deficits in the medium run.[12] An economic downturn is characterized

---

7 It has been pointed out that the relevant issue is not the level or size of debt as such, but its relation to economic growth. As long as the economy grows faster than the debt, the debt burden is in fact decreasing. See E. Domar, 'The "Burden of the Debt" and the National Income' (1944) 34 *Am. Economic Rev.* 798. However, the experience of the peripheral European countries during the crisis made the precarious position of debtor countries manifest, which policy makers will likely try to evade. In this sense, see H. Thompson, 'Austerity as ideology: The bait and switch of the banking crisis' (2013) 11 *Comparative European Politics* 729, at 733.

8 J. Keynes, 'How to Avoid a Slump' in *The Collected Writings of John Maynard Keynes, Vol. XXI*, ed. D. Moggridge (1982) 390.

9 See, for example, Blyth, op. cit., n. 6, who, in the preface, defines austerity as 'a form of voluntary deflation in which the economy adjusts through the reduction of wages, prices, and public spending to restore competitiveness, which is (supposedly) best achieved by cutting the state's budget, debts, and deficits.'

10 For a version of this argument in the context of the current crisis, see J. Stiglitz et al., 'A Call for Policy Change in Europe' (2014) 57 *Challenge* 5, at 7; in this section I specifically refer to Keynesian, rather than heterodox schools in general, because the essential characteristic of Keynesianism is its analysis of the economic downturn and its strategy to overcome it.

11 See, for example, id., p. 9.

12 For a succinct overview, see A. Sen, 'The economic consequences of austerity' *New Statesman*, 4 June 2015.

by falling private demand, which leads to a rise in public debt as tax receipts fall and unemployment increases. If the state reacts to the crisis by cutting spending, by increasing taxation or deflating wages (for exaple, via labour market deregulation), the economic downturn will be aggravated, and public debt will ultimately increase, and not fall. By contrast, increased public expenditure during a crisis has the potential to limit or end the downturn because the lacking private demand is replaced by public expenditure. This can kick-start the economy, which in turn reduces public deficit when tax receipts increase and social expenditure falls as a consequence of increased economic activity. Once the economy has recovered, the government may enact (upturn-) austerity measures if necessary. This essentially constitutes the case against austerity policies during a downturn. By contrast, the alternative view – which belongs to the realm of neoclassical and new classical economic theory – assumes that spending cuts during a downturn can actually reduce public debt, and that they may also facilitate economic recovery.[13] This idea, which can be traced back almost three centuries,[14] re-emerged in the current crisis under headlines such as 'expansionary fiscal consolidation'.[15] Different theories have been put forward as to how this effect is supposed to materialize. One mechanism that has been proposed is that the investment climate is supposedly improved when the government cuts expenses, as individuals will assume that no higher taxes will be levied in the future.[16]

The concept of austerity is liable to ideological misuse because it is, as shown, connected to ethical notions that are held across the political spectrum, and yet also describes a specific, contested socio-economic strategy. Referring to the Keynesian position as 'anti-austerity' and to the alternative view as 'austerity politics,' as it is frequently done, is liable to misrepresent the respective positions and the precise nature of their disagreement: it could be assumed that the Keynesian position would ignore or downplay the potential negative effects of high public debt, when this, in fact, is not the case. This, in turn, can (and frequently did and does) become part of an ideologically coded narrative, in which the Keynesian position is charged with profligacy, whereas the neoclassical position is represented as prudent. This is also the case when terms such as 'fiscal consolidation', 'tight fiscal policy' or 'wage moderation' are employed to describe the downturn-austerity position, as it implies that the Keynesian counter-view would weaken the fiscal stance of a state, and its policies would be loose and

---

13 See, for example, A. Alesina and S. Ardagna, 'Large Changes in Fiscal Policy: Taxes versus Spending' in *Tax Policy and the Economy*, ed. J. Brown (2010) 37.
14 See Blyth, op. cit., n. 6, ch. 6.
15 id., ch. 3.
16 A. Alesina, 'Fiscal adjustments: lessons from recent history' (2010), paper prepared for Ecofin meeting, Madrid, 15 April 2010, at <http://scholar.harvard.edu/files/alesina/files/fiscaladjustments_lessons-1.pdf> 4.

37

immoderate. To avoid such misrepresentation, I will from now on speak of the '*downturn*-austerity' position to describe the alternative view, and – if necessary – '*upturn*-austerity' for the Keynesian position. While these terms are uncommon in scholarly or public debate, I believe that their obvious benefit lies in evading the problematic effects deriving from the double meaning of the term austerity just discussed.

The two strategies of dealing with public spending, taxation, and wages in times of economic crisis are rooted in different economic theories, which in turn derive from a variety of different axioms, for example, about human behaviour or the predictability of future developments, and thus ultimately from two different worldviews. Claiming that the Treaties would legally prescribe downturn-austerity thus implies that they make a legally binding choice for a socio-economic programme shaped by a specific ideology or worldview. Whether this is in fact the case will be discussed in the next section. It should be added that describing the two views as ideologically informed positions does not, of course, mean that, in scientific terms, both positions are equally valid: an ideologically informed position can still be true or false, and be empirically confirmed or falsified. Today, to my knowledge, the significantly larger part of macroeconomists subscribes to some form of the Keynesian perspective, and rejects downturn-austerity.[17] The relevance of this from a legal perspective will be discussed in a later section.

THE THESIS OF THE CONSTITUTIONALIZATION OF DOWNTURN-AUSTERITY

The thesis of the European constitutionalization of downturn-austerity holds that the European Treaties, understood as the Union's constitution, compel member states and the Union institutions to enact downturn-austerity policies in some form, the nature of which is to be established. I propose that two versions of the constitutionalization thesis can and should be distinguished. The first, which conceptualizes 'constitutionalization' in legal terms and which I describe as its 'normative' dimension, holds that downturn-austerity policies are a legal obligation established by the Treaties. It can easily be seen that the normative constitutionalization thesis is incorrect, and

---

17 Regarding the majority views among macroeconomists, see S. Wren-Lewis, 'The academic consensus on the impact of austerity' (2015), at <https://mainlymacro.blogspot.nl/2015/06/the-academic-consensus-on-impact-of.html>; see, also, T. Fricke, 'How German Economists Really Think' (2015), at <http://bit.ly/2cUkKXd>. Already, in the early 2000s, Gill had identified a similar agreement on the EMU among economists: S. Gill, 'Constitutionalising Capital: EMU and Disciplinary Neo-Liberalism' in *Social Forces in the Making of the New Europe*, eds. A. Bieler et al. (2001) 48.

quite obviously so. While it is occasionally put forward in legal (as well as non-legal) discourse in the form of a positive assertion,[18] in practice it is mainly operational as an *implicit assumption*. This assumption is effective because it remains essentially unchallenged. Challenging the normative constitutionalization thesis would require critiquing its manifest incon-sistencies (which we will discuss more extensively below) in a systematic form, but also developing a comprehensive interpretation of the Treaties that proves their openness to alternative socio-economic strategies. The absence of such challenge in legal discourse leaves the normative constitutionali-zation thesis as the only developed interpretation of the Treaties, not because it is convincing, but because it appears void of alternatives.[19] This hege-monic position, in turn, makes it easier to ignore the manifestly implausible character of the normative constitutionalization thesis. Scholarship often marginalizes Treaty provisions and interpretations that contradict the normative constitutionalization thesis, most notably by interpreting them in an overly restrictive way, or by denying them any autonomous function altogether.[20] The evidence for the influence and effectiveness of the normative constitutionalization thesis in both legal and non-legal discourse thereby lies in the manifest absence of alternative Treaty interpretations.

The second variant of the constitutionalization thesis proposes that the legal and institutional structure of the Treaties in the present economic and political context tends to advance downturn-austerity-oriented policies, or undermine the viability of alternative socio-economic programmes. It can be distinguished from the first version because it does not conceptualize this relationship in normative terms alone (that is, downturn-austerity as a legal obligation) but, rather, as a factual, observable relationship (that is, downturn-austerity as the effect of a certain legal and institutional setup). I will term this view the 'causal' version of the constitutionalization thesis, as it aims to describe causal (in the sense of establishing contributing factors rather than in a mechanistic sense) relationships between the Union's constitutional structure on the one hand and the downturn-austerity-oriented outcomes on the other. The general idea – which exists in a left (for example,

18 For an example from non-legal discourse see J.-P. Fitoussi and F. Saraceno, 'European economic governance: the Berlin-Washington Consensus' (2013) 37 *Cambridge J. of Economics* 479; for examples from legal discourse, see M. Nahtigal and B. Bugaric, 'The EU Fiscal Compact: Constitutionalization of Austerity and Preemption of Democracy in Europe' (2012), at <https://ssrn.com/abstract=2194475> 1–2; I. Glivanos, 'Law's Empire of Austerity: De-Politicisation of Economic Decisionmaking in the Twilight of European Democracy' (2015), University of Westminster School of Law research paper, no. 16-04, 4.

19 For a similar argument, see R. Hirschl, 'The origins of the new constitutionalism: lessons from the "old" constitutionalism' in Gill and Cutler, op. cit., n. 3, p. 96.

20 For a particularly blatant example of such interpretation, see U. Häde, 'Artikel 126 AEUV' in *EUV/AEUV Kommentar*, eds. C. Calliess and M. Ruffert (2016) para. 11.

neo-Gramscian) and a right (for example, public choice) version[21] – is that political actors mobilize legal and institutional frameworks in some form in order to lock in a specific socio-economic policy, and thereby insulate it from future challenges. Depending on the ideological vantage point, these challenges are conceptualized either as driven by popular movements or by 'rent-seeking interest groups'. This lock-in of a specific socio-economic policy is assumed to be realized via national constitutional, European or international law, but it may also extend to 'regular' national law, soft law or legal practices.[22] Scholars advancing a version of the causal constitutionalization thesis tend to understand the term 'constitution' as including, but extending beyond, the binding force of higher-ranking law. Stephen Gill, who coined the term 'new constitutionalism,' defined it as follows:

> New constitutionalism is an international governance framework. It seeks to separate economic policies from broad political accountability in order to make governments more responsive to the discipline of market forces, and correspondingly less responsive to popular-democratic forces and processes. New constitutionalism is the politico-legal dimension of the wider discourse of disciplinary neo-liberalism.[23]

According to Gill, the Treaties and, in particular, the provisions on the European Monetary Union (EMU) should be understood along these lines:

> Maastricht and EMU seek to minimise the threat of currency turbulence by moving to a single currency and by 'locking in' political commitments to orthodox market-monetarist fiscal and monetary policies that are perceived to increase government credibility in the eyes of financial market players.[24]

It can be seen that the concept of 'new constitutionalism' centres on law ('the politico-legal dimension ...'), but locates it in the broader context of a hegemonic discourse that is the object of study ('... of the wider discourse of disciplinary neo-liberalism.'). To Gill, '[l]egal or administrative enforcement is required, since the power of normalising discourse or ideology is not enough to ensure compliance with the orthodoxy.'[25] The central ambition of scholars advancing a version of the *causal* constitutionalization thesis is, to reiterate, to describe a process in which socio-economic choices shall, by means of higher-ranking law, be insulated from challenges, and thereby enforce a specific socio-economic paradigm, or disable the pursuit of alternative programmes.[26] The narrow legal question as to whether there is an

---

21 For a neo-Gramscian account, see Gill, op. cit., n. 17; for a public choice version, see R. Rotte and K. Zimmermann, 'Fiscal restraint and the political economy of EMU' (1998) 94 *Public Choice* 385.
22 Gill and Cutler, op. cit., n. 3, p. 6.
23 Gill, op. cit., n. 17, p. 47.
24 id., pp. 47–8.
25 id., p. 59.
26 See, for example, H. Radice, 'Enforcing Austerity in Europe: The Structural Deficit as a Policy Target' (2014) 22 *J. of Contemporary European Studies* 318, at 322–3. See, however, the analysis and gentle critique of the implicit assumptions of the

unambiguous *obligation* to implement such policies is one aspect of this, but not the only one.[27] For example, institutions may also, knowingly or unknowingly, interpret the law incorrectly (for instance, as prescribing a specific socio-economic programme when the constitution is in fact undetermined in that regard); they may apply their discretion in a consistently biased form; furthermore, hegemonic legal, economic, and political discourse may legitimate such incorrect interpretation or biased application of the law; institutional or political dynamics (for example, the composition of a decision-making body) may be liable to consistently produce biased outcomes despite the law's formal neutrality, and so on.[28] In principle, the narrow legal dimension and the broader institutional dynamic may point in the same direction (that is, the European constitutional framework facilitates downturn-austerity outcomes and also legally requires them), but they may also stand at odds (that is, the European constitutional framework may facilitate downturn-austerity outcomes in some form despite the fact that it does not require them in a narrow legal sense). This article will argue that the latter is in fact the case, and that emphasizing the tension between the two is necessary in order to avoid an unwarranted equation of the law on the one hand with its hegemonic interpretation on the other.

A specific, currently particularly influential variant of the causal constitutionalization thesis argues, correctly in my view, that the architecture of the EMU has not only exacerbated the crisis (it is frequently spoken of the EMU's 'structural' or 'design flaws',[29] and its 'deflationary bias'[30]), but also facilitated the implementation of downturn-austerity-oriented measures in the Union and the member states.[31] Stockhammer gives the following reasons why the EMU architecture facilitates downturn-austerity:

scholarship forwarding the 'New Constitutionalism' thesis provided by Anderson, op. cit., n. 3, p. 372.

27 Scholars forwarding a causal constitutionalization thesis often emphasize that the legal obligation as such is not relevant. McBride, for example, after explaining that the process of constitutionalization may be pursued via international, constitutional, and/or 'regular' national law, and may also include institutions and practices, holds: 'If successful, such measures can create a kind of quasi-constitutional convention, not legally enforceable but a habitual and accepted practice with which there is general compliance': S. McBride, 'Constitutionalizing Austerity: Taking the Public out of Public Policy' (2016) 7 *Global Policy* 5, at 7.

28 See, for example, M. Bartl, 'Internal Market Rationality, Private Law and the Direction of the Union: Resuscitating the Market as the Object of the Political' (2015) 21 *European Law J.* 572.

29 Thompson, op. cit., n. 7, p. 730.

30 Gill, op. cit., n. 17, p. 64.

31 The fact that the United States was initially hit harder by the crisis, but then recovered much faster than the Eurozone is an important indicator of the EMU's 'design flaws'. On this, see Stiglitz et al., op. cit., n. 10, p. 6; see, also, Stockhammer, op. cit., n. 6, pp. 2 and 6; Blyth, op. cit., n. 6, preface.

41

First, fiscal policy is essentially national policy. The EU budget, restricted to 2% of GDP, is too small and too inflexible to serve a macroeconomic function. It is simply not designed to provide a countercyclical stimulus in case of crisis. Second, national fiscal policies are restricted in the short term as the budget deficit must not exceed 3% of GDP (except in severe recessions) and they must aim at a balanced budget in the medium term. Third, monetary policy is centralized at the EU level and it is effectively inflation targeting, with the independent ECB having set the inflation target close to or below 2%. Fourth, financial markets are liberalized, internally as well externally. Thus the EU foregoes instruments of controlling credit growth or allocating credit. Fifth, there was a no bail-out clause, stating that neither other national governments nor the ECB will support individual countries which are facing problems in financing themselves (this is the only area where we will see fundamental changes in the policy setup). Sixth, labour markets are supposed to be flexible. The European Commission (EC) and the ECB regard wage flexibility as the cure to economic imbalances. By this they mean downward wage flexibility (they have not called for higher wages in Germany). But this anti-labour bias should not hide the fact that within the economic policy regime of EMU there is an economic logic to the argument: with fiscal policy restrained, exchange rate policy abolished and monetary policy centralized, the standard economic policy tools are all paralyzed. The burden of adjustment has thus to be carried by the labour market and wage policy.[32]

It is thus argued that the Treaty rules, in conjunction with the Union's institutional setup, the institutions' practices, and neoliberalism as the hegemonic ideology, effects downturn-austerity-oriented outcomes. With a nod to the ESM it is recognized, however, that the legal rules are not fully determined in that regard, and that their hegemonic interpretation can change over time. Authors forwarding the causal constitutionalization thesis usually recognize that, given the ambiguities of the Treaties and the discretionary choices granted by various Treaty provisions (for instance, in regard to the debt and deficit rules, as we will discuss below), the European macro-economic constitution cannot be considered to be fully determined.[33] This implies that European law could, at least potentially, be mobilized in support of alternative socio-economic objectives, and would support challenges to the Union's neoliberal program.[34]

The implication of recognizing the underdetermined character of Euro-pean law is that the normative constitutionalization thesis cannot be taken at face value; as a narrow legal claim, it must be considered to be incorrect. This, in turn, has important implications for the *causal* constitutionalization

---

32 Stockhammer, id., pp. 5–6.
33 See, for example, Rotte and Zimmermann, op. cit., n. 21, p. 392; see, also, Gill, op. cit., n. 17, p. 61. For example, Gill argued that '[u]nder different political conditions EMU might allow the possibility of a more democratic form of surveillance and potential political control and channelling of global movements of capital.' (p. 63).
34 Speaking generally, Gill and Cutler emphasized that constitutional frameworks may provide opportunities for contestation. Gill and Cutler, op. cit, n. 3, p. 4; see, also, C. Cutler, 'New constitutionalism and the commodity form of global capitalism', id., p. 58.

thesis. If the law is, in principle, open towards different socio-economic paradigms, other factors – including those just discussed – must explain the Union's bias towards downturn-austerity-oriented outcomes. This may, of course, include legal provisions (for example, the decision-making procedure or composition of European institutions) in conjunction with current political or economic dynamics. However, the relation between the law and the outcomes is not straightforward: what needs to be explained is the tension between the fact that the European economic constitution is pluralist in legal terms, and the biased outcomes that can nonetheless be observed in practice. But while, as just discussed, many authors recognize the potentially pluralist character of European law, the implication – namely, that socio-economic strategies other than downturn-austerity could potentially be pursued – is virtually never spelled out. This leaves, as argued above, the normative constitutionalization thesis in place, albeit in the form of an uncontradicted implication. This, it could be argued, is characteristic of many hegemonic assumptions. Because they appear as obvious or self-evident, they do not have to be asserted explicitly in order to be effective, nor do they actually have to be plausible or overly convincing. This means that the counterview has to be spelled out explicitly.

THE PLURALIST CHARACTER OF THE EUROPEAN MACROECONOMIC CONSTITUTION

In this section I will scrutinize the plausibility of the normative constitutionalization thesis, and reject it as incorrect. The thesis resembles the ordoliberal claim as to the alleged orientation of the 'European economic constitution'. It proposed that the Treaty of Rome, even though it did not state so explicitly, would nonetheless exhibit a 'Gesamtentscheidung' (a comprehensive choice) in favour of a specific socio-economic paradigm, in the light of which ambiguous Treaty provisions should be interpreted and discretionary choice be exercised.[35] It has long been held that the ordoliberal claim constituted a strategic attempt of a specific group of academics and policy makers to impose its preferred socio-economic views on the European legal system.[36] This strategy has been successful insofar as it has significantly shaped the hegemonic view of European law over the past decades, and still does so today. This is remarkable, in particular as the ordoliberal claim is so manifestly implausible, given that it built on a fundamentally contradictory assumption. The 'Gesamtentscheidung' is not explicitly laid down in the Treaty and is yet assumed to be obvious and precise enough to

35 See Kaupa, op. cit., n. 1, pp. 3–4; D. Gerber, 'Constitutionalizing the Economy: German Neo-liberalism, Competition Law and the "New" Europe' (1994) 42 *Am. J. of Comparative Law* 25.
36 Gerber, id., pp. 69–83.

provide clear guidance for the interpretation of ambiguous Treaty provisions. Such legal argumentation is hardly plausible and is therefore unconvincing, as it assumes the Treaties to be ambiguous and fully determined at the same time. Not unlike the ordoliberal claim, the normative constitutionalization thesis asserts that the Treaties hold a legal requirement, which, while not explicitly stated, is nonetheless sufficiently manifest in the Treaties, and also sufficiently determined as to guide the interpretation of a broad spectrum of Treaty provisions relevant from a perspective of macroeconomic governance. As such, it is as implausible and therefore as unconvincing as the ordoliberal claim.

The normative constitutionalization thesis, as a claim about the normative content of the Treaties, must be assumed to be falsifiable. I posit that this can be assumed to be the case if it can be shown that alternative interpretations of the Treaties are possible (and not completely implausible). If such an alternative reading is possible, the normative constitutionalization thesis can obviously no longer be upheld. Lacking explicit Treaty support, the thesis of the normative constitutionalization of downturn-austerity must be based on the assumption that a number of provisions of the Treaties, in conjunction with the Union's legal history and regulatory objectives, would express a normative choice in favour of a specific socio-economic paradigm which is in turn relevant in the interpretation of ambiguous provisions. I have already analysed this claim extensively on a more general level elsewhere:[37] I argued that the Treaties are pluralist in the sense that they support, in principle, the implementation of a variety of very different socio-economic policies, and do not prescribe any specific socio-economic paradigm as the interpretative standard. Arguing deductively, this also implies that the normative thesis of the constitutionalization of austerity is incorrect. I now present a few examples to substantiate this.

The key issue that has to be addressed is, of course, the Treaty rules concerning the public deficit and debt (the Stability and Growth Pact, or SGP).[38] The SGP was enacted during the global neoliberal turn of the 1990s and must therefore be understood in this context.[39] It is well documented that the EMU convergence requirements have led to the adoption of downturn-austerity measures in all member states.[40] However, I assert that, while there

37 Kaupa, op. cit., n. 1.
38 id., pp. 294–308; apart from the TFEU and Protocol No. 12 on the excessive deficit procedure, the relevant secondary law acts discussed here are Council Regulation No. 1466/97 on the strengthening of the surveillance of budgetary positions and the surveillance and coordination of economic policies (1997) OJ L 209/1, as amended by Regulation No. 1175/2011 (2011) OJ L 306/12; and Council Regulation No. 1467/97 on speeding up and clarifying the implementation of the excessive deficit procedure (1997) OJ L 209/6, as amended by Council Regulation No. 1177/2011 (2011) OJ L 306/33.
39 See Gill, op. cit., n. 17.
40 See Rotte and Zimmermann, op. cit., n. 21.

44

certainly is a relationship between the SGP rules and downturn-austerity-oriented measures to be explored, this relationship may not be of a direct *legal* nature. I claim that, insofar as the Treaties involve open provisions (be they ambiguous, or providing for discretionary choice), there is no *obligation* to interpret them along the lines of downturn-austerity. It should be reiterated in this context that an argument such as the normative constitutionalization thesis (just like the ordoliberal '*Gesamtentscheidung*') implies a logical fallacy: the need for arguing that the Treaty interpretation should be guided by the socio-economic paradigm that is the subject of a comprehensive choice allegedly inherent in the Treaties arises precisely because many Treaty provisions are in fact ambiguous, and could be interpreted otherwise. But if these provisions are in fact ambiguous, then, logically, other interpretations are possible as well. Consequently, the very existence of ambiguous or discretionary provisions tend to undermine an understanding of the Treaties as requiring the interpretation of these very provisions along the lines of a specific socio-economic paradigm. And the SGP, when it comes to its debt and deficit limits, indeed grants discretionary choices at numerous instances, and relies on ambiguous provisions.[41] Most notably, the SGP regime can essentially be suspended in case of major economic crises[42] – and it is precisely at this point, as we discussed, where Keynesians disagree with neoclassical theorists' view on debt, not on the desirability of avoiding high public debt as such. Keynesians argue that, during an economic downturn, deficit reduction should not be the primary objective: instead, pursuing an active growth policy during an economic downturn will be the best solution for the debt problem in the medium run. Thus, at the very point where Keynesians and neoclassical scholars disagree, the SGP provides for the possible suspension of its regime, meaning that a Keynesian crisis programme could very well be implemented.

The situation is similar for the balanced budget requirement, which forms part of both the SGP and of the Fiscal Compact.[43] The requirement relies on the ability to distinguish between deficits that are caused by a downturn in the business cycle on the one hand, and those which would have occurred even in the absence of such downturn on the other, the latter being called the 'structural deficit'. However, establishing the structural deficit depends on

---

41 Article 126 TFEU in conjunction with Article 2 Reg 1467/97 grants the Commission discretion in establishing whether a deficit is 'excessive', or whether it is 'exceptional,' 'temporary' or 'sufficiently diminishing', and requires the Commission to take a holistic, 'overall assessment.' Within the excessive deficit procedure, deviations from the proposed annual improvement path are possible in 'special circumstances,' and a 'severe economic downturn' allows it to revise the prescribed path. According to Article 11 of the Regulation, fines are prescribed 'as a rule', which similarly implies the possibility of exceptions. For a more extensive discussion, see Kaupa, op. cit., n. 1, pp. 294–308.
42 Article 2(1) and Article 3(5) Reg 1467/97.
43 Article 3(1)(b) TSCG, Article 2a Reg 1466/97.

45

the economy's performance potential in the absence of a downturn which, as a counterfactual assumption, is impossible to establish unambiguously.[44] Consequently, the question of whether a structural deficit exists depends on how the Commission calculates the output gap. A similar ambiguity exists in regard to another contentious point, namely, whether there should be a qualitative difference made between debt taken up for productive investment on the one side, and debt to fund current expenses on the other. Keynesians tend to believe that the two should be treated differently, as the former constitutes an investment into the future.[45] And indeed, Article 126 TFEU allows the Commission to 'take into account whether the government deficit exceeds government investment expenditure' which consequently would allow for such a distinction. The current accounting standards are laid down in the ESA2010, which was passed as a Regulation, and can be changed via the ordinary legislative procedure.[46] This would allow, for example, the implementation of the much-demanded 'golden rule', which would exclude productive investment from the debt that counts towards the SGP limits.[47]

Moving to another contentious question, a brief discussion of Article 125 TFEU will further illustrate the pluralist character of the Treaties. Article 125 TFEU has frequently been referred to as the 'no bail-out clause,' even though the provision itself does not actually speak of bail-outs, and is instead much narrower in its wording.[48] Despite this, commentators have frequently claimed that a contextual, historical, and functional reading of the provision would clearly establish a prohibition much broader than that which the provision's wording suggests, namely, a prohibition of any form of financial support for member states, despite its explicit authorization in Article 122 TFEU.[49] This, in turn, was assumed to be an expression of a specific, essentially downturn-austerity-oriented, socio-economic paradigm allegedly implicit in the Treaties. This view has ultimately outlived itself after the CJEU's decision in *Pringle*, where the Court provided an alternative inter-

---

44 Z. Darvas, 'Mind the gap! And the way structural budget balances are calculated' (2013), at <http://bruegel.org/2013/10/mind-the-gap-and-the-way-structural-budget-balances-are-calculated/>; this point is also addressed by Menéndez in this volume.

45 See, for example, Stiglitz et al., op. cit., n. 10, p. 9.

46 Regulation No. 549/2013 of the European Parliament and of the Council on the European system of national and regional accounts in the European Union (2013) OJ L 174/1.

47 See European Parliament Resolution of 8 October 2013 on effects of budgetary constraints for regional and local authorities regarding the EU's Structural Funds expenditure in the member states, 2013/2042(INI); see, also, F. Barbiero and Z. Darvas, 'In sickness and in health: protecting and supporting public investment in Europe' (2014), at <http://bruegel.org/2014/02/in-sickness-and-in-health-protecting-and-supporting-public-investment-in-Europe/>.

48 For an extensive discussion, see Kaupa, op. cit., n. 1, pp. 318–24.

49 See, for example, G. Beck, 'The Court of Justice, the Bundesverfassungsgericht and Legal Reasoning During the Euro Crisis: the Rule of Law as a Fair-Weather Phenomenon' (2014) 20 *European Public Law* 539, at 549.

pretation of Article 125 TFEU allowing for financial support via the ESM.[50] This further illustrates the fact that the Treaties do not unambiguously pursue any specific socio-economic paradigm, and certainly not a downturn-austerity-oriented one.

While more cases could be cited (for example, regarding the ECB's mandate or the Macroeconomic Imbalance Procedure[51]), these examples suffice to falsify the normative constitutionalization thesis: if a Keynesian programme could, in principle, be implemented under the SGP, it is simply impossible to uphold the claim that downturn-austerity would be normatively required. Of course, the various Treaty provisions establish numerous limitations on policy makers: potentially, this could indeed make the pursuit of certain socio-economic programmes more difficult. However, these limitations do not unambiguously conform to or prescribe any specific socio-economic paradigm, and it thus can be asserted that the normative thesis of the constitutionalization of downturn-austerity is incorrect. The Treaty can be interpreted on the basis of different socio-economic paradigms, and is thus open to different socio-economic projects. This pluralist character of the Treaty, which resembles the significant openness regarding the various socio-economic paradigms observable in other constitutional frameworks, is unduly obscured by the normative constitutionalization thesis.[52]

THE NON-TRIVIAL TRANSLATION OF ECONOMIC ASSUMPTIONS INTO LAW: WHAT DOES IT EVEN MEAN TO CLAIM THAT DOWNTURN-AUSTERITY HAS BEEN 'CONSTITUTIONALIZED'?

The normative constitutionalization thesis implies a straightforward relation between a concept of economic discourse on the one side and legal norms on the other. It assumes that law can clearly and unambiguously prescribe a specific socio-economic paradigm (as *downturn-austerity* has been constitutionalized), and, logically preceding this, that such a paradigm is also unambiguously translatable into legal rules (as downturn-austerity has been *constitutionalized*). In the previous section we saw that the first part of this assumption is not true. In this section we will see that the second part implies significant difficulties as well.

---

50 Case C-370/12, *Thomas Pringle* v. *Government of Ireland, Ireland and The Attorney General* (2012) ECLI:EU:C:2012:75.
51 For an extensive discussion of further examples, see Kaupa, op. cit., n. 1, pp. 277–336.
52 American constitutional history provides a useful analogy here: over the course of the last century, the United States Supreme Court interpreted the same constitutional text as allowing or prohibiting very different socio-economic regimes. This becomes manifest when the case law of the so-called 'Lochner era' is compared with that of the New Deal era that followed: see Kaupa, id., p. 10, fn. 32.

On an abstract level, these difficulties can be described as translation problems between the economic and the legal discourse, which constitute two different epistemic systems. In terms employed by Luhmann, a scientific discourse operates on the basis of a true/false binary.[53] By contrast, the legal discourse employs a code based on the binary legal/illegal.[54] It is quite obvious that the first does not readily translate into the second, and vice versa: the fact that a certain view is deemed correct by a specific scientific discipline does not imply that it is also legally prescribed, and the law may prescribe something with which scientists disagree. However, this problem of translation remains unacknowledged by the normative constitutionalization thesis, which holds that the implementation of a specific socio-economic programme, that is, downturn-austerity, is legally required. The specifics of this obligation would presumably follow from and are legitimated by academic research. The necessary translations – from science to policy prescription to legal requirement to the application of the law – pose non-trivial problems of translation, which will be briefly described here. It will be argued that these problems are obscured by the normative constitutionalization thesis, and this, in turn, facilitates ideological, unwarranted claims about the law. The translation problems are illustrated by reference to two economic texts that have been highly influential in the socio-economic debate of the past few years, frequently cited as academic support for downturn-austerity policies.

The first text, a 2010 article by Alberto Alesina and Silvia Ardagna, was based on historical case studies and argued that spending cuts could be successful in reducing large deficits in a downturn, and suggested that they could also foster economic growth.[55] The proposal was popular among European policy makers under terms such as 'expansionary fiscal consolidation'.[56] An article by Carmen Reinhart and Kenneth Rogoff, published the same year, was equally influential, and was frequently referenced as academic evidence of the need for downturn-austerity policies. For example, a 2013 commentary in the *Financial Times* claimed that Reinhart/Rogoff's work would support 'the case for austerity', and 'a tough line on debt'.[57] In their article, Reinhart/Rogoff had argued that high public debt of more than 90 per cent of GDP is correlated to lower economic growth. The first problem we encounter when we think about downturn-austerity as a legal obligation is that the policy, and the supporting scholarship, is extremely contested within the economic discipline itself. Reinhart/Rogoff's

---

53 N. Luhmann, *Die Wissenschaft der Gesellschaft* (1990) 85.
54 N. Luhmann, *Das Recht der Gesellschaft* (1995) 60.
55 Alesina and Ardagna, op. cit., n. 13, p. 37.
56 In 2010, Alesina even presented his arguments to the European finance ministers: Alesina, op. cit., n. 16.
57 A. Aslund, 'Reinhart-Rogoff austerity case still stands' *Financial Times*, 19 April 2013, at <https://next.ft.com/content/2df58ce0-a8ba-11e2-bcfb-00144feabdc0>.

48

findings were undermined when significant calculation errors were uncovered,[58] and Alesina/Ardagna's article was challenged because its methodical selection of historical cases severely overstated the authors' argument.[59] Regarding the substance of the claim, it is, as previously seen, the very core argument of the Keynesian economic school that downturn-austerity exacerbates rather than alleviates the debt problem. But the normative constitutionalization thesis essentially ignores the contested nature of downturn-austerity in economic scholarship: it assumes that a concept that is highly contested in its own scientific field should nonetheless be understood as normatively required by the Treaties, even though they do not even state this explicitly. This is obviously a problematic legal claim.

The second problem is that, even if we ignore the scientifically contested nature of downturn-austerity for a moment, it is far from clear which legal obligations would actually follow from it. This is because the key assumptions of downturn-austerity, namely, that spending cuts and (less so) tax increases during an economic downturn may reduce public debt and induce growth, do not apply unconditionally and are instead highly dependent on the circumstances. This issue was explained, for example, by Mike Konczal as follows:

> What we found when we dug into the OECD data was that you can cut your way out of a recession as long as you can lower interest rates. Or export your way out of the recession. Or if you are comfortable blowing up your debt-to-GDP ratio. Or if you let unemployment skyrocket further. Or if you are a really small country. The big two are interest rates and exports, and neither are available at the zero bound or in a global recession. And without being able to put this in motion an austerity measure would be very, very ugly.[60]

Such conditionality in downturn-austerity has also been explicitly acknowledged by Reinhart/Rogoff themselves. In an op-ed from 2013, tellingly titled 'Austerity is not the only answer to a debt problem', they argued: 'We must remember that the choice is not simply between tight-fisted austerity and freewheeling spending. Governments have used a wide range of options over the ages. It is time to return to the toolkit.'[61] According to the two scholars, strategies available to governments, besides fiscal stimulus (about which the two are cautious), include debt write-downs, non-transparent forms of taxes (for example, for savers) as well as increasing inflation. This

58 T. Herndon et al., 'Does high public debt consistently stifle economic growth? A critique of Reinhart and Rogoff' (2013) 38 *Cambridge J. of Economics* 257.
59 D. Leigh et al., 'Will it Hurt? Macroeconomic effects of Fiscal Consolidation' in *IMF World Economic Outlook* (2010).
60 M. Konczal, 'IMF, Economist and Roosevelt Institute on Alesina and Ardagna' (2010), at <https://rortybomb.wordpress.com/2010/10/05/imf-economist-and-roosevelt-institute-on-alesina-and-ardagna/>.
61 K. Rogoff and C. Reinhart, 'Austerity is not the only answer to a debt problem' *Financial Times*, 1 May 2013, at <http://www.ft.com/cms/s/0/cca28c2e-b1a4-11e2-9315-00144feabdc0.html>.

leads them to state that '[...] no one should be arguing to stabilise debt, much less bring it down, until growth is more solidly entrenched – if there remains a choice, that is.' But if not even those scholars hailed as the academic support for downturn-austerity actually support it in an unconditional form, how could it be argued that spending cuts and tax increases constitute an unconditional legal requirement under European law?[62] Even if the Treaties should really require the implementation of downturn-austerity policies, this cannot – at least from the perspective of some of its main scientific proponents – be held to mean unconditional spending cuts regardless of the circumstances. Rather, in order to implement downturn-austerity as imagined by its academic supporters, the legal framework would presumably have to allow for considerable flexibility to adapt to the specific situation. Thus, if the Treaties were assumed to be a diligent implementation of downturn-austerity as understood by its academic torchbearers, this would essentially exclude their interpretation as an unconditional prescription of spending cuts.[63] Let us assume for a moment, however, that the Treaties implemented a strict downturn-austerity rule that required spending cuts along the lines of the SGP thresholds at all times, regardless of the circumstances, and regardless of the adverse effects this might have, and despite the fact that academic support for such rigid policy is weak. We would encounter the absurd situation that, according to the normative constitutionalization thesis, the implementation of a policy is prescribed in the name of an economic approach whose very proponents do not support such a form of implementation.

It can thus be seen that unconditional, strictly rule-based prohibitions on deficit spending regardless of the context will not lead to outcomes envisioned by the intellectual supporters of downturn-austerity; and, conversely, if the intellectual supporters of downturn-austerity had their way, this would necessitate a legal framework that allowed for significant discretionary choices.[64] More generally, it can be argued that a fully rule-based system of budgetary control pre-determined to effect outcomes preferred by a specific socio-economic paradigm is impossible.[65] The same

62 As a side-note, it can be mentioned that Reinhart/Rogoff's text appeared in the *Financial Times* only two weeks after it had published a commentary, discussed above, which had attempted to instrumentalize their work for the very position that the two rejected, thereby providing an unintended illustration of the translation problems between scientific and non-scientific discourse.

63 For a similar argument, see Nahtigal and Bugaric, op. cit., n. 18, pp. 15–16.

64 A similar point was made by Laurence Tribe in the discussion on the enactment of a constitutional amendment in the United States requiring a balanced federal budget. Here, Tribe argued: '[T]he goal of a balanced budget would have to be couched either in such flexible and general terms as to be meaninglessly lax, or in such rigid terms as to be unthinkably harsh': L. Tribe, 'Issues Raised by Requesting Congress to Call a Constitutional Convention to Propose a Balanced Budget Amendment' (1979) 10 *Pacific Law J.* 627, at 629.

65 For a similar argument, see Menéndez's contribution in this volume.

50

argument can be made based on purely practical considerations: no law makers could foresee all future developments, nor could a legal system possibly provide for all such eventualities. Consequently, it would be absurd to assume that a macroeconomic regulatory framework would completely preclude the ability of policy makers to make discretionary choices in the face of new, unforeseen developments or unintended outcomes. More speculatively, it can be argued that a very rigid legal system will motivate policy makers to exploit all available possibilities in order to reconstruct space for discretion if necessary.[66] The Union's development over the past years – as expressed, for example, in CJEU judgments like *Pringle* and *Gauweiler* – supports this claim, and shows that, even in a macroeconomic constitutional system that has commonly been perceived to be very rigid, scope for discretionary choices can in fact be constructed if necessary.[67]

THE NORMATIVE CONSTITUTIONALIZATION THESIS AS AN IDEOLOGICAL COMMUNICATION

The previous two sections have shown that the normative constitutionalization thesis is incorrect as a description of the legal obligations arising from the European constitution, as well as being problematic in epistemological terms. It has already been hinted that both characteristics make it liable to ideological misuse. This argument will be further developed in this section. Despite being incorrect, the normative constitutionalization thesis has been shaping the hegemonic understanding of European law over the past years, prominently featuring not only in the legal debate proper, but also in political and economic discourse. For example, Jean-Paul Fitoussi and Francesco Saraceno – two prominent left-leaning economists – argued in a 2013 article that by '[e]mbedding neoliberal principles in the treaties defining its governance, the EU has enshrined a peculiar doctrine within its constitution.'[68] It can be posited that the normative constitutionalization thesis, though incorrect, still plays an important role in facilitating downturn-austerity-oriented outcomes in the EU, insofar as it shapes the hegemonic understanding of European law. Drawing on a remark made by Kelsen in a different context, the normative constitutionalization thesis could be conceptualized not as a proper legal statement, but as a communicative strategy.[69] In this section I will describe what appears to be the content of this communication, and briefly speculate about its effect. I will suggest that

---

66 Menéndez describes the current practice of the European system of budgetary control, correctly in my view, as 'Cloaking (pseudo-)technocratic discretion' (p. 75).
67 Gill and Cutler, op. cit., n. 3, p. 13.
68 J.-P. Fitoussi and F. Saraceno, 'European economic governance: the Berlin-Washington Consensus' (2013) 37 *Cambridge J. of Economics* 479.
69 H. Kelsen, 'On the Theory of Interpretation' (1990) 10 *Legal Studies* 127, at 135.

it obscures the extent to which the Treaties could allow for alternative socio-economic strategies, as well as the fact that the measures enacted after 2008 and their distributive effects are the result of political choice, rather than of legal necessity.

As a communication, the normative constitutionalization thesis appears to have at least two elements: first, it suggests that the Treaty should be read *as if* it required the implementation of downturn-austerity, even though this is not actually true. The constitutionalization thesis thereby proposes a reductionist interpretation of the Treaties: it is claimed that *less* is possible under the Treaties than is actually the case. It thus obscures the pluralist character of the European macroeconomic constitution, and instead puts forward an ideological reading, in which the Treaties seemingly allow only the implementation of one specific socio-economic programme. This communication could be understood to be addressed to a legal as well as a non-legal audience: for a legal audience, the communication delimits the scope of discretion seemingly available to those acting within the constraints of European law. For a non-legal audience, it delimits the scope of political action: as constitutions are commonly understood as binding and difficult to reform, an unchallenged claim about the normative content of the Treaties establishes an effective limit to what is perceived as politically possible.

The second suggestion implied by the normative constitutionalization thesis is that the post-crisis measures would conform to downturn-austerity as an intellectually coherent policy approach, however contested, which, in turn, would find academic support in the economic literature. It thereby provides political and academic legitimacy to the crisis measures. However, the measures enacted over the past years do not actually conform to one single socio-economic paradigm, and instead have a plurality of different intellectual pedigrees.[70] Consequently, they cannot find justification as belonging to one specific coherent policy approach. More practically speaking, as they were relying on deficit spending in an economic downturn, they certainly do not conform to the premises of downturn-austerity. Moreover, the normative constitutionalization thesis, as discussed, assumes a straightforward connection between economic theory, policy, and the legal framework, and obscures the various translational problems that arise. It thus ultimately suggests that the measures enacted under the European Treaty framework should be understood *as if* they were justified by an intellectually coherent policy that is backed up by economic science, even though this is not in fact the case. Thus, the communication obscures the extent to which European law is, as a pluralist framework, open to the pursuit of different socio-economic policies, that the measures enacted over the past year are not merely the implementation of a coherent policy

70 See Menéndez, op. cit., n. 2; for a comparable argument, see Thompson, op. cit., n. 7, p. 731.

52

programme and, instead, constitute political choices which are, moreover, maybe partly motivated, but hardly coherently supported, by academic theory. The apparent effect of the normative constitutionalization thesis is that it cloaks the enacted policies in an unwarranted aura of legal necessity, political coherence, and academic support, and obscures the political nature of these choices.[71]

The measures enacted in the wake of the crisis have been found to have significant distributive consequences:[72] the costs of the banking crisis, the origin and core of the economic crisis, were shifted from the bank share-holders to the general public, from small to large businesses, and from capital and high-income earners to labour and low-income earners, particularly in the peripheral member states.[73] The normative constitutionalization thesis obscures this important distributive dimension of the crisis because it represents the result of political choices as a side-effect of a legal require-ment. It thereby plays a highly problematic ideological role, obscuring what are *political choices* by the European institutions and national governments in favour of measures leading a specific distributive outcome.[74]

CONCLUSION

The fact that the Treaties do not contain a *legal* obligation to enact downturn-austerity does not imply that member states are *factually* free to enact alternative socio-economic policies. The political and economic history of the Union shows that member states were significantly restricted in their ability to pursue autonomous macroeconomic policies long before the EMU was enacted. The single most important influence was and continues to be the United States and its socio-economic policies.[75] As long as the United States pursued a broadly social-democratic macroeconomic policy, European governments could do so as well. However, the neoliberal turn in America put pressure on the European governments to follow similar policies.[76] Within the Union, the size and strength of the German economy constitutes another important factor shaping and limiting the policy choices

---

71 This can be related to a broader argument by Gill and Cutler (who, in turn, refer to authors like Polanyi) who argue that market capitalism requires constant political intervention to ensure its continued functioning. Gill and Cutler, op. cit., n. 3, p. 16; Cutler, op. cit., n. 34, pp. 57 and 59.
72 Blyth, op. cit., n. 6, preface.
73 id.; however, the landscape of winners and losers is, of course, a complex one. On this see, for example, Stockhammer, op. cit., n. 6, p. 2; Thompson, op. cit., n. 7, p. 733.
74 Gill and Cutler, op. cit., n. 3, p. 3.
75 See W. Streeck, *Gekaufte Zeit* (2013).
76 For a discussion of the development of the EMU within the broader global context, see G. Ross, 'European Integration and Globalization' in *Globalization and Europe*, ed. R. Axtmann (1998) 176–9.

of the other member states. Especially after the breakup of Bretton Woods, the German mark became the lead currency in Europe.[77] This had the effect, for example, of forcing the peripheral member states to follow German interest-rate policy, even though it did not necessarily conform to their own specific socio-economic needs. The measures of currency coordination adopted since the 1970s (the 'snake', the EMS, and the EMU) can in part be understood as attempts to mitigate German influence on the other member states which, at the same time, further reduced the space for autonomous policy making. The example of France in the early 1980s, especially after the EMS rules came into force, illustrates the significant limits that even the Union's second-largest economy was subjected to. Faced with an untimely recession triggered by the Volcker-shock which led to a trade deficit and to capital flight, the Mitterand government was forced to abort much of its socio-economic strategy, and essentially had to mirror German macroeconomic policies.[78] Clearly EMS rules (Germany had to consent to a franc depreciation) played a significant part in this dynamic: however, member states would face significant limitations on their ability to decide on their domestic macroeconomic policies even in absence of such rules.

While the EMU and the post-2008 reforms exacerbated the legal and factual restrictions the member states face, I have argued in this article that the Treaties remain pluralist in nature, and do not, as such, prescribe any specific socio-economic paradigm. The *normative* thesis of the constitutionalization of downturn-austerity is therefore incorrect. However, it is of course possible that the legal and institutional framework, within the existing economic and political context, is still structured in a way that is liable to undermine the enactment of alternative socio-economic policies in practice. This is the core argument of the *causal* constitutionalization thesis; its validity does not as such depend on the correctness of the *normative* claim. However, and this has been the central argument of this article, failing to emphasize the tension between the Union's factual political orientation on the one hand, and the openness of its legal framework on the other, has problematic implications. On an abstract level, these can be described as an is/ought confusion: the fact that member states are factually restricted in their ability to enact beneficial macroeconomic policies is conceptualized as a requirement set by the legal framework. This, in turn, gives rise to a number of misconceptions with problematic implications: European institu-

---

77 R. McKinnon, 'Optimum Currency Areas and Key Currencies: Mundell I versus Mundell II' (2004) 42 *J. of Common Market Studies* 689, at 698–9.

78 See, for example, Ross, op. cit., n. 76, p. 176; however, the member states certainly retained a degree of discretion. Bibow describes, for example, how countries like France and the United Kingdom could deviate from the German downturn-austerity strategy after 1992, and pursue more expansionary strategies: J. Bibow, 'Germany in crisis: the unification challenge, macroeconomic policy shocks and traditions, and EMU' (2005) 19 *International Rev. of Applied Economics* 29, at 38.

tions and member states may incorrectly be assumed to be legally barred from enacting policies that deviate from the downturn-austerity prescriptions; and measures enacted since 2008 may incorrectly be assumed to conform to, and therefore be legitimated by, downturn-austerity as a coherent and academically grounded policy programme. The enacted measures are cloaked in an aura of legal necessity, political coherence, and academic legitimacy. All this obscures the fact that, because the measures enacted in the wake of the crisis are not actually legally required, they thus constitute *political* choices by the various European institutions and member states. For this reason, it has been proposed that the *normative* constitutionalization thesis could be conceptualized as a strategic communication that serves an ideological purpose.

Of course, the economic and political environment within which these choices are made can still exercise important constraints. However, whether the restrictions faced by the member states or by the Union institutions are of a legal, political or economic nature is significant. The recognition that the measures enacted constitute *political* choices within a pluralist constitutional framework allows us to focus on their political implications, most notably their distributive effects, and also to challenging them politically. There are, of course, numerous obstacles to the implementation of, for example, a Keynesian growth and investment programme; but the European economic constitution is not one of them, at least not in the sense of unambiguously prescribing downturn-austerity.[79] Consequently, I propose that the *causal* constitutionalization thesis should be sharpened or rephrased as follows: there has been an attempt to lock in a specific socio-economic paradigm in the European constitutional framework, but it failed insofar as it continues to be pluralist. Yet, the incorrect *claim* that downturn-austerity has become a legal obligation still remains a powerful resource in political debate.

---

79 For examples of a Keynesian reading of the crisis, and proposals for Keynesian reform steps, see S. Storm and C. Naastepad, 'Europe's Hunger Games: Income Distribution, Cost Competitiveness and Crisis' (2015) 39 *Cambridge J. of Economics* 959; see, also, Stiglitz et al., op. cit., n. 10.

JOURNAL OF LAW AND SOCIETY
VOLUME 44, NUMBER 1, MARCH 2017
ISSN: 0263-323X, pp. 56–78

The Crisis of Law and the European Crises: From the Social and Democratic *Rechtsstaat* to the Consolidating State of (Pseudo-)technocratic Governance

AGUSTÍN J. MENÉNDEZ*

Europe has been badly hit by several overlapping crises. This article explores how they were triggered by and, in turn, aggravated a structural crisis of European law. It spells out the concrete implications of 'austerity' in constitutional terms. First, the crises have led to ad hoc decisions and structural reforms honouring European constitutional norms in the breach. Secondly, the governance of the crises has facilitated the radicalization of the ongoing mutation of European constitutional law, in particular, changes to the structural and substantive constitutional law which have locked in a constitutional vision of sorts at odds with the regulatory ideal of the Social and Democratic Rechtsstaat. *Thirdly, the very nature of European law, and in particular its role as the grammar of democratic law, has been endangered: European law is in the process of becoming an instrument of authoritarian governance.*

William Roper: So, now you give the Devil the benefit of law!
Sir Thomas More: Yes! What would you do? Cut a great road through the law to get after the Devil?
William Roper: Yes, I'd cut down every law in England to do that!
Sir Thomas More: Oh? And when the last law was down, and the Devil turned 'round on you, where would you hide, Roper, the laws all being flat? This country is planted thick with laws, from coast to coast, Man's laws, not God's! And if you cut them down, and you're just the man to do it, do you really think you could stand upright in the winds that would blow then? Yes, I'd give the Devil benefit of law, for my own safety's sake!

Robert Bolt, *A Man for all Seasons*

* *Faculty of Law, University of León, Campus de Vegazana, s/n., 24071 León, Spain; ARENA Centre for European Studies, PO Box 1143, Blindern, 0318 Oslo, Norway*
agustin.menendez@unileon.es

56

The various, overlapping, and mutually reinforcing crises that have hit the European Union since 2007 have accelerated the transformation of the constitution and organization of power both within European states individually and at European Union level. The financial crisis was followed by an economic crisis, and these, in their turn, have resulted in fiscal crises, which have become as of late intertwined with the refugee crisis and a 'national security' crisis (in the wake of several major terrorist attacks).

In this article, I focus on the impact that the crises have had on the law, and argue that we are undergoing a three-fold crisis of European law. First, the governance of the crises has led to breaches of a number of constitutional norms, something that has eroded the rule of law in Europe (Section I). Secondly, the crises have propelled major changes in the substantive and structural constitutional law of the European Union, thus radicalizing the mutation of national and supranational constitutional law which was already under way well before the crises, and, in the process, remoulding the post-war regulatory ideal of the Social and Democratic *Rechtsstaat* into the consolidating state, the institutional counterpart of so-called 'austerity' politics. (Section II). Thirdly, European law has been widely used as a tool of (pseudo)-technocratic governance, as it has become detached not only from democratic politics, but from politics in general; this is transforming the kind of *law* that European law is (Section III), a phenomenon much facilitated by a certain narrative and understanding of European law (as analysed by Kaupa in the previous article).

I. THE GOVERNANCE OF THE CRISES AND THE RULE OF LAW: AD HOC BREACHES OR SYSTEMATIC SIDE-LINING OF LAW?

The constitutional soundness of quite a number of legal norms and practices through which the European Union has aimed at containing and overcoming the crises has been contested. An exhaustive list of the controversial decisions and reforms would push this article beyond its word limit in just its first section. Still, a sample of the most relevant points of 'friction' between constitutional standards and the ways in which the crises have been governed is necessary (and hopefully sufficient) to prove the first thesis of this article, namely, that the governance of the crises has resulted in the erosion of the rule of law in Europe. In the remainder of this section, I provide that sample, focusing first on the governance of the financial crisis and then on the governance of the fiscal crisis.

1. *The governance of the financial crisis*

It is well-known that since the late 1970s the financial sector has grown at a far more rapid pace than the non-financial sector, resulting in the 'financialization' of Western economies,[1] and in the inflation (at some points, hyperinflation) of financial assets.[2]

Doubts regarding the real value of financial assets were bound to pop up sooner or later. The day of financial reckoning finally came in 2007, leading to the major financial crisis of September 2008, aptly described as an 'accident waiting to happen'.[3] The collapse of financial institutions which were reputed to be fully solvent not only cast doubts on the solvency of all other financial institutions and assets, but, given the massive intertwinement of financial markets and financial actors, on the solvency of the financial system as a whole. When financial markets came very close to freezing in the autumn of 2008, economists rightly spoke of a 'systemic' crisis, one that is far from over at the time of writing. Regulatory changes have been far too little, far too late. The ghost of the collapse of major financial institutions triggering a new systemic collapse is very much alive.

The European governance of the financial crises has been structured around two key sets of policies. First, the European Central Bank (ECB) has adopted several 'non-conventional' monetary measures formally aimed at dispelling the (allegedly irrational) doubts about the solvency of financial institutions, so as to return financial markets to 'normality'. Since August 2007, massive amounts of liquidity have been injected into Eurozone financial institutions at fixed (and low) rates, at the very same time that the criteria by reference to which the eligibility of the guarantees (collateral) that banks have to provide have been much relaxed. At some points, banks have been offered as much liquidity as they demanded, as was the case in the two massive refinancing operations of late 2011 and early 2012. Secondly, member states have implemented massive programmes of public aid to financial institutions, by means of capital injections, acquisition of 'toxic' assets or the extension of more or less conditional guarantees.

Each of these measures raises serious constitutional concerns. Massive injections of liquidity at fixed rates are hardly compatible with capital allocation by competitive markets, as required by Article 127.1 of the Treaty on the Functioning of the European Union (TFEU) when read in the light of Article 120 TFEU. At some points (for example, in the autumn of 2008 or the autumn of 2011), the ECB has come very close to substituting for financial markets. Since 2007, the ECB has constantly shaped the operation of financial markets through its unconventional refinancing operations (in the usual jargon, the ECB has been a market maker), with the result that the

---

1 C. Lapavitsas, *Profiting without Producing* (2013).
2 Presciently, R. Triffin, 'How to End the World "Infession": Crisis Management or Fundamental Reforms?' in *Europe's Money: Problems of European Monetary Coordination and Integration*, eds. R.S. Massera and R. Triffin (1984) 13. See, also, P. Coggan, *Paper Promises* (2011).
3 Parliamentary Commission on Banking Standards, *'An accident waiting to happen': The failure of HBOS* (2013), at <http://www.publications.parliament.uk/pa/jt201213/jtselect/jtpcbs/144/144.pdf> 3.

58

ECB has come to determine to a rather large extent the terms according to which markets allocate capital within the Eurozone and beyond. This influence has been strengthened through the other 'non-conventional monetary' policies of the ECB, to which we will return below, including the acquisition of Eurozone sovereign debt in secondary markets (through the Securities Markets Programme, the Outright Monetary Transactions (OMT) programme, and last but not least, quantitative easing as practised by the ECB).

In turn, state aid to financial institutions seems to run afoul of Article 107 TFEU. The fact that the European Commission weakened the rules it regarded as applicable *after* massive amounts of aid were granted in late 2008 is regarded by some as an indicator that Article 107 TFEU has actually been bent.

Taken together, 'non-conventional' refinancing and massive state aid constitute a huge departure from the regulatory ideal of 'free markets' as enshrined in the Treaties. If indeed the financial system is at the core of contemporary capitalist economies, these public interventions thoroughly and systematically alter 'competitive markets'. One may well discuss the soundness of the normative choices which underlie the Treaties as they stand (as I for one am willing to do), but as long as these are the choices enshrined in the Treaties, it is hard to escape the conclusion that the policies followed by the ECB and the member states are in breach of the Treaties. The fact that the breaches favour the interest of financial institutions (and, unavoidably, of some more than others) makes the breach even more problematic.

2. *The governance of the fiscal crisis*

The launching of a peculiarly asymmetric economic and monetary union in 1999 paved the way to the growth of structural imbalances within the Eurozone.[4] Such imbalances largely shaped the form that financialization took in Europe.[5] The Eurozone core (led by Germany) radicalized its reliance on trade surpluses as the driver of (rather modest) economic growth, a strategy much facilitated by the locking in of the currency exchange rate. German surpluses were to a large extent the result of a very favourable trade balance with the Eurozone periphery.[6] The growing trading gap between Eurozone core and Eurozone periphery was financed by means of recycling the resulting Eurozone core profits into Eurozone periphery private debt.[7]

---

4 A. Bagnai, *Il Tramonto dell'euro* (2012) 93 ff.
5 J. Beeler, J. Jäger, and R. Weissenbacher, 'Uneven and dependent development in Europe' in *Asymmetric Crisis in Europe*, eds. J. Jäger and E. Springler (2015) 81, at 86.
6 Bagnai, op. cit., n. 4, pp. 80 ff.
7 Among many others, Y. Varoufakis, *The Global Minotaur* (2013, 2nd edn.) 165 ff.

The geometrical growth of private debt in the periphery fostered real estate speculation (Spain, Ireland) and very unequal and unbalanced consumption booms (Greece, to a lesser extent Portugal).[8]

The financial crisis of 2007–8 resulted in a sudden stop of the massive financial flows from Eurozone core to Eurozone periphery, revealing the shaky grounds on which the apparent catching up between core and periphery was built, as well as casting serious doubts about the solvency of the piles of cross-border debt cumulated in the first decade of monetary union. This posed a new *systemic risk*, not only due to the amounts of money involved, but also due to the fact that the euro was a *stateless* currency, in the double sense that monetary union was not grounded on political union (so there was no *lender of last resort* of national sovereign states), and monetary union did not come hand-in-hand with *banking union* (so it was far from clear who was the *guarantor of last resort* of cross-border financial credit transactions). As a result, the massive risks stemming from cross-border financial transactions were 'widow' risks, as it was unclear who would be the said guarantor of last resort, generating uncertainty about the solvency of the European (and global) financial system.

From the autumn of 2008 to the spring of 2009, several decisions were taken, leading to the three-fold policy which the Eurozone applied to contain the risks stemming from the massive pile of 'non-performing' cross-border loans. First, widow risks were nationalized or, similarly, exchequers pledged to absorb them. Private debt was thus transformed into public debt, and in the process, creditor financial institutions were cleared of any responsibility for their flawed risk assessment. Secondly, the costs of absorbing widow risks were imposed on 'debtor' countries, that is, the countries where the debtor financial institutions were established which, in practice, were those of the Eurozone periphery. Thirdly, the debt absorbed by periphery exchequers was transformed into loans extended by the Eurozone (in a coordinated fashion or collectively) to 'debtor' countries, on condition that 'assisted' states applied specific economic, fiscal, and social policies. Thus Eurozone 'conditionality' was born, and spelled out in the several Memoranda of Understanding at the core of 'financial assistance' programmes. At the same time, the 'liquidity' of 'assisted' member states was further supported by the acquisition of their debt in secondary markets by the ECB, through the afore-mentioned Securities Markets Programme and OMT Programme.[9]

The granting of financial assistance to states experiencing acute fiscal crises raises constitutional concerns to an extent that is hard to reconcile with

8 F. Bogliacino and D. Guarascio, 'La crisis del euro en perspectiva' (2016), at <https://papers.ssrn.com/sol3/papers.cfm?abstract_id=2833322>.

9 For details on the three steps I refer to: A.J. Menéndez, 'Neumark Vindicated' in *The End of the Eurocrat's Dream*, eds. D. Chalmers, M. Jachtefuchs, and C. Joerges (2016) 78.

Articles 125.1 TFEU and Article 122.2 TFEU. Financial assistance is argued to be in breach of Article 125.1 TFEU because it implies a clear break from the principle of absolute national fiscal independence and its corollary, strict national responsibility for national debt, as enshrined in Article 125.1 TFEU (the so-called *no bail-out* clause). No matter how strict the conditions imposed upon member states, the decision to grant assistance to a Eurozone member state implies accepting the risk of the assisted state being incapable or unwilling to repay the loan, which would de facto result in the original debt having been shifted to the creditor states. If we go beyond forms and consider substance, extending credit to a Eurozone state in fiscal crisis implies the risk of debts being, factually, if not formally, mutualized. Moreover, the fiscal crises experienced by assisted Eurozone states might be characterized as an 'exceptional occurrence beyond [their] control', or the same kind of situation in which the no bail-out clause enshrined in Article 125.1 TFEU is excepted by virtue of Article 122.2 TFEU. However, the very narrative of the crisis endorsed by most, if not all, Chancellors of the Exchequer and supranational officials is hard to reconcile with the characterization of the crisis as an exceptional occurrence beyond the control of the governments of Eurozone periphery states. Either the crises are the product of 'irresponsible' fiscal policies (as was sustained, and is still claimed) or the crises are due to 'occurrences' beyond the control of the states in fiscal crisis. If the former, Article 122.2 TFEU cannot be the foundation of financial assistance. If the latter, the specific financial assistance provided to countries experiencing fiscal crises could not have taken the form of loans at far from concessionary rates, and under the referred strict conditionality, because Article 122.2 TFEU foresees solidaristic, not punitive, assistance.

By the same token, the Securities Markets Programme and the (not yet implemented) OMT Programme are criticized on account of their breaching not only Article 123.1 TFEU, which forbids the ECB from acting as the lender of last resort of the Eurozone's member states, but for being in general incompatible with the strict division of labour between member states and the ECB as the basis of the independence, and consequently strictly defined mandate, of the ECB, restricted to the implementation of monetary policy. As Harm Schepel explains in detail in his contribution to this volume, the ECB has claimed that both programmes were needed to ensure the capacity of the ECB to implement its monetary policy. Doubts about the 'irreversibility' of the euro did not only generate 'excessive' interest rates for some member states, but also damaged the key lever through which the ECB implements its monetary policy, as changes in the interest rate will fail to affect interest rates in countries in fiscal crises (assuming that markets will keep on demanding much higher interest rates, no matter which monetary decisions the ECB takes). As Schepel argues, the argument is far from persuasive on many counts. For our present purposes, it is important to stress that no matter what the aims of the decisions might be, their necessary and

61

unavoidable consequence is that the ECB has bought considerable amounts of the debt of some states, and not others; in so doing, it has muddied the independence of both the ECB vis-à-vis the member states, and of the member states vis-à-vis the ECB (as the several letters penned by Trichet during his very literary spell at the presidency of the ECB abundantly prove). Whether the ECB's independence *was* bound to be frustrated is an even more relevant but still different question.

Finally, the key instruments spelling out conditionality, that is, the Memoranda of Understanding, have been subject to severe constitutional criticism on two main accounts. For one, the latitude and concreteness of the Memoranda are said to be incompatible with the necessarily attributed character of the competences of the European Union (Article 5 TEU). The Memoranda include, among many others, measures regarding public health, the organization of the administration of justice, civil procedural law, and the sale of specific assets within specific deadlines – all issues regarding which the Union is simply not competent. For another, the substantive conditions imposed through the Memoranda are regarded as being in breach of international, supranational and national fundamental rights standards. Not only have several reports by international organizations detailed quite a number of specific breaches, but some national constitutional courts have rendered judgments which substantially, if not formally, imply the unconstitutionality of several of the decisions and norms enshrined in or resulting from Memoranda of Understanding.[10]

3. *Taking stock*

It is far from extraordinary that crisis governance raises major constitutional concerns. Indeed, all crises seem to result in similar controversies and debates. To a certain extent, this is so because crises reveal the structural limits (and flaws) of the pre-existing constitutional order. In the case of the Eurozone, it is hard to escape the conclusion that some of the norms being breached were simply *impossible to comply with*, either in themselves, or within the specific overall structure of the European Union, and in particular, of the asymmetric economic and monetary union. Assuming, as the original design of the Eurozone did, that the stability of the currency area could be ensured without either a central bank acting as lender of last resort, with the mutualization of the debts of states strictly forbidden, and without any political scheme of redistribution of economic resources across monetary union, was bound to be proven an illusion.

Still, it would be too hasty to downplay the constitutional controversies around crisis governance. There is more to it than the painful pangs of the

---

10 Compare the rulings of the Portuguese Constitutional Court: see *The Key Legal Texts of the European Crises* (2014), at <http://www.sv.uio.no/arena/english/research/publications/publications-2014/menendez-losada-legal-texts-v1-170914.pdf>.

'evolution' of European law. For one thing, if we move beyond the analysis of specific breaches, and consider the justification for the contested measures, we will notice that the advocates of crisis governance have no *consistent* understanding of European law, either before or after the crisis measures breaching European constitutional law. Not only are we denied access to some of the key opinions of the legal services of the European institutions arguing for the constitutional soundness of the reforms (and thus cannot know *why* the said services found the reforms *constitutionally sound*), but the arguments that have been made in public reveal a pattern of ad hoc justification, lacking any consistency both across different disputes and with the constitutional theory that underlies the institutional interpretation of European law.[11] Just to illustrate the point: a narrow reading of Article 122.2 TFEU may lead to the conclusion that the Greek fiscal crisis was an occurrence beyond the control of the Greek state, and thus the granting of assistance to Greece was covered by the said article. But the literal, narrow reading of Treaty articles is not the standard way in which European law has been interpreted by European institutions. Why is a narrow reading justified in this case and not in *Van Gend en Loos* or *Costa*?[12] If, moreover, financial aid is covered by Article 122.2 TFEU, the *specific kind* of aid granted to Greece, as already indicated, should be coherent with Article 122.2 TFEU, and in particular, with the association of this type of aid with the aid provided in case of natural disasters. Solidarity, not punishment, should be offered when Article 122.2 TFEU is invoked.

For another, the fact that the crises have revealed the limits of some rules does not result in a licence to reshape the European constitution at will in the name of an underlying emergency, thus bypassing not only the processes of constitutional reform, but also any requirement of consistency. It matters not only whether emergency governance is in line with pre-existing constitutional law, but also *what actual practices or conventions* are followed to fill the resulting gaps. This by itself suggests the need to move on to the second set of questions put forward in the introduction, namely, the impact that the governance of the crises has had on the substantive and structural constitution of the European Union.

---

11 As Kaupa stresses in his contribution to this volume, the inconsistency of the standard EU law narrative on the crisis is hard to reconcile with the alleged determinacy of EU law which would *require* austerity policies to be implemented.

12 C-26/62, *NV Algemene Transport – en Expeditie Onderneming van Gend & Loos* v. *Netherlands Inland Revenue Administration* ECLI:EU:C:1963:1; C-6/64, *Flaminio Costa* v. *E.N.E.L.* ECLI:EU:C:1964:66.

II. THE TRANSFORMATION OF THE EUROPEAN CONSTITUTION: THE (UN)CONSTITUTIONAL MUTATION OF THE EUROPEAN UNION

The governance of the European crises has transformed the constitutional setup of the European Union. Ad hoc decisions, ordinary legislative reforms, and constitutional conventions have de facto altered the structural and substantive constitutional law of the European Union, with the case law of the Court of Justice and 'quasi' European Treaties (the so-called Fiscal Compact, the peculiar Treaty establishing the European Stability Mechanism, the ESM) having formally 'locked-in' the changes.[13] Constitutional change has proceeded not only through the ordinary process of European Treaty amendment (which presupposes ratification by all member states, and would have required in many instances national constitutional reforms), but also through a process of de facto *transformation* of the organization of power in Europe.[14] It is in this sense that I have argued that the crises have accelerated and radicalized the process of *constitutional mutation*[15] of European Union law that started well before the 2007 crises, and indeed can be dated back to a previous set of crises, those of the 1970s.[16]

In this section I consider the main changes in both the *substantive constitution* of the European Union (and very specifically on its socio-economic constitution, sub-section 1) and in the *structural constitution* of the European Union, in the allocation of power across levels of government, between member states, and among supranational institutions (sub-section 2).

1. *Substantive constitution: from the social and democratic* rechtsstaat *to the consolidating state*

The substantive content of European supranational constitutional law has been deeply transformed through the crises. Three key objectives of public action (financial stability, full faith and credit[17] of public debt, and economic growth)

---

13 It seems to me that this supports rather than contradicts Kaupa's argument, because the narrative which supports the constitutional mutation is deeply Münchausenan: it presupposes that the changes that result from a new practice are justified by the new practice.
14 For the conceptual framework, see S. D'Albergo, *Costituzione e organizzazione del potere nell'ordinamento italiano* (1991).
15 A.J. Menéndez, 'A European Union in Constitutional Mutation?' (2014) 20 *European Law J.* 127.
16 See W. Streeck, *Buying Time* (2014).
17 The unconditional guarantee or commitment by one entity to back the interest and principal of another entity's debt, typically employed by a government to help lower the borrowing costs of a smaller, less stable government or a government-sponsored agency. When this occurs, the smaller government or agency takes on the backer's credit quality.

have been turned into free-standing ends of public action and meta-principles of European law. In the process, such meta-principles have been redefined as constant financial liquidity, fiscal soundness, and competitiveness.

(a) From financial stability to financial liquidity

Financial stability was long understood as the capacity of the financial system to perform its key social functions in a constant manner, and very especially, as intermediation between savers and investors. Public action was expected to foster financial stability through the regulation and supervision of financial institutions. Financial stability was not an end in itself, but a *means* to achieve other key socio-economic *ends*, including full employment and rising living standards.

By the time the Maastricht Treaty was signed, the understanding of financial stability had changed. The focus of public action shifted from actions aimed at ensuring the actual discharge of the social functions of the financial system, to lighter intervention limited to fostering and guaranteeing deep financial markets capable of pricing all assets, and thus ensuring that all financial assets could be bought and sold *at any moment*. It is revealing that in the constitutional framework of monetary union, as enshrined in the Maastricht Treaty, we can find reference to *monetary stability* (the 'price stability' at the core of the mandate of the ECB), but not to *financial stability* or to the *stability of the financial system*. This was partially due to the fact that financial regulation and financial supervision were competences which remained in the hands of member states (as pointed out, monetary union would not only be asymmetric, not leading to full fiscal and political union, but would also proceed without a banking union) but also partially attributable to the strength (in the immediate aftermath of the collapse of the Berlin Wall) of economic theories and visions that financial markets tended to self-stabilization. These views fostered deregulation and the weakening of prudential supervision *assuming they were the proper ways to encourage* the emergence and reproduction of *deep financial markets.*[18]

The governance of the crises has contributed to entrenching the identification of financial stability with financial liquidity. The non-conventional monetary policy of the European Central Bank has indeed aimed at ensuring financial liquidity, even if doing so required *standing in* for money markets, or the ECB becoming a market maker (something which, as noted in the first section, casts doubts on whether we can speak of allocation of capital through competitive markets, as required by Article 127.1 TFEU). Similarly, the ECB's buying of public debt in secondary markets was justified in the name of ensuring the 'proper functioning' of sovereign debt markets and, in particular, in avoiding an escalation of borrowing rates for (some) Eurozone

---

18 M. Amato and L. Fantacci, *The End of Finance* (2013) and *Saving the Market from Capitalism* (2014).

states. The latter would have resulted in those states having no access to financial markets, and eventually public debt becoming impossible not only to issue, but also to negotiate. Such an outcome, it was said, would render the ECB incapable of implementing its monetary policy; quite certainly, it constituted a major threat to the liquidity of the public bonds of Eurozone states. Finally, the Eurozone provision of financial assistance resulted in assisted states being offered alternative funding to that provided by financial markets, with a view to ensuring not only the full faith and credit of their standing debt (which implied preserving the liquidity of underlying financial assets, because only if there is an expectation of debt repayment can secondary markets in public bonds function smoothly) but also with a view to ensuring that assisted states would eventually be capable of 'returning' to financial markets.

It can thus be said that a strong constitutional convention on both the new understanding of financial stability, and the place that financial stability as financial liquidity has in European constitutional law, underpins some of the key elements of European governance of the crisis. This new understanding of the principle and of its systemic hierarchy has been entrenched in the Fiscal Compact, the Treaty Establishing the ESM, and European Court of Justice case law, in particular in *Pringle*, a ruling in which the Luxembourg judges explicitly characterize financial stability as liquidity as the 'higher principle' underpinning the European socio-economic constitution.[19]

It is important to note that financial liquidity entails the protection of the value of financial assets. This is reflected in the emergence of constitutional conventions according to which Eurozone states not only cannot default on their sovereign debts, but should also act as the guarantors of last resort of their financial institutions. This, however, does not rule out that the interests of the holders of specific assets may have to be sacrificed for the sake of protecting the integrity of the financial system as a whole, and thus the liquidity of most assets. In other terms, the concrete rights to private property of specific financial assets holders are subordinated to 'financial liquidity' as a *collective good* of sorts. This was argued to be the case, for example, regarding the Memorandum of Understanding at the core of the provision of financial assistance to Cyprus.[20] It is important to note that the subordination of the right to private property to fiscal liquidity is not an expression of the post-war constitutional subordination of the right to private property to the social function of property (and consequently to the whole set of goals of the Social and Democratic *Rechtsstaat*), but a consequence of the fact that financial liquidity is not an intrinsic part of *markets* as much as of *capitalism*

---

19 C-370/12, *Pringle*, ECLI:EU:C:2012:756 , s. 135.
20 See now C-8 to 10/15, *Ledra*, ECLI:EU:C:2016:701, ss. 69, 71, 72, 74. The conflict between financial stability and the protection of the value of some financial assets is also at the core of the 2014 Bank Recovery and Resolution Directive.

(which moreover benefits specific capitalists).[21] Indeed, the Eurozone crisis has empirically shown that ensuring liquidity in financial markets (as the ECB has constantly done) does not by itself lead to the financial system providing funding opportunities for non-financial economic activities. Similarly, the policies through which liquidity has been restored and guaranteed have had massive distributive implications, benefitting in a clearly disproportionate manner (some of) the (big) holders of financial assets. This is clearly at odds with the goals of the Social and Democratic *Rechtsstaat*.

(b) From full faith and credit of public debt to fiscal probity

Full faith and credit of public debt is intrinsically related to the democratic legitimacy of government, and in particular, to sovereign democratic control over the shape of the tax system and over monetary policy. The soundness of public debt is guaranteed by the capacity of the state to issue currency and to allocate the financial burdens resulting from public policies through a democratically decided and constitutionally framed tax system. The constitutional discipline of fiscal policy was flexible in all post-war European constitutions. Only the original text of the German Fundamental Law (and the Swiss Constitution) contained a rule which was open to be constructed as constituting a hard fiscal rule. The German Fundamental Law was reformed in 1966, and the German 'fiscal' constitution accordingly brought in line with other European constitutions.

The present generation of fiscal rules is a stepchild of asymmetric monetary union, and indeed, of the transfer of monetary competence to an intentionally depoliticized Central Bank, which is explicitly forbidden from acting as the lender of last resort of the Eurozone states. The Maastricht Treaty debt (60 per cent GDP) and deficit (3 per cent GDP) ceilings were intended as means both to ensure the coordination of fiscal policy in an asymmetric monetary union and to guarantee fiscal solvency in the absence of a lender of last resort which underpinned sovereign bonds. The Stability and Growth Pact accentuated the latter role of fiscal rules by means of introducing a procedural and substantive operationalization of the deficit ceiling that explicitly aimed at *limiting* the margin of discretion of member states by reference to a regulatory ideal of 'fiscal probity' structurally biased in favour of *structural reforms* resulting in lower public expenditure (for example, by means of favouring private pension systems).[22]

The massive growth of private debt, and the resulting artificial growth of tax revenue, cloaked in plain sight the structural consequences of the affirmation of fiscal probity as a key principle of European constitutional law.

---

21 Amato and Fantacci, op. cit., n. 18.
22 For an insider's criticism, insightful even if lacking in nuance, see G. Guarino, *Ratificare Lisbona?* (2008).

The crises and the governance of the crises have radically altered the effective bite of fiscal rules. As pointed out above, a constitutional convention has emerged according to which no Eurozone state may default on its debts.[23] Similarly, the 2012 Spanish constitutional reform made the full credit of public debt a paramount constitutional objective, subordinating any state expenditure to there being monies left to refund principal and pay interest on sovereign debt. By the same token, the different Memoranda of Understanding have been firmly based on the assumption that the reduction of public expenditure could have an expansionary effect by means of generating confidence in public policy (growth through austerity).[24] Not only have fiscal rules been tightened, but new ones have been introduced, establishing compulsory deficit reduction and debt reduction 'trajectories' and automatic correction mechanisms (or, similarly, automatic stabilizers in reverse, automatic cuts in expenditure once a certain deficit threshold is reached). More conspicuously, the Fiscal Compact requires member states to patriate fiscal rules, and in particular, to introduce a deficit ceiling either in the national constitution or in norms of equivalent status and force (Article 3.2 of the Fiscal Compact).

Still, it should be noted that neither the Memoranda of Understanding nor the recommendations of the Commission have equated fiscal probity with the actual reduction of deficits and debts (quite fittingly, given that debt has not fallen but, rather, increased in all member states that have introduced debt ceilings in their constitutions), but with the 'sustainability of debt'. This entails that public policy as a whole is subordinated to guaranteeing the full faith and credit of public debt. The latter is no longer a means, but an end, as it has to be guaranteed even if states lack the means to provide such a guarantee. In the absence of any supranational effective coordination of tax policy, member states are de facto hampered in making effective use of tax policy to increase revenues in order to underwrite their debt if their solvency is questioned. The European Central Bank is thus the gatekeeper of probity, but is unwilling to act as such unless member states are committed to the kind of policies that make up conditionality, and which require fiscal probity. The circle is thus closed.

(c) From economic growth to competitiveness

Economic growth was regarded as a key means of reconciling the different aims of the post-war European states and the European Communities. This *instrumental* character of economic growth is clearly reflected in the Pre-

---

23 Whether or not the threat is a credible one, the Euro Summit seems to have suggested that it would consider the expulsion of any defaulting state from the Eurozone.

24 Very influential was the presentation by the 'father' of austerity through growth, Alberto Alesina, to the Economic and Financial Affairs Council, 15 April 2010, 'Fiscal Adjustments: Lessons from Recent History', at <http://scholar.harvard.edu/alesina/publications/fiscal-adjustments-lessons-recent-history>.

amble to the 1957 Treaty establishing the European Communities, where growth is defined as the means to achieve the goals of 'constant improvement of the living and working conditions of [European] peoples' and 'economic and social progress'.

European economies grew constantly and intensively during the thirty years following the war (the *treinte glorieuses*). By the late 1960s, however, growth slowed down. During the 1970s, the monetary shock following the collapse of the international monetary system in 1971 and the oil crises of 1973 and 1979 pushed European economies into recession. Since then, growth has come to be regarded as an *end*, something that has led to a different understanding of the *means* through which growth is to be achieved.

It was at this point that the present mutation of the way in which power is organized in Europe was unleashed. The radical reinterpretation of economic freedoms as the ultimate parameter of the validity of law in Europe, first put forward by the European Commission, then supported by the European Court of Justice (*Cassis de Dijon*), and then partially endorsed by the European Council in the form of the Single European Act, resulted in economic integration being emancipated from political integration, and consequently, from ordinary legislation. Economic freedom and undistorted competition were defined as free-standing meta-constitutional principles. Their holders thus should be unencumbered by any national law which could be regarded as an obstacle to the exercise of the said freedoms. Asymmetric economic and monetary union dented state capacities further. Not only was monetary union (even monetary cooperation under the ESM) conditioned to the renunciation of key macroeconomic levers (monetary policy, control over state borrowing rates) but came hand-in-hand with the transformation of free movement of capital, the only economic freedom the application of which was to extend *beyond* the EU borders.

It is in this context (and thus well before the present crises) that the 'competitiveness' of the national economy emerged as a key end of public action. Indeed, the move towards the single market shifted the relationship between member states quite radically, as European law, instead of creating the conditions for national autonomous policy choices, unleashed a dynamics of competition between legal systems, under which systems more protective of socio-economic rights quickly came to be perceived as *non-competitive*. The Lisbon Strategy codified to a large extent the premises of such dynamics. But it was through the governance of the crises that the imperative became so strong and so powerful as to empower European institutions to undertake the structural transformation of national socio-economic models

This was first reflected in the economic programmes upon which the granting of financial assistance was conditional. Such programmes aimed very explicitly at turning around the economies of the assisted states by means of increasing their exports. While in 'classical' International Monetary Fund (IMF) programmes the national currency is devalued, such an option was not available to assisted states as long as they remained within the Eurozone. Instead, 'internal devaluations' were to be implemented, that is, policies aimed at reducing wages and social benefits. The governance of the crises, however, has not aimed at eliminating the imbalances within the Eurozone that accumulated during its first decade but, rather, to render the *whole Eurozone* more competitive, pushing *every Eurozone state* into *constant surpluses* with the rest of the world. The aim is not *internal rebalancing*, but *generalizing the German (and Dutch) net external surplus position to the Eurozone as a whole.* This is why competitiveness is not an end *only* for states in fiscal crisis, but for the Eurozone and the European Union as a whole. Consequently, constant pressure in favour of the reduction of wages and social benefits is found in the recommendations of the Commission apropos of national stability and convergence plans, multi-annual financial perspectives, and annual budgets. Constant gains in competitiveness are required because the rest of the world, quite obviously, is not in a monetary union with the Eurozone, so any competitive advantage is likely to be diluted by the exchange rate. Indeed, macroeconomic stability criteria assume that macroeconomic stability is fostered by trade surpluses.[25] By the same token, the Five Presidents' Report takes for granted that external competitiveness is a founding principle of European constitutional law, so much so that the report can largely be seen as a reflection on how effectively to achieve that objective (and in the process, reshape the national economies of member states that used to have an economic model where *domestic demand* was the key driver of economic activity into export-led economies).[26]

2. The structural constitution: powers shifted to the centre, to non-representative institutions and to 'creditor' states

The governance of the crises has led to power being shifted in three directions: to the centre (with many socio-economic competences allocated to the supranational level of government), to non-representative institutions, and to 'creditor' states (as a result of the marked relativization of the principle of equality among member states).

---

25 As reflected in the asymmetric rule regarding current account balance. A more than 4 per cent deficit is indicative of an imbalance, but only a more than 6 per cent surplus is regarded as reflecting a macroeconomic imbalance. Compare European Commission, 'Scoreboard for the Surveillance of Macroeconomic Imbalances' (2012) European Economy Occasional Papers 92.
26 What was a rather vague objective in the 2000s (Lisbon Strategy) is now the alpha and omega of economic policy.

(a) Centralization of power

The supranational level of government has been assigned the power to both *monitor and ensure the stability of the financial system as a whole* (macroprudential supervision being now in the hands of the ECB as 'leader' of the Systemic Risk Board) and *to supervise all major financial institutions* (the 'second pillar' of the ECB is in charge of the micro-prudential supervision of all the Eurozone's major financial institutions).[27]

European institutions have been assigned new powers to *monitor and discipline national fiscal policy*. For one, an emerging constitutional convention forbids Eurozone states from defaulting on their debts. For another, the Eurozone has acquired the financial means and has set up the decision-making process necessary to provide financial assistance to member states experiencing fiscal crises. The acceptance of financial assistance is subject to the assisted state's acceptance of the troika (the ECB, the Commission, and the IMF)[28] placing conditions on national economic and social policy as a whole. Thirdly, the European Central Bank has assumed the role of the lender of last resort of Eurozone states, a power that it has pledged to exert by reference to the terms of the financial assistance provided by the Eurozone, and consequently, by reference to their underlying *conditionality*. Fourthly, the Commission (particularly the Commissioner for Economic and Financial Affairs) has seen its powers to monitor and discipline national fiscal policy strengthened, as a result of the introduction of new fiscal rules, and the increased authority given to proposed decisions it puts forward to the Council (approved if a qualified minority, not a majority, of the member states agree with them). Finally, member states are obliged to insert a deficit ceiling into their constitutions (or constitutional laws). The European Court of Justice has the power to review the 'European constitutionality' of eventual national (including constitutional) reforms adopted to comply with the new obligation.

European institutions are acknowleged to have the power to require member states to *bring their economies into (macroeconomic) equilibrium*, in other words, to stabilize their economies. The Commission is recognized as having the power to define the set of macroeconomic indicators which

27 And member states which may decide to transfer such competence to the ECB.
28 Quite obviously, the oddest institution out of the three that make up the troika is the IMF, because it is not only independent from the EU as such, but also rather external to it. A full assessment of the actual role of the IMF in Eurozone financial assistance would require access to documents that remain reserved for the time being. But, contrary to what might be expected taking into account the IMF involvement in multilateral financial assistance (but see López and Nahón in this issue), there is clear evidence that the Commission and the ECB have been stronger advocates of much more intrusive policies regarding national policy autonomy than the IMF itself. See IMF's Independent Evaluation Office, 'The IMF and the Crises in Greece, Ireland and Portugal', 8 July 2016, at <http://www.ieo-imf.org/ieo/files/completedevaluations/EAC__REPORT%20v5.PDF>.

71

help determine whether national economies are or are not in equilibrium, and then to monitor and enforce national compliance, so that macroeconomic imbalances, particularly 'excessive' macroeconomic imbalances, are prevented or corrected.

Finally, a constitutional convention has emerged according to which the *remit* of monetary policy is to be as wide as necessary to achieve the *goals* of monetary policy, independently of the (narrow) legitimacy basis of the European Central Bank. This implies that the ECB can decide on the shape of its monetary policy independently of whether or not this affects the conduct of national fiscal policies, while the reverse does not hold.

(b) Power to non-representative institutions

Power has not only shifted across levels of government, but also (and crucially) along the supranational level of government. The new competencies attributed to the European Union have all resulted in gains by institutions whose legitimacy is indirectly democratic (to be pedantic, whose 'chain' of democratic legitimacy is long, with many links) while the competencies and authority of both the European Parliament and of national parliaments (with the rather more formal than substantive exception of some national parliaments, as just indicated) have largely stalled. Most new powers are assigned to the European Central Bank, the Commission, and the European Court of Justice. The other clear institutional winner is the Eurozone Council (the so-called Euro Summit). While, on the face of it, this seems to point to a deepening of the 'intergovernmentalization' of the Union, the fact of the matter is that the 'formalization' of the unequal positions of creditor and debtor countries makes this 'new intergovernmentalism' less a guarantee of the transmission of democratic legitimacy from the national to the supranational level than a serious risk to the democratic legitimacy of Eurozone collective actions. By contrast, the European Parliament has been assigned no substantive powers in the reformed European 'economic governance'.

(c) Power to creditor states

The move from majority to minority voting on the monitoring, and especially, the disciplining of national fiscal policy results, de facto, in empowering creditor/surplus states (a minority within the Eurozone) against debtor/deficit states. Given the interplay of the rules assigning votes in the Council and the national interests at stake, it is not too far-fetched to see that a Commission seeking to sanction a debtor/deficit state (say Greece) will look for the votes of the creditor/surplus states, namely, Germany, Austria, Finland, and the Netherlands, which happen to make up a qualified minority. Similarly, while the European Stability Mechanism can only act by unanimous consent when taking important decisions (including the decision to provide financial assistance to one Eurozone state), there is one exception,

72

which allows decisions by 85 per cent of the votes when there is urgency. Votes have been attributed in a rather peculiar fashion (according to democratic standards), as the voting weight of each state depends on the ESM capital it has subscribed. This means that some, but not all states, have formal *solo* veto power: Germany, France, and Italy, of which perhaps only Germany can effectively make use of it without setting a precedent that may apply in the long run to itself.

3. *Taking stock*

In substantive terms, we can observe that the governance of the crisis has inverted the relationship between ends and means in the Social and Democratic *Rechtsstaat*. Financial stability, full credit of public debt, and economic growth have been turned from means to ends, and in the process, have been redefined as constant liquidity of financial markets, fiscal probity, and competitiveness. The ends of the social state (providing public goods and services, redistributing income, and ensuring macroeconomic steering with a view to guarantee full employment and rising living standards) have not only been turned into means, but detached from the old ends. It should be noticed that purposive fiscal, monetary, and macro-economic policy are not regarded, as in orthodox neo-classical economics, as self-defeating, but have been recovered as key means of transforming national socio-economic structures, and indeed defined to the smallest detail in some Memoranda of Understanding. Now, however, purposive policies are aimed at realizing the very different goals of the 'consolidating state'. All substantive policies, from social policy to education policy, from health policy to urban planning, are decided in the shadow of fiscal policies that guarantee the eternal rolling over of public debt. If a ghost is haunting the national exchequers, it is the ghost of internal devaluation, that is, the phantom of further wage reductions and worsening of working conditions in the name of competitiveness. The prospect of new rounds of internal devaluation is the bigger evil that renders palatable the lesser evil of pre-emptive wage moderation and a further weakening of social rights.[29] The consolidating state cannot but be a Social and Democratic *Rechtsstaat* in reverse.

In structural terms, as we saw, power has been centralized, leading to both the empowerment of supra-national non-representative institutions and the abandonment of the principle of equality between member states. As a result, the Union has been transformed from a (weak) quasi-federal polity into a rump centralized, hierarchical, and deeply asymmetric *state,* the actual strength of which is only fully revealed in crisis moments, when it can bring to bear its power over money (the Eurozone as member states' lender of last

29 See Christodoulidis in this volume.

73

resort, the ECB as lender of last resort to national financial institutions).[30] But the long shadow of such emergency powers leaves is bound to leave its mark on *ordinary* European politics.

III. THE STRUCTURAL CRISIS OF THE LAW

In this section, I turn to third dimension of the crisis of European law, namely, the structural transformation of the role that law plays in the process of European integration. Or, in other words, to the impact that the crises have had on the *kind of law* that European *law* is.

My claim in a nutshell is that the European law that is emerging from the crises is detached not only from democratic politics, but also from politics as such, and has become a tool of (pseudo)-technocratic governance. *Integration through a law that poses itself as pure* (beyond political conflict) cannot but turn out to be a means of authoritarian governance. To prove the thesis, I consider the extent to which formal legal arguments have played a key role in (i) undermining pre-existing European constitutional law, through discovering or, more frequently, manufacturing empty constitutional spaces, and the re-characterization of breaches of legal norms as conflicts between legal systems; (ii) providing cover to the pseudo-technocratic discretionality by means of which the substantive contradictions at the core of the new understanding of substantive European law are avoided.

1. *Decoupling governance from democratic constitutional law through law*

European law as it has emerged from the crises has played a key role in justifying the radical alteration of pre-existing, democratically legitimated, European constitutional law. Or to put it differently, constitutional limits have been transcended through *formal* legal arguments.

The bite of democratic constitutional law has been avoided by means of 'finding' spaces[31] beyond the reach of constitutional law (and which could be labelled as empty constitutional spaces) or by means of reconstructing breaches of law as *conflicts* between legal orders. At the core of both arguments is the rejection of any form of hierarchical relationship between national, European, and international law (contrary to what is indeed assumed in both national and European constitutional law) or, in other

---

30 While this structural transformation has been fuelled by the governance of the Eurozone crisis, there are signals of similar trends in the governance of other crises (particularly the refugee crisis, with the creation of the embryo of a supranational police force, the European Border Guard): compare A.J. Menéndez, 'The Refugee Crisis' (2016) 22 *European Law J.* (forthcoming).
31 'Finding', rather obviously, means the characterization of a given situation as lacking a legal framework, whether this is the case or not.

words, a peculiar variant of radical constitutional pluralism. Ad hoc decisions (the provision of 'financial assistance' to Greece in May 2010) and structural reforms (the establishment of the European Financial Stability Facility in the spring of 2010), the constitutionality of which was regarded as dubious under either European or national law, were said to be valid because adopted on the basis of public international law. Similarly, troika officials have tended to justify actions in clear breach of national or European law by claiming that when acting they are neither bound by national law, as 'supranational agents', nor by Union law, as they are not implementing mandates under EU law. By the same token, the decision to expel one finance minister from a Eurogroup meeting was justified on the basis of the Eurogroup's not being formally established in the Treaties, and consequently, not being subject to EU law.

The *escape* into *empty constitutional spaces* has further relied on the alleged state of emergency in which the European Union found itself, so that either circumstances would render it necessary to set aside (temporarily) some legal norms, or would reveal the shortcomings of existing norms, leading to a quasi-constitutional moment in which *there was no option* but to remould the constitution.

2. *Cloaking (pseudo-)technocratic discretion*

Massive changes in European secondary law have resulted, as pointed out above, in a much denser set of fiscal rules framing fiscal and economic policy. Such a transformation results not only in the centralization of power, but at the same time alters the very nature of European law, turning the law into a cloak of arbitrariness disguised as (pseudo-)technocratic governance.

First, it is simply impossible to constrain fiscal policy by means of rules. Even if we were to reduce fiscal policy to a means of cutting the sharpest corners of economic cycles (that is, to a lever of macroeconomic policy), a rule-based fiscal policy would remain a contradiction in terms. The Treaties define the European economy as a market economy based on free competition. Market economies do not self-stabilize but, rather, move from one disequilibrium to another. Stability is not only created through collective action, that is, through state action, but through state action defined by reference not only to long-term goals, but also to the specific socio-economic conjuncture in which the economy and the polity find themselves. This implies that macroeconomic policy cannot but be discretionary. Consequently, either all the key levers of macroeconomic policy (fiscal policy, monetary policy, social policy) are open to being used in discretionary fashion, or at least some of them are. The Eurozone has formally committed to non-discretionary monetary policy (by making price stability the first and foremost mandate of the ECB, renouncing the setting of any macroeconomic objective as part of its mandate, as is the case with other central banks), and has now committed, through fiscal rules, to an (almost) non-discretionary

75

fiscal policy. As a matter of fact, however, European *monetary policy* and *fiscal policy* are both discretionary, only that the discretion is cloaked by the appearance of technocratic governance. Consider first fiscal policy and fiscal rules. The Spanish government implemented a major income tax reform in 2015. This led to a major drop in tax revenue. As a result, Spain failed not only to honour the 'old' Maastricht deficit ceiling, but also failed to comply with the commitments it had entered into in its stability plan under the new fiscal rules. This seemed a clear-cut case in which a fine was due. And indeed the Commission proposed sanctioning Spain in July 2016. But not only did the Commission propose a fine of zero euros,[32] but the Economic and Financial Affairs Council did not endorse even such a purely symbolic fine. My point is not whether it was a wise or unwise decision to sanction Spain but, rather, that the non-application of the sanction proves the illusion that non-discretionary fiscal policy is. As several of the institutional actors involved in the issue rightly pointed out, political discretion trumped an 'automatic application' of the new fiscal rules.[33] But if the rules can only be applied *discretionally*, then the rules are not really rules, but the mere *semblance* of rules, or pseudo-rules. The *semblance* of rules is not only ineffective, but perverse because it cloaks the exercise of discretion, which can be presented as the technocratic implementation of a rule. This creates a serious risk of *arbitrariness*, as the existence of a formal rule empowers the Commission and the Council to decide when and when not to apply the rule (indeed, arbitrary selectiveness of application is inbuilt into pseudo-rules). What if next time the Commission and the Council regard it as convenient to sanction a state which finds itself in a similar situation to that of Spain? Less obviously, but equally problematic, is the arbitrariness at the core of the understanding of monetary policy as defined by reference to its goals, not the basis of the legitimacy of the ECB, which underpins the OMT ruling of the European Court of Justice. The ECB has made use of its discretion to implement non-conventional monetary policies that not only have a massive impact on fiscal policy, but which can serve as functional equivalents of discretionary fiscal policy. This is clearly the case of the different instruments through which the ECB has implemented *quantitative easing*. This is problematic for many reasons, but for our present purposes, it is a further instance of discretion being cloaked and presented as the technocratic implementation of rules.

---

32 In the words of President of the Commission Juncker: 'We must not be more Catholic than the Pope, but please make it known that the Pope wanted a fine of zero', at <http://www.politico.eu/article/wolfgang-schauble-bails-out-spain-portugal-sanctions-juncker-german-finance-minister/>.
33 See <http://www.politico.eu/article/wolfgang-schauble-bails-out-spain-portugal-sanctions-juncker-german-finance-minister/>; <http://elpais.com/elpais/2016/07/28/inenglish/1469704242_546729.html>.

Secondly, the fiscal rules at the core of the new 'European economic governance' are *false rules*, because they are constructed around a *radically indeterminate concept*, that is, 'structural deficit'. The *syntax of fiscal rules* (the concrete and clear-cut way in which they are written) and the *compliance-inducing* mechanisms attached to them (the European Semester, the new sanctioning procedure) make them *look like* rules in the strict sense of the term. However, if fiscal rules define the framework within which member states, and particularly Eurozone states, are to implement their fiscal policy, the concept of 'structural deficit' is the concept by reference to which the new fiscal rules are defined (new fiscal rules set limits to public action by reference to a percentage of the 'structural deficit'). And here lies the problem. The structural deficit is not the *actual* deficit (which is itself not a brute figure, but a figure obtained after the elaboration of raw fiscal data), but the figure that results from 'discounting' the positive or negative effects that the *economic cycle* has on the national exchequers. What is said to be the 'structural deficit' depends on which model of the 'economic cycle' is the correct one. There are however *many* possible models. This entails that different *opinions* on what is the 'structural deficit' can emerge, and that the judgement on which model is *best* is not final, but depends on the future performance of the economy. Moreover, given the degree of economic interdependence within the European Union, particularly within the Eurozone, any serious model of the business cycle of each member state has to take into account the evolution of the economy of the EU as a whole and, in particular, that of each member state (if not that of the *world economy* as a whole, or at least, the conjuncture of the main non-European trading partners of the member state in question).[34] So, while the structural deficit may be a useful concept in terms of policy making, it is totally inadequate as a concept on which to base the legal discipline of national fiscal policy, particularly the eventual imposition of sanctions on a member state, for two reasons. The first is that defining the rule by reference to a radically indeterminate concept gives the European Commission a massive margin of discretion, as it suffices to tweak the underlying economic model to obtain the desired result. The second is that an indeterminate concept cannot be the ground on which to take transcendental decisions, including the imposition of fines on Eurozone states. This is clearly illustrated by the shifting estimation of Ireland's and Spain's structural deficit by the IMF.[35] In 2008, the IMF calculated that during the period 2000–2007, Ireland had run an annual

---

34 The more growth is made to depend on external/international competitiveness, as has been clearly the case since 2010, the more the business cycle model of each member state becomes dependent on the performance of Eurozone and non-Eurozone economies, rendering things even more complex, and consequently, less amenable to precise calculation. And, alas, constant trade surpluses result in importing the socio-economic problems of the countries buying them.

35 M. Wolf, *The Shifts and the Shocks* (2015) 85.

surplus at an average of +1.3 per cent GPD, and Spain of +0.5 per cent GDP. In 2012, the IMF revised these figures on the basis of a different model of both economies. Ireland was now said to have run an average deficit of 2.7 per cent GDP, Spain of 1.2 per cent GDP.

The pretence is that discretion can be kicked out of the Eurozone window by means of the 'rulification' of Eurozone economic governance. The reality is that discretion is merely cloaked, and in the process, turned into arbitrariness, as the Commission is empowered to define the economic model by reference to which structural deficits are to be calculated, and the ECB is given the power to take decisions that are formally monetary but objectively fiscal. The consequences of these transformations are heightened by the additional new rules (the sanctioning procedure) or constitutional conventions (the ECB as lender of last resort to both member states and national financial institutions). Discretion denied is arbitrariness cloaked.

CONCLUSION

In this article I have claimed that the European financial, economic, and fiscal crises have resulted in a triple crisis of law. First, the governance of the crises has resulted in the taking of decisions and the adoption of reforms of dubious constitutional validity, thus undermining the predictability of law, the core of the rule of law. Secondly, the governance of the crises has accelerated and radicalized a long-term process of mutation of European constitutional law, resulting in major changes to the way in which power is organized in Europe (which I detailed by reference to changes in both structural and substantive European constitutional law). Thirdly, the governance of the crises has transformed the very essence of the kind of law that European law is, turning it into a means of (pseudo-)technocratic governance.

No polity emerges unchanged from a major crisis. At the time of writing, it has become almost self-evident that the European financial, economic, and fiscal crises were but manifestations of a deeper *existential* crisis of European integration. The refugee crisis and the semi-latent security crises seem to indicate that the Union has become incapable of meeting major challenges before they become open crises. It is far from obvious whether the European Union will survive the crises. The more the Union mutates, the less clear it is whether the price of overcoming the crises would not be unacceptable in normative, social, and cultural terms. Only exiting the crises in a way that allows us to be at the same time loyal to the ideal of the Social and Democratic *Rechtsstaat* constitutes a real way out.

JOURNAL OF LAW AND SOCIETY
VOLUME 44, NUMBER 1, MARCH 2017
ISSN: 0263-323X, pp. 79–98

The Bank, the Bond, and the Bail-out: On the Legal Construction of Market Discipline in the Eurozone

Harm Schepel*

The 'logic of the market', so holds the Court of Justice, is the standard of legality of financial assistance to indebted member states under EU law and, ultimately, the legal justification for strict conditionality and the imposition of austerity. This logic of the market, though, is different from actual market behaviour. Austerity, it turns out, is not the inevitable response to market pressures but a function of political substitutes for market discipline (Pringle) and technocratic truth seeking about the 'correct' price of debt (Gauweiler) which the Court has frozen into law. The perverse consequence of making the modalities of financial assistance dependent on the 'logic of the market' is, moreover, to render the assistance as ineffective and expensive as possible. 'The logic of the market' in the Court's case law is best seen as punitive and cynical politics masquerading as inept economics.

We must not simply abandon interest rates as a disciplinary mechanism. Governments need the markets. Markets tell governments things that governments don't want to hear. And they force governments to do the right thing.

Wolfgang Schäuble[1]

* Kent Law School and Brussels School of International Studies, University of Kent, Espace Rolin, Boulevard Louis Schmidt 2a, 1040 Brussels, Belgium
hjcs@kent.ac.uk

1 W. Schäuble, 'A Comprehensive Strategy for the Stabilization of the Economic and Monetary Union', speech at the Brussels Economic Forum, 18 May 2011, at <http://ec.europa.eu/economy_finance/bef2011/media/files/speech-brussels-economic-forum-schauble.pdf>.

INTRODUCTION

The power of market discipline to constrain spendthrift states is, by now, widely seen as an indispensable complement – or alternative – to the legal mechanisms in the Treaty and beyond to enforce the limits on member states' debts and deficits in Economic and Monetary Union.[2] Its legal anchoring is said to be in the 'no bail-out' clauses of Articles 123 and 125 TFEU, prohibiting monetary financing of national debt by the European Central Bank (ECB) and national central banks, and the assumption of liability for the debts of any member state by other member states and the Union. In one of its least contested observations in *Pringle*, the Court of Justice of the European Union held that the purpose of these 'no bail-out' clauses is to ensure that member states 'remain subject to the logic of the market when they enter into debt, since that ought to prompt them to maintain budgetary discipline.'[3] Accordingly, the 'logic of the market' is the standard of legality of financial assistance to indebted member states under EU law and, ultimately, the legal justification for strict conditionality and the imposition of austerity. This *logic* of the market, though, is something different from actual market behaviour. This was necessarily so in the two grand Euro-crisis judgments of the Court. The European Stability Mechanism (ESM) gives assistance only to member states who have lost access to markets in the first place, leaving the Court in *Pringle* with the task of deciding whether the conditions the ESM imposed on beneficiaries prompted budgetary discipline according to the logic of the market. The Outright Monetary Transactions (OMT) of the ECB were explicitly meant to correct the 'excessive' interest rates charged on indebted member states in the sovereign debt market, leaving the Court in *Gauweiler* with the arduous task of deciding whether the market behaved according to the logic of the market.[4] The *logic* of the market also has little bearing on the history of the cost of debt in the Eurozone; the markets have clearly got it 'wrong' time and again,[5] which makes the proposition that they can 'force governments to do the right thing' tenuous at best.

---

2 On the hardening of these legal constraints, see, for example, M. Adams, F. Fabbrini, and P. Larouche (eds.), *The Constitutionalization of European Budgetary Constraints* (2014).

3 C-370/12 *Thomas Pringle* EU:C:2012:756, para. 135. Compare M. Herdegen, 'Price Stability and Budgetary Restraints in the Economic and Monetary Union: The Law as Guardian of Economic Wisdom' (1998) 35 *Common Market Law Rev.* 9, at 22: '[T]he no bail-out provision of the EC Treaty cannot sweep away the fact that the euro area will constitute a solidarity compact, the members of which are under a *de facto* obligation to rescue defaulting members.'

4 C-62/14 *Peter Gauweiler* EU:C:2015:400.

5 'The story of the Eurozone is also a story of systematic mispricing of the sovereign debt': P. de Grauw and Y. Ji, 'Mispricing of Sovereign Risk and Macroeconomic Stability in the Eurozone' (2012) 50 *J. of Common Market Studies* 866, at 879.

This article is not concerned with the implications of the judgments in *Pringle* and *Gauweiler* on the constitutional structure and legal integrity of the European Union.[6] It focuses, instead, on the way the Court constructs 'market discipline' in its very absence as a legal requirement. It is a case of obscene politics masquerading as bad economics making for terrible law, rendering any financial assistance in the Eurozone both as ineffective and as painful as possible.

THE MARKET IN SOVEREIGN DEBT IN EUROLAND, PART I

The logic of the market in sovereign debt is cruel and clear. The worse a state's economic policy, the higher the debt, and the greater the risk of default. The higher that risk, the costlier borrowing becomes, and the more expensive the debt. The only way for states to get out of this vicious cycle is to pursue 'sound' budgetary policies, lower the debt, and be rewarded with lower interest rates. For this virtuous mechanism of market discipline to work, it is vital that government debt is priced 'correctly', which necessitates markets processing information about 'market fundamentals' to estimate credit risk. The importance of the 'no bail-out' clauses lies there: if the market expects states to be bailed out in case of trouble, they will price government debt accordingly and create 'moral hazard' for debtors: borrowing will be cheap, and governments will pile up debt rather than making the hard and politically unpopular choices required under 'sound' budgetary policy. In sum: disaster can only be avoided if disaster is a credible prospect. This price formation takes place on secondary markets: bonds from sovereigns considered under risk will get sold at lower prices than their nominal value. Since the interest on these cut-price bonds remains the same, the return on investment, the yield, goes up. To be able to attract investors for new bonds, states will naturally have to offer interest rates that match the yield. Figure 1 plots the debt-to-GDP ratios of Germany and the PIIGS[7] in relation to long-term yields on their sovereign bonds in the years leading up to the introduction of the Euro and the 'good years' thereafter until 2007.

6 See, for example, M. Dawson and F. de Witte, 'Constitutional Balance in the EU after the Euro-crisis' (2013) 76 *Modern Law Rev.* 817; E. Chiti and P. Teixeira, 'The constitutional implications of the European response to the financial and public debt crisis' (2013) 50 *Common Market Law Rev.* 683; K. Tuori and K. Tuori, *The Eurozone Crisis: A Constitutional Analysis* (2015); B. de Witte, 'Euro crisis responses and the EU legal order: increased institutional variation or constitutional mutation?' (2015) 11 *European Constitutional Law Rev.* 434; M. Ioannidis, 'Europe's New Transforma- tions: How the EU economic constitution changed during the Eurozone crisis' (2016) 53 *Common Market Law Rev.* 1237; and, especially, Menéndez in this volume.
7 Portugal, Italy, Ireland, Greece, and Spain.

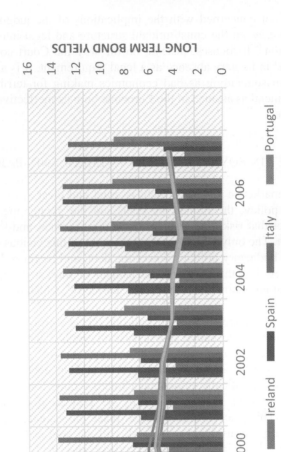

Figure 1. The Price of Debt, Part I

Source: Ameco

For all the crudeness of the measures, it is obvious that the figure shows exactly the opposite of what the market was supposed to do. Convergence of yields started before the introduction of the Euro, and by 2002 the spread of yields between member states with vastly divergent debt burdens steadied on scant decimals of percentage points. Greek and Italian debt ratios remained perilously close to double the 60 per cent prescribed by EMU, and yet the cost of their debt was nearly identical to that of Germany. Spanish and Irish debt went down significantly, and significantly below German debt levels, and yet the cost of their debt was nearly identical to that of Germany. Whatever else the markets may have been punishing or rewarding, 'budgetary discipline' or lack thereof was clearly not on their minds.[8]

If the markets were creating moral hazard among debtor states, one of the causes was clearly the moral hazard created among creditors by European banking regulation. Banks operate under capital requirements limiting their leverage and exposure. The capital ratio is expressed as a percentage of the regulatory capital banks are to hold in relation to their lending and investment. That lending and investment, in turn, is 'risk-weighted', forcing banks to have higher capital ratios for 'riskier' assets. Exposure limits seek to diversify risk by limiting the proportion of lending and investment to particular assets. These regulatory requirements have proven spectacularly ineffective, of course, with banks and other financial institutions finding ways above, beyond, and around almost any regulatory limit imposed on them.[9] For sovereign debt, however, there has never been any need at all to be creative. Exposure to member states' central governments is assigned a risk weight of 0 per cent.[10] Limits to exposure to sovereign debt are non-existent. Banks can pile up as much sovereign debt as they please.

Regulating risk away from sovereign debt seems a strange way to ensure that markets correctly price risk. And yet, perversely, the rationale behind the regulatory treatment of sovereign debt seems to have been to render markets more, not less, attuned to the risk of insolvency of member states. One of the factors polluting price formation, so the theory goes, is 'liquidity risk': if investors fear that they will not be able to re-sell their bonds, their

---

8 But see C. Rommerskirchen, 'Debt and Punishment: Market Discipline in the Eurozone' (2015) 20 *New Political Economy* 752 (finding that membership of EMU reduces market punishment but increases policy makers' responsiveness).

9 See, for example, A. Admati and M. Hellweg, *The Bankers' New Clothes – What's wrong with banking and what to do about it* (2013).

10 Article 114 (4), Regulation 575/2013 on prudential requirements for credit institutions and investment firms, (2013) OJ L 321/6. Frankfurt has had enough: see J. Weidmann, 'Stop encouraging banks to load up on state debt' *Financial Times*, 1 October 2013; C. Buch, M. Koetter, and J. Ohls, 'Banks and sovereign risk: a granular view' (2013), Deutsche Bundesbank Discussion Paper 29/2013; and Deutsche Bundesbank, *Annual Report: Reducing the privileged regulatory treatment of sovereign exposures* (2014). See, also, European Systemic Risk Board (ESRB), *ESRB Report on the regulatory treatment of sovereign exposures* (2015).

appetite for sovereign bonds will go down and the cost of debt will go up. The zero-risk weighting, by increasing demand for sovereign debt, will increase liquidity and hence 'free' markets to price risk 'correctly'. With a bit of effort, one could still see 'the logic': that demand for the asset *class* of sovereign debt will go up and the return on the asset *class* of sovereign debt will go down does not necessarily mean that financial institutions will not be able to distinguish between the sovereign debt of Germany and that of, say, Greece or Italy. Except that banks will want to make some money even on zero-risk-weighted assets. As long as there is some spread left between Italian and Greek bonds and German bonds, periphery debt will be the more rewarding. As the spread decreases, banks will need more and more of periphery debt for it still to be worthwhile, thus increasing demand further, and decreasing the yield further still until the spread is all but gone. At this point banks find themselves with enormous leveraged exposure to sovereigns whose budgetary policies are blissfully unaffected by any market discipline. It is here that the final perversity kicks in: in what Mark Blyth has called 'the mother of all hazard trades', banks decided to buy up still more periphery debt at still higher leverage (and at still lower yields) until they became so big as to virtually ensure that they would be 'too big to fail' and be bailed out in case their sovereign assets should lose value and the house of cards come tumbling down.[11] A few odd rogue banks that are 'too big to fail' can, of course, be bailed out without getting states into insurmountable trouble. An entire banking system that is collectively 'too big to fail' will, however, become 'too big to bail'.[12] And so the banking crisis transforms into a sovereign debt crisis.[13]

---

11 M. Blyth, *Austerity – The History of a Dangerous Idea* (2013) 81. See, also, more formally, V. Acharya and S. Steffen, 'The "greatest" carry trade ever? Understanding Eurozone bank risks' (2015) 115 *J. of Financial Economics* 215. The plot thickens when one factors in the repo market, or the way banks use sovereign debt as collateral in borrowing cash: see D. Gabor and C. Ban, 'Banking on Bonds: The New Links Between States and Markets' (2016) 54 *J. of Common Market Studies* 617.

12 See, for example, A. Mody and D. Sandri, 'The Eurozone crisis: how banks and sovereigns came to be joined at the hip' (2012) 27 *Economic Policy* 199, and V. Acharya, I. Drechsler, and P. Schnabl, 'A Pyrrhic Victory? Bank Bailouts and Sovereign Credit Risk' (2014) 69 *J. of Finance* 2689.

13 Cumulated support measures to banks in the Eurozone as a whole amounted to 8 per cent of GDP. See ECB, *The fiscal impact of financial sector support during the crisis*, ECB Economic Bulletin, Issue 6/2015, at <https://www.ecb.europa.eu/pub/pdf/other/eb201506_article02.en.pdf>. This is a common pattern in history. Even without large-scale bail-outs, Reinhart and Rogoff estimate that government debts 'typically' rise about 86 per cent in the three years following a systemic financial crisis, largely owing to collapsing revenues: C. Reinhart and K. Rogoff, 'From Financial Crash to Debt Crisis' (2011) 101 *Am. Economic Rev.* 1676.

In an attempt to address the ensuing crisis, the European Stability Mechanism was set up to provide financial assistance to member states in severe difficulties. Not unreasonably, the matter of the compatibility of financial assistance with the 'no bail-out clause' was raised widely, and came before the Court of Justice in *Pringle*.[14] The Court derived from Articles 122 and 123 TFEU that the purpose of Article 125 TFEU cannot be to prohibit *all* financial assistance by one member state to another.[15] To divine the precise meaning of the prohibition, then, the Court decided to look at the purpose of the provision, which it formulated as follows:

> The prohibition laid down in Article 125 TFEU ensures that the Member States remain subject to the logic of the market when they enter into debt, since that ought to prompt them to maintain budgetary discipline. Compliance with such discipline contributes at Union level to the attainment of a higher objective, namely maintaining the financial stability of the monetary union.[16]

From this, the Court held it to follow logically that the reach of the 'no bail-out' clause is limited to forms of financial assistance that 'diminish' the 'incentive' for member states to pursue sound budgetary policies.[17] From that, in turn, it follows for the Court that bail-outs are perfectly compatible with Article 125 TFEU as long as the beneficiary member state 'remains responsible for its commitments to its creditors' and if they are subject to 'strict conditions'.[18]

The aim of Article 125 TFEU is thus to ensure the proper working of the market in sovereign debt. Now, as such, the link between the 'no bail-out' clause and correct price formation on sovereign bond markets is fairly straightforward: unless default is a credible prospect, the risk of default is never to going to be priced properly, and the market will not be able to provide the correct incentives to indebted states. In other words, for the 'logic of the market' to exert its magic, it is vital that creditors live in fear of losing their money,[19] and that debtors live in fear of full-blown disaster. If

---

14 See, generally, for example, T. Beukers and B. de Witte, 'The Court of Justice approves the creation of the European Stability Mechanism outside the EU legal order: *Pringle*' (2013) 50 *Common Market Law Rev.* 805; P. Craig, '*Pringle*: Legal Reasoning, Text, Purpose and Teleology' (2013) 20 *Maastricht J. of European and Comparative Law* 3; G. Beck, 'The Court of Justice, legal reasoning, and the *Pringle* case-law as the continuation of politics by other means' (2014) 39 *European Law Rev.* 234.
15 *Pringle*, op. cit., n. 3, para. 132.
16 id., para. 135.
17 id., para. 136.
18 id., para. 137.
19 See Q. Peel and R. Atkins, 'Financial Markets "do not understand the euro"', interview with Wolfgang Schäuble, *Financial Times*, 6 December 2010. ('Mr. Schäuble warned that if private bondholders did not bear some risk, as well as the reward, of investing, it could destroy the legitimacy of the market economy and even "our political order".')

we take the Court seriously, then, we are to believe that a credible threat of financial instability in the monetary union contributes to the 'higher objective' of financial stability in the monetary union. For the compatibility of the ESM with Article 125 TFEU, the disastrous implication of the 'logic of the market' is that a bail-out is only lawful if everyone behaves as if there were no bail-out. That, in turn, leads to an obligation on the ESM to be as ineffective as possible, and to inflict as much pain and misery on the populations of debtor states as feasible.

The distributional consequences of the requirement that any financial assistance may not intervene in the relationship between the debtor state and its creditors are clear enough: by granting loans to debtor states with which these are then to service their debt to private creditors in full, taxpayers from creditor states are effectively transferring money to (their) banks. This may not be fair, but it could still conceivably be useful to citizens from debtor states if the loans were plentiful enough to guarantee creditors payment: in that case, risk premiums would disappear, debt would become cheaper, and the debtor state could perhaps start thinking about allocating some of its very scarce resources to purposes other than paying off banks. But Article 125 TFEU will not actually allow loans to be *that* useful. Advocate General Kokott explains:

> Direct support of the creditors is prohibited, while indirect support, which arises as a result of the support to the debtor Member State, is not prohibited. The creditors of a Member State will therefore as a rule benefit from support given to that Member State. There remains however for the potential creditors of a Member State an additional uncertainty as to whether possible financial assistance to a Member State may actually lead to the satisfaction of their demands. To that extent, the voluntary support of a Member State need not inevitably be accompanied by either a complete or even partial satisfaction of the Member State's creditors. *That uncertainty is intended to promote the objective that Member States have differentiated interest rates on the capital markets.*[20]

It is an astonishing piece of logic that will make the legality of a financial assistance programme conditional upon its being useless.

The Court itself is much less candid, or just less clear. For loans and purchases of bonds on primary markets, the requirement poses no problem: here, the beneficiary member state contracts new debt, and remains responsible to its original creditors for existing debt.[21] Article 18 of the ESM Treaty, however, also makes provision for the purchase of sovereign bonds on secondary markets. If it does not exactly or necessarily constitute 'support', such a transaction surely does at least 'benefit' the original bond-holder: after all, if she couldn't see any benefit in the sale, she wouldn't be selling. In addressing this, the Court pens one of the more mysterious passages in *Pringle*:

20 *Pringle*, op. cit., n. 3, view of A.G. Kokott, para. 148 (emphasis added).
21 id., paras. 139–140.

86

Next, as regards the purchase on the secondary market of bonds issued by an ESM Member, it is clear that, in such a situation, the issuing Member State remains solely answerable to repay the debts in question. The fact that the ESM as the purchaser on that market of bonds issued by an ESM Member pays a price to the holder of those bonds, who is the creditor of the issuing ESM Member, does not mean that the ESM becomes responsible for the debt of that ESM Member to that creditor. *That price may be significantly different from the value of the claims contained in those bonds, since the price depends on the rules of supply and demand on the secondary market of bonds issued by the ESM Member concerned.*[22]

The Court obviously thinks it is important that the price of the bonds be determined under normal market conditions, but it is a little cryptic as to why this is. Thankfully, the Advocate General provides some help in the exegesis:

Although in the event of such a purchase of bonds the funds of the ESM flow directly to the creditor, in my opinion the prohibition on directly benefiting creditors continues to be observed if the bonds are acquired on normal market terms. The reason is that, in that case, the previous bondholder obtains his money as he would from any ordinary third party and does not derive any specific advantage from the capacity of another Member State. When an ordinary purchase is made on the securities market the creditor would also be unaware that the purchaser of the bond is a Member State. Such a bond purchase is therefore not designed to build up the confidence of potential creditors of a Member State in the capacity of another Member State.

It is not evident that the deployment of financial assistance instruments under Article 18 of the ESM Treaty would necessarily deviate from the circumstances described. The purchase of bonds by the ESM in accordance with that provision therefore is not a priori necessarily incompatible with Article 125 TFEU; rather there exists in any event the possibility of effecting those purchases in a way that complies with its provisions.[23]

If this is really the reasoning behind the Court's reference to the laws of supply and demand, it is easy to see why it wouldn't necessarily want to spell it out more clearly. By the time the ESM is triggered, the threat of insolvency of a state in need of help will be such that bond holders are selling off to save what they can. The price will be down, and the yield will be up. This is vulture fund territory: at a few cents to the Euro, investment in junk bonds is very risky, but potentially very profitable *if* the state should be able and willing (or forced) to pay the full nominal value of the claim. According to the Court's logic, purchases of bonds in such circumstances are perfectly fine under Article 125 TFEU: the debtor state will still have to repay its debt, and the previous bond holders do not derive any benefit up and above 'normal' market prices. As long as the ESM conducts these purchases by stealth and without upsetting the market, the transactions may conceivably be considered compatible with the no bail-out clause.

Assuming that the ESM wasn't set up as a vulture fund, however, it is hard to see what the benefit would be to anyone for it to act the way the

22 id., para. 141 (emphasis added).
23 id., view of A.G. Kokott, paras. 158–159.

Court instructs it to conduct its business: a financial assistance programme that is not allowed to make either creditors or debtors better off is not likely to be of much use to anyone. The very purpose of purchasing bonds on secondary markets is to upset 'normal market conditions': restore confidence, increase demand, get the price up, get the yield down, and get the cost of debt down. And as Mario Draghi would show to dramatic effect in the OMT saga, this is best done not in secret but by waving a bazooka around.

If the 'logic of the market' makes the ESM as ineffective as feasible, it also makes its assistance as painful as possible on the recipient state and its population. It may be worth recalling how the Court gets from a 'no bail-out clause' to a requirement of strict conditionality – and thereby freezes the enactment of austerity measures into a legal obligation for states in financial distress. On the Court's construction, Article 125 TFEU does not actually prohibit financial assistance, it exists only to preserve 'the logic of the market' in sovereign debt. Article 125 TFEU does not actually impose budget discipline; the impetus to pursue sound policies is merely a contingent by-product of 'the logic of the market'. That logic, in turn, depends on price formation not being polluted by expectations of bail-outs. Once a facility is in place to in effect 'bail out' debtor states, that logic is obviously out of the window, and the markets are not going to exert any disciplinary power. The Court's fundamental move, then, is to sanction the substitution of political decisions on austerity for the 'logic of the market' and to force assisted states to behave *as if* they were headed for insolvency. The purpose of this exercise is not to work out the most sensible path to the restoration of growth and financial health for the assisted state but to restore some semblance of 'the logic of the market' to the sovereign debt markets of *other* member states: if not by the discipline of unpolluted markets themselves, states will have to be deterred from pursuing unsound budgetary policies by the prospect of having to live through the same amount of pain and misery inflicted on states assisted by the ESM. The measure of punishment inflicted, then, is not a matter of market forces but of a political decision whose legality is bounded by theoretically contested and empirically unfounded assumptions about the 'the logic of the market' and about the sacrifices the markets *would have demanded* of debtor states had they not been unable to meet the demands of the markets in the first place.[24] All of this comes totally unhinged when the Court will have to admit, as a matter of EU law, that the markets get it 'wrong'.

---

24 As Michelle Everson puts it: 'the most disturbing feature of crisis-busting jurisprudence is its legal ossification of a violently disputed economic theory of market-disciplined structural renewal at a time of radicalized protest against austerity at national level.' M. Everson, 'A Technocracy of Governing: Power without the State; Power without the Market' in *The European Crisis and the Transformation of Transnational Governance*, eds. C. Joerges and C. Glinski (2014) 229. See, also, Kaupa in this volume.

After the collapse of Lehman Brothers, sovereign debt markets in the Eurozone woke up from their slumber and for the fateful years between 2008 and 2012 seemed to be doing what the 'logic of the market' would predict. As Greek sovereign debt spiralled out of control, so did the yield on Greek bonds. Rapidly rising Portuguese debt was duly punished with increased borrowing costs. As Spain and Ireland recapitalized their banks and turned a financial crisis into a sovereign debt crisis, they too were hit hard. [25] And even Italy – which largely remained as sluggish and indebted as it had been for a long time – came in for harsh treatment. As Figure 2 shows, whatever the markets woke up from or to, the reaction was abrupt and violent. The disciplinary power of the market was finally unleashed.

With the power of financial markets acutely felt, it became an article of faith that discrimination between member states was a good thing, and that the spread was a vital mechanism to have spendthrift states live up their responsibility and engage in the austerity policies of 'adjustment' and 'consolidation'. The *Bundesbank* rejoiced: 'market discipline – *if actually exercised by market actors* – offers a decisive incentive to guarantee sustainable long-term finances in the euro area.'[26]

The moral, political, and macroeconomic argument was won so decisively that the only space for viable contestation of austerity politics seemed to become econometrics. It was not the power of financial markets in itself that was questioned, but their wisdom: what if they got it 'wrong'? An enormous literature spawned fairly soon from central banks and think tanks on the question of whether the markets were 'right', or more modestly, whether the 'correction' or 'revaluation' could plausibly be explained by 'market fundamentals'[27] or rather at least partly also by

---

25 There are, of course, enormous differences between banking systems in the various member states, which go a long way in explaining the different paths towards sovereign debt crises (or not). See, for example, I. Hardie and D. Howarth, '*Die Krise* but not *La Crise*? The Financial Crisis and the Transformation of German and French Banking Systems' (2009) 47 *J. of Common Market Studies* 1017; I. Hardie and D. Howarth (eds.), *Market-Based Banking and the International Financial Crisis* (2013); and L. Quaglia and S. Royo, 'Banks and the political economy of the sovereign debt crisis in Italy and Spain' (2015) 22 *Rev. of International Political Economy* 485. The bigger the banking sector, the greater the effect on sovereign bond yields: S. Gerlach, A. Schulz, and G. Wolff, 'Banking and sovereign risk in the Euro area' (2010) Deutsche Bundesbank Discussion Paper 09/2010. The bigger the bail-out, the greater the effect on sovereign bond yields: see M. Fratzscher and M. Rieth, 'Monetary policy, bank bailouts and the sovereign-bank risk nexus in the Euro area' (2015) Centre for Economic Policy Research (CEPR) Discussion Paper 10370.
26 Deutsche Bundesbank, *Monthly Report* (June 2011) 44 (emphasis added).
27 The econometric models are complex, largely because of the need to avoid the almost inevitable endogeneity of nearly every conceivable set of correlating variables. See, for example, M.-G. Attinasi, C. Checherita, and C. Nickel, 'What explains the surge

---

89

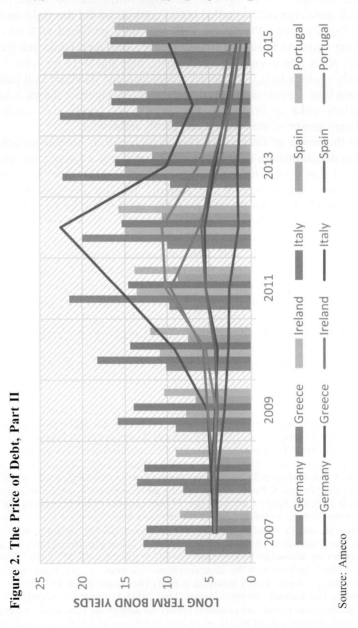

Figure 2. The Price of Debt, Part II

Source: Ameco

panic and fear.[28] A lot hinged on the matter: after all, 'if markets can stay irrational longer than a country can stay insolvent, their disciplinary power is considerably weakened.'[29] Dominant theory for quite some time held on to the central role of country-specific weak fundamentals, and of increased scepticism regarding peripheral states' solvency – rather than contagious fears of a contagious break-up of the Eurozone. The *Bundesbank* at one point even suggested that the financial markets were sophisticated enough to price sovereign bonds according to the now infamous thesis of the 90 per cent debt-to-GDP 'cliff' above which growth was nigh impossible:[30]

> The at times abrupt and massive revaluations can also be explained by the nonlinear relationship between the credit risk and the aforementioned fundamentals... There could be a type of threshold value with regard to fundamentals such as the debt ratio where – once surpassed – the markets are especially critical of any further increase.[31]

The debate settled when the European Central Bank espoused the theory of a 'bad equilibrium' – 'namely an equilibrium where you have self-fulfilling expectations that feed upon themselves and generate very adverse scenarios' – and Mario Draghi announced the OMT programme in September 2012 with the assurance of doing 'whatever it takes' to reverse these expectations.[32] As can be gleaned readily from Figure 2, it worked rather well, and spreads were brought down despite periphery debt levels rising unper-

in Euro area sovereign spreads during the financial crisis of 2007–2009?' (2009) ECB Working Papers 1131; S. Barrios, P. Iversen, M. Lewandowska, and R. Setzer, 'Determinants of intra-euro area government bond spreads during the financial crisis' (2009) European Economy Economic Papers 388/2009; M. Arghyrou and A. Kontonikas, 'The EMU sovereign-debt crisis: Fundamentals, expectations and contagion' (2012) 22 *J. of International Financial Markets, Institutions and Money* 658; J. Beirne and M. Fratzscher, 'The pricing of sovereign risk and contagion during the European sovereign debt crisis' (2013) ECB Working Papers 1625; C. Chiarella et al., 'Fear of Fundamentals? Heterogenous beliefs in the European sovereign CDS market' (2015) 32 *J. of Empirical Finance* 19.

28 A thesis brought to prominence by Paul de Grauwe. See, for example, P. de Grauwe and Y. Ji, 'Self-fulfilling Crises in the Eurozone: An Empirical Test' (2013) 34 *J. of International Money and Finance* 15.

29 C. Favero and A. Missale, 'Sovereign spreads in the eurozone: which prospects for a Eurobond?' (2012) 27 *Economic Policy* 231, at 267.

30 C. Reinhart and K. Rogoff, 'Growth in a Time of Debt' (2010) 100 *Am. Economic Rev.* 573, notoriously undermined by T. Herndon, M. Ash, and R. Pollin, 'Does high public debt consistently stifle economic growth? A critique of Reinhart and Rogoff' (2014) 38 *Cambridge J. of Economics* 257 and, perhaps even more painfully, by A. Pescatori, D. Sandri, and J. Simon, 'Debt and growth: is there a magic threshold?' (2014) IMF Working Paper 14/34.

31 Deutsche Bundesbank, op. cit., n. 26, pp. 40–1.

32 ECB, Introductory statement to the press conference (with Q&A), 6 September 2012, at <http://www.ecb.europa.eu/press/pressconf/2012/html/is120906.en.html>.

turbedly. So much for 'fundamentals'.[33] Yet, spreads remained decidedly higher than they had been before the crisis, leading to contentment in Frankfurt. In 2014, the Bundesbank reiterated its hardwiring of the EMU rulebook, proclaiming that spreads are not 'proof of a lack of integration but represent an acceptable, if not to say highly desirable state of affairs which re-affirms the central role played by individual national responsibility within the euro area's regulatory framework.'[34]

The debate about the markets' rationality played out differently in different policy contexts. Fears of 'moral hazard' were enough to stifle any serious discussion about the mutualization of debt through the issuing of Eurobonds.[35] When first launched in the early days of the Euro, the idea was driven by worries about market fragmentation and lack of liquidity.[36] Latter-day iterations, on the other hand, bent over backwards to devise schemes, mechanisms, and institutional arrangements to square the circle of mutual-ized debt, market discipline, and individual responsibility.[37] The Com-mission's own short-lived proposal of 'stability bonds' is a good example of this. The proposal admits to 'possibly some degree of overshooting' on the part of the markets, but puts such faith in their disciplining power none-theless, that 'moral hazard' is to be avoided at all cost.[38] And thus:

> While yields of Stability Bonds would be market-based, funding costs might be differentiated across Member States depending on their fiscal positions or fiscal policies, or their market creditworthiness, as reflected by the risk-premium of national issuances over common issuances. This would provide an incentive for sound fiscal policies within the system and would mimic market discipline though in a smoother, more consistent fashion than markets. Such an incentive ... could be further enhanced with 'punitive' rates in case of slippages from plans.[39]

33 See, for example, P. de Grauwe and Y. Ji, 'Disappearing government bond spreads in the Eurozone: Back to normal?' (2014) CEPS Working Document 396; and M. Chang and P. Leblond, 'All In: Market expectations of Eurozone integrity in the sovereign debt crisis' (2015) 22 *Rev. of International Political Economy* 626.

34 Deutsche Bundesbank, *Monthly Report* (January 2014) 75.

35 See M. Matthijs and K. McNamara, 'The Euro Crisis' Theory Effect: Northern Saints, Southern Sinners, and the Demise of the Eurobond' (2015) 37 *J. of European Integration* 229.

36 Report of the Giovannini Group, 'Co-ordinated Public Debt Issuance in the Euro Area' (2000), at <http://ec.europa.eu/economy_finance/publications/publication6372_en.pdf>. The report, remarkably for post-crisis sensitivities, does not once mention the concepts of 'moral hazard' or even 'market discipline.'

37 See, for example, J. Muellbauer, 'Conditional Eurobonds and the Eurozone sovereign debt crisis'(2013) 29 *Oxford Rev. of Economic Policy* 610; A. Hild, B. Herz, and C. Bauer, 'Structured Eurobonds: Limiting Liability and Distributing Profits' (2014) 52 *J. of Common Market Studies* 250; R. Beetsma and K. Mavromatis, 'An analysis of eurobonds'(2014) 45 *J. of International Money and Finance* 91.

38 European Commission, *Green paper on the feasibility of introducing Stability Bonds*, COM(2011)818 final, 7.

39 id., p. 23.

With conditional financial assistance functioning as *ersatz* 'logic of the market', the problem over the last few years has been that financial markets have been defeating the economic theory behind austerity policies.[40] Periphery countries are caught in a spiral of fiscal contraction, lower growth, higher debt, higher borrowing costs, more fiscal contraction, and so on. This may seem perfectly intuitive, but it was not supposed to be like this. Ecofin ministers, the European Commission, and the ECB have all been under the spell of the theory of 'expansionary fiscal consolidation' according to which serious spending cuts and deep structural reform may lead to short-term contractions, but will, after a year or so, actually return indebted countries to sustained growth.[41] The blatant failure of austerity policies to deliver anything of the kind has led to a fierce debate between institutional creditors. For a chastened IMF, exaggerated growth forecasts and projections stem from a radical underestimation of the 'fiscal multiplier'.[42] The European Commission will have none of that, however. For them, the problem is simply that financial markets are 'short-sighted', with sovereign debt spreads and borrowing costs frustrating any gains from fiscal consolidations.[43] In other words, the financial markets just don't 'get it'.

---

40 Markets do not welcome austerity: I. McMenamin, M. Breen, and J. Muñoz-Portillo, 'Austerity and credibility in the Eurozone' (2015) 16 *European Union Politics* 45.

41 The groundwork of the theory lies in F. Giavazzi and M. Pagano, 'Can Severe Fiscal Contractions be Expansionary? Tales of Two Small European Countries' in *NBER Macroeconomics Annual 1990, Vol. 5*, eds. O. Blanchard and S. Fischer (1990) 75; A. Alesina and S. Ardanga, 'Tales of Fiscal Adjustment' (1998) 13 *Economic Policy* 489. On how Alesina swayed the powers that be, see M. Blyth, *Austerity – The History of a Dangerous Idea* (2013) 169–77; S. Dellepiane-Avellaneda, 'The Political Power of Economic Ideas: The Case of "Expansionary Fiscal Contractions"' (2015) 17 *Brit. J. of Politics and International Relations* 319; and O. Helgadóttir, 'The Bocconi boys go to Brussels: Italian economic ideas, professional networks and European austerity' (2016) 32 *J. of European Public Policy* 392. Incredibly, the European Commission is still a fan: see European Commission, *Report on Public Finances in EMU 2014* (2014), rehearsing episodes of successful consolidations, concluding that revenue-based consolidations do not work nearly as well as expenditure-based consolidations, and recommending, on p. 134, that 'cuts should concentrate on the more rigid and persistent components of government expenditure, namely compensation of employees and social benefits.'

42 See O. Blanchard and D. Leigh, 'Growth Forecasts and Fiscal Multipliers' (2013) IMF Working Paper 13/1. On the development of policy in the IMF, see C. Ban, 'Austerity versus Stimulus? Understanding Fiscal Policy Change at the International Monetary Fund since the Great Recession' (2014) 28 *Governance* 167.

43 See, for example, European Commission, *Report on Public Finances in EMU 2012* (2012) 115; J. Boussard, F. de Castro, and M. Salto, 'Fiscal Multipliers and Debt Dynamics in Consolidations' (2012) European Economy Economic Papers 460/2012; K. Berti, F. de Castro, and M. Salto, 'Effects of fiscal consolidation envisaged in the 2013 Stability and Convergence Programmes on public debt dynamics in EU Member States' (2013) European Economy Economic Papers 504/2013. The plot thickens in a theory that holds that the large presence of public creditors with real or perceived seniority pushes up yields in the market: S. Steinkamp and F. Westerman, 'The role of creditor seniority in Europe's sovereign debt crisis' (2014) 29 *Economic Policy* 495.

With the OMT programme, the ECB signalled its readiness to buy up massive quantities of government bonds of periphery countries from secondary markets. Not unreasonably, the compatibility of the programme with the ECB's mandate and Article 123 TFEU was raised widely, and came to the Court of Justice via an extraordinarily didactic preliminary reference from the Bundesverfassungsgericht in *Gauweiler*.[44]

The first task at hand was to find a way to classify OMT as falling within the ECB's mandate as an instrument of 'monetary', rather than 'economic' policy. Since the Court had stated categorically in *Pringle* that 'financial assistance to a member State clearly does not fall within monetary policy',[45] the imperative was to cast the ECB's intervention – which rather obviously had as its immediate objective to lower spreads and rates and so to lower refinancing costs for indebted member states – as something other than 'assistance'.

To this end, the Court had little choice but to side with the ECB against both the Bundesverfassungsgricht and the Bundesbank. It thus took over the ECB's theory of having to clear noise from the system: since the effectiveness of monetary policy depends on the transmission of 'impulses' sent out across the money market to the various sectors of the economy, the concept of 'monetary policy' has to include any measures designed to repair that transmission mechanism in case it is disrupted.[46] The Court also accepted the ECB's analysis that the economic situation in the euro area was characterized by 'high volatility and extreme spreads', spreads that:

> were not accounted for solely by macroeconomic differences between the States concerned but were caused, in part, by the demand for excessive risk premia for the bonds issued by certain Member States, such premia being intended to guard against the risk of a break-up of the euro area.[47]

The next step was, then, simply, to classify 'excessive' interest rates as noise:

> It is undisputed that interest rates for the government bonds of a given State play a decisive role in the setting of interest rates applicable to the various economic actors in that State, in the value of the portfolios of financial institutions holding such bonds and in the ability of such institutions to obtain

---

44 See, generally, D. Adamski, 'Economic Constitution of the Euro area after the *Gauweiler* preliminary ruling' (2015) 52 *Common Market Law Rev.* 1451; M. Wilkinson, 'The Euro is Irreversible! ... Or Is It?: On OMT, Austerity and the Threat of "Grexit"' (2015) 16 *German Law J.* 1049; V. Borger, 'Outright monetary transactions and the stability mandate of the ECB: *Gauweiler*' (2016) 53 *Common Market Law Rev.* 139; P. Craig and M. Markakis, '*Gauweiler* and the legality of outright monetary transactions' (2016) 41 *European Law Rev.* 4.

45 *Pringle*, op. cit., n. 3, para. 57.

46 *Gauweiler*, op. cit., n. 4, para. 50.

47 id., para. 72.

liquidity. Therefore, eliminating or reducing the excessive risk premia demanded of the government bonds of a member State is likely to avoid the volatility and level of those premia from hindering the transmission of the effects of the ESCB's monetary policy decisions to the economy of that State and from jeopardizing the singleness of monetary policy.[48]

This is not the kind of economic engineering that finds much favour in Frankfurt and Karlsruhe. Probably the most significant argument against the ECB's theory is the one the Court of Justice completely ignores. As the German constitutional court points out, it is hard to conceive of *any* debt crisis where the 'monetary policy transmission mechanism' is not disrupted:

> A critical deterioration of the solvency of a state typically coincides with a corresponding deterioration of the solvency of the national banking sector (so-called bank-state nexus). As a result, in this situation, the lending practices of the banks tend to hardly reflect the reductions in the key interest rate anymore; the monetary policy transmission mechanism is disrupted. If purchases of government bonds were admissible every time the monetary policy trans-mission mechanism is disrupted, it would amount to granting the European Central Bank the power to remedy any deterioration of the credit rating of a euro area Member State through the purchase of that state's government bonds. [49]

Even if the argument here seems unaffected by the question of the rationality of spreads and rates, the more visible and notorious disagreement between the two Courts consisted largely of a rehearsal of the econometric debate about the role of 'fundamentals' in the spreads. The Bundes-verfassungsgericht had no trouble working this seamlessly into an argument about the role of 'market discipline' in the incentive structure of EMU, and throwing *Pringle* back in the face of the Court of Justice:

> According to the European Central Bank, these spreads are partly based on fear – declared to be irrational – of investors of a reversibility of the euro. However, according to the convincing expertise of the *Bundesbank*, such interest rate spreads only reflect the skepticism of market participants that individual Member States will show sufficient budgetary discipline to stay permanently solvent. Pursuant to the design of the Treaty on the Functioning of the European Union, the existence of such spreads is entirely intended. As the Court of Justice of the European Union has pointed out in its *Pringle* decision, they are an expression of the independence of national budgets, which relies on market incentives and cannot be lowered by bond purchases by central banks without suspending this independence.[50]

The Bunderverfassungsgericht surely opens itself up to justified criticism embracing a theory that is demonstrably false: the convincing expertise of Paul de Grauwe and his collaborators does a fine job undermining the

---

48 id., para 78.
49 BVerfG, Order of the Second Senate of 14 January 2014, 2 BvR 2728/13, BVerfGE 134, 366, para. 97.
50 id., para. 71.

assertion that spreads are *only* a function of public debt ratios.[51] But this criticism ignores the way the constitutional court later on develops a stance separate from the 'convincing expertise' of the Bundesbank that is rather more interesting. Where the court first references 'explanations' given by the Bundesbank according to which 'one cannot, in practice, divide interest rates into a rational and an irrational part',[52] it subsequently dismisses the distinction entirely as not just 'impossible to operationalise', but as 'irrelevant' and 'meaningless':

> Spreads always only result from the market participants' expectations and are, *regardless of their rationality*, essential for market-based pricing. To single out and neutralise supposedly identifiable individual causes would be tantamount to an arbitrary interference with market activity.[53]

The Bundesverfassungsgericht, in other words, has no difficulty at all in conceiving of markets as social and political institutions consisting of operators and participants with hopes, fears, and interests. It may be 'market fundamentalist', but its faith and loyalty is to markets as they actually behave. What the Court of Justice does is altogether more insidious: this is market fundamentalism loyal not to actual market behaviour, but to some mysterious equilibrium reached by hypothetical markets that we have never actually witnessed in real life, that we have no particularly compelling theoretical reason to believe could ever materialize, and that we have to accept on the force of our faith in the expertise of the ECB.[54] By accepting the theory of 'excessive' interest rates, the Court also embraces the concept of 'right' and 'proper' interest rates that can be discerned and engineered by technicians. This is not just an academic exercise: this elusive equilibrium is the dividing line between admissible monetary policy and prohibited economic policy, and the exact measure of how much austerity is legally required of debtor states.

When the ESM buys up bonds on secondary markets, it is 'economic policy.' When the ECB does the same, and makes these purchases conditional on compliance with the ESM's 'macroeconomic adjustment' demands, it is 'monetary policy.' In this regard, the Court holds, it is the difference between the objectives of the respective operations which is decisive.[55] By accepting the ECB's objective of 'repairing' a 'disrupted' monetary policy transmission mechanism, and by demanding that OMT

---

51 See P. De Grauwe, Y. Ji, and A. Steinbach, 'The EU debt crisis: testing and revisiting conventional legal doctrine' (2016) LSE 'Europe in Question' discussion paper 108/2016.

52 BverfGE, op. cit., n. 49, para. 71.

53 id., para. 98 (emphasis added).

54 *Gauweiler*, op. cit., n. 4, para. 75 ('nothing more can be required of the ESCB apart from that it use its economic expertise and the necessary technical means at its disposal to carry out that analysis with all care and accuracy').

55 id., para. 64.

cease 'as soon as these objectives have been achieved',[56] the magical moment when 'the market' will be restored to its purified 'logic' is the precise boundary of the legality of the programme.[57]

That equilibrium is also the the measure of exactly the right amount of 'market discipline' member states ought to be subjected to. Pulling the plug on OMT as soon as the noise has been cleared means

> (i) that the Member States cannot, in determining their budgetary policy, rely on the certainty that the ESCB will at a future point purchase their government bonds on secondary markets and (ii) that the programme in question cannot be implemented in a way which would bring about a harmonisation of the interest rates applied to the government bonds of the Member States of the euro area regardless of the differences arising from their macroeconomic or budgetary situation.
>
> The adoption and implementation of such a programme thus do not permit the Member States to adopt a budgetary policy which fails to take account of the fact that they will be compelled, in the event of a deficit, to seek financing on the markets, or result in them being protected against the consequences which a change in their macroeconomic or budgetary situation may have in that regard.[58]

Before that moment is reached, however, we still need conditionality and austerity, lest OMT should be perceived 'as an incentive to dispense with fiscal consolidation'.[59]

More disastrously still, the Court demands – as it did in *Pringle* – that the ECB's intervention – which has as its objective to return irrational markets to the 'logic of the market' – takes place according to the 'logic of the market'. And that means – as it did in *Pringle* – that the legality of the intervention depends on its being as ineffective as possible. This comes out clearly in the Court's treatment of Article 123 TFEU's prohibition of monetary financing. This outlaws purchases on primary markets, but not purchases on secondary markets. The Court, however, in view of the objective of 'encouraging' sound budgetary policies, will not allow the ECB to go on a buying spree that would have 'an effect equivalent to that of direct purchases of government bonds'.[60] That means, in turn, that the ECB will have to disrupt the functioning of the irrational market according to the logic of the irrational market. And thus 'safeguards' have to be built in to OMT: enough time should be left between issues on primary markets and purchases on secondary markets for 'normal' price formation to take place; there may not be any prior announcement of whether and how much the ECB plans to buy where, lest 'normal' price formation is corrupted;[61] the ECB may not

---

56 id., para. 82.
57 id., paras. 82 and 112.
58 id., paras. 113–114.
59 id., para. 120.
60 id., para. 97.
61 id., paras. 104–107.

claim seniority creditor status lest OMT would affect 'normal' price formation.[62] In one of the most startling passages of the judgment, the Court notes with apparent regret that 'it is true that, despite those safeguards, the ESCB's intervention remains capable of having … some influence on the functioning of the primary and secondary sovereign debt markets', only to remember, almost as an afterthought, that such an effect is the very purpose of the OMT programme.[63]

CONCLUSION

At the time of writing, the ECB has purchased, through its Public Sector Purchase Programme, close to a *trillion* Euros' worth of central government bonds, almost a quarter of which from Germany.[64] The only Eurozone country excluded from the extravaganza is Greece, whose 'credit quality' does not meet the Bank's exacting standards. It is inherent in 'the logic of the market' that credit is readily available and cheap for those who don't really need it, that it gets more expensive the more you need it, and that it slides out of reach altogether for those who cannot do without it. In theory, one can see how a well-functioning sovereign debt market (if such a thing could ever exist) might exercise some discipline that could be useful to keep states from getting themselves into trouble. As a recipe to get states out of the trouble they did not cause themselves, however, 'the logic of the market' is just punitive and cynical politics masquerading as inept economics. To freeze political substitutes for market discipline (ESM) and technocratic truth-seeking about the 'correct' price of debt (OMT) into law as the standard of permissible assistance and as the measure of austerity is rather worse than just bad law. This is how we live in Euroland.

62 Cryptically, id., para. 126.
63 id., para. 108.
64 See <https://www.ecb.europa.eu/mopo/implement/omt/html/index.en.html>.

JOURNAL OF LAW AND SOCIETY
VOLUME 44, NUMBER 1, MARCH 2017
ISSN: 0263-323X, pp. 99–122

The Growth of Debt and the Debt of Growth: Lessons from the Case of Argentina

Pablo J. López* and Cecilia Nahón**

Argentina's case is a 'game changer' in the discussion about sovereign debt across the globe, particularly regarding debt restructuring. This article reviews Argentina's sovereign debt and economic growth process over the last 25 years and draws lessons from the country's trajectory. Alternating austerity and heterodox economic policies resulted in different outcomes throughout this period. One lesson, in particular, stands out: sustainable debt has been a necessary condition for sustainable growth. Conversely, austerity policies combined with a lax approach toward debt have led to economic recession and debt unsustainability alike. Argentina's case underscores that the only way to overcome the debt-recession trap is a timely and big-enough debt restructuring that provides an economy with a fresh start. Neither austerity policies nor debt roll-overs have done the job. That is why an orderly, predictable, fair, and balanced sovereign debt restructuring system is such a relevant – still pending – component of the international financial architecture.

* University of Buenos Aires, Av. Córdoba 2122, Buenos Aires, Argentina. Secretary of Finance at the Argentine Ministry of Economy, 2013–2015. palopez77@gmail.com
** Model G20 Initiative, School of International Service, American University, 4400 Massachusetts Avenue, NW, Washington, DC 20016, United States of America. Argentine Ambassador to the United States, 2013–2015.
cnahon@gmail.com

We are grateful to Martín Guzman, Sebastián Soler, Ana Adelardi, Marija Bartl, and Markos Karavias for their valuable comments on an earlier draft of this article. Though their feedback contributed to improving the article, we alone are responsible for its final content.

99

INTRODUCTION

Argentina made headlines around the world in June 2014 when, after debt litigation lasting a decade, the United States Supreme Court let stand a ruling in favour of distressed-debt hedge funds known as 'vulture funds'. The judicial system ruled against the arguments put forth by the United States government, Brazil, France, and Mexico as amici curiae in support of the Argentine position throughout the litigation. While Argentina had faced debt problems in the past,[1] this time the situation was unique in domestic and international terms alike.

Following a successful debt restructuring voluntarily accepted by 92.4 per cent of Argentine bondholders, New York Federal Judge Griesa stated – in an unprecedented ruling – that the country had violated a standard *pari passu* clause in its un-restructured sovereign bonds that the country had stopped paying in December 2001. Argentina was ordered to refrain from making any payments on the new performing bonds until it made a ratable payment to the holders of the old defaulted bonds (the so-called holdouts). When Argentina payed its exchange bondholders in June 2014 as it had done since 2005, Judge Griesa blocked these overwhelming majority of good-faith creditors – unrelated to the litigation – from collecting their payment by prohibiting financial intermediaries from distributing the funds. The payment chain was abruptly interrupted. Argentina denounced this unprecedented negative ruling and rallied overwhelming international support.

In April 2016, the country once again made headlines when a newly elected government decided to quickly put an end to the debt litigation by paying off vulture funds through a multi-millionaire bond issuance, once again under New York law. This decision is part of an 'austerity' and structural reform package currently being implemented in the country, with foreseeable consequences: higher poverty and unemployment rates. At the same time, after 15 years outside the international bond markets, Argentina is now 'back in business,' a return celebrated by many Wall Street bankers.[2]

The case of Argentina has been a game changer in the sovereign debt world, exposing the enormous obstacles that sovereign countries face within the current international system to attaining and maintaining sustainable debt levels compatible with sustainable growth. Debt overhang continues to be a major threat to many advanced and developing economies alike. The goal of

---

1 Argentina defaulted seven times between 1825 and 2001: see E. Basualdo, *Estudios de Historia Económica Argentina* (2013).
2 Indeed, Wall Street is not only celebrating but, according to Bloomberg, 'Wall Street Is in Charge in Argentina (Again)' (2016) as 'President Mauricio Macri, a former businessman himself, has loaded his administration up with traders, financiers, entrepreneurs, economists and corporate executives': see <http://www.bloomberg.com/news/articles/2016-03-09/jpmorgan-and-deutsche-bank-boys-are-running-the-new-argentina>.

this article is to broadly review Argentina's sovereign debt and growth process over the last 25 years, particularly focusing on Argentina's successive debt restructurings and the litigation with the vulture funds in the United States, and draw lessons from this trajectory.

HOW ARGENTINA GOT TO THE BIGGEST DEFAULT IN HISTORY (1990–2001)

1. The Brady plan: 'too little, too late'

The 1980s are known as the 'lost decade' for Latin America. But it was not all about 'loss'. A decisive transference of power from nation states to its international creditors – mainly Wall Street banks – took place throughout the decade.

After a period (1974–1981) of lavish and loose loans to Latin American economies – mostly channelled through international banks' syndicates – as a result of the excess of liquidity in global financial markets, the 'debt crisis' exploded in 1982 after an abrupt hike in United States interest rates. Cornered by over-indebtedness, most Latin American countries were unable to meet upcoming debt maturities, even after the implementation of painful adjustment programmes. Likewise, creditors, mostly United States commercial banks, were reluctant to acknowledge the losses on their balance sheets, which would have forced many into bankruptcy and expose the fragility of the international financial system. The structural insolvency problem was not addressed until the end of the decade, when it became apparent that the persistent debt burden on the sluggish fiscal budgets required debt-restructuring actions.

United States Treasury Secretary Nicholas Brady led the push for a restructuring scheme that was accepted by – and most likely designed with – international banks. The so-called 'Brady Plan' consisted of an exchange of old banking debt for newly issued sovereign bonds – with a haircut on the face value and an extension of maturities – guaranteed by United States securities. In order to secure the funds to acquire the United States collateral, debtor countries would receive direct loans from international financial institutions that were conditional upon the implementation of structural adjustment programmes and reform packages. Mexico was the first to sign a Brady deal in 1989. Many Latin American countries and other developing economies followed, implementing their own Brady-type deals.[3] The World Bank and the IMF eagerly backed the scheme because it furthered the then-

---

3 See J. Schumacher, C. Trebesch and H. Enderlein, 'Sovereign Defaults in Court: The Rise of Creditor Litigation 1976–2010' (2013), at <http://papers.ssrn.com/sol3/papers.cfm?abstract_id=2189997>.

revered 'Washington Consensus' throughout the South. According to former Colombian Finance Minister José Antonio Ocampo, this scheme was 'an excellent way to deal with the US banking crisis, and an awful way to deal with the Latin American debt crisis.'[4]

Argentina reached an agreement with its creditors in 1992. In exchange for debt amounting to around $30 billion ($21 billion in capital plus interest in arrears), the country issued new securities in April 1993 with a face value of $25.6 billion, partially guaranteed by United States securities and a deposit at the Federal Reserve.[5] Different analysts calculated the haircut on this transaction to be between 20 and 35 per cent.[6]

There were two important consequences of the Brady plan in Argentina, in particular, but also in Latin America in general. First, the nature and profile of countries' creditors changed, as sovereign bonds – mostly issued under New York law – began to circulate on a large scale in international capital markets. As the banking sector was in practice 'bailed-out', bond-holders became highly atomized, anonymous, and widespread across the globe, including a growing number of hedge funds increasingly specializing in such bonds. Whereas sovereign bonds represented 27 per cent of the total public debt before the Brady deal (in December 1992), their weight rose to almost 70 per cent of the total Argentine public debt after the plan's implementation a year later. Debt with international financial institutions also increased, although modestly. Conversely, commercial banks reduced their participation as creditors of the country from 34 per cent before the Brady plan to roughly 2 per cent after the restructuring.[7] A second result of the Brady plan – arguably its main goal – was to get debtors ready to regain access to international capital markets.

Briefly, the Brady restructuring was the pillar of a new debt cycle in Argentina and throughout the region, setting the basis for a new phase of over-indebtedness a decade later. Although it involved certain haircuts in face value, it turned out to be a clear example of the so-called 'too little, too late' problem in debt restructurings.[8] In the case of Argentina, just a few months after the Brady deal's implementation, total public debt was already

---

4 Cited by J. Roos, 'Since the Mexican Debt Crisis, 30 years of neoliberalism' *ROAR Magazine*, 22 August 2012, at <https://roarmag.org/essays/mexican-greek-debt-crisis-neoliberalism/>.
5 For the Brady Plan in Argentina, see R. Lavagna and L. Sigaut, 'Un análisis del ingreso argentino al Brady' (1992) 2(16) *Nuestros Bancos de Provincia*; M. Sangermano, 'Los planes Baker y Brady. Alternativas de solución a la crisis de la deuda de argentina y países latinoamericanos' (2005) Fundación EGE Working Paper.
6 For a discussion on different methodologies to estimate haircuts in debt restructuring processes, see J.J. Cruces and C. Trebesch, 'Sovereign Defaults: The Price of Haircuts' (2013) 5(3) *Am. Economic J.: Macroeconomics* 85.
7 Data from the Ministry of Economy of Argentina.
8 See M. Guzman, J.A. Ocampo, and J. Stiglitz, *Too Little, Too Late: The Quest to Resolve Sovereign Debt Crises* (2016).

higher than before the agreement ($71 billion in December 1993 as opposed to $63 billion in December 1992).

2. *The convertibility regime: lots of austerity and lots of debt*

Re-entering the debt cycle was necessary to finance Argentina's structural reform package, which included capital deregulation, market liberalization, and privatization of public utilities and the pension system.[9] In April 1991, the Menem administration passed the 'Convertibility Law,' which established a currency board that pegged the Argentine peso to the US dollar to stabilize the economy and bring back economic growth. Under this regime, the monetary base had to be backed by foreign reserves, so monetary policy was basically eliminated as an economic tool. Initially, the convertibility regime was effective in controlling hyperinflation, and the economy experienced a few years of positive economic growth as a consequence of new investments in some specific sectors and a consumption boom financed by foreign capital. Argentina's 'success' was then showcased around the world.

However, as early as 1994, the Mexican 'Tequila' crisis hit Argentina and revealed the artificial and fragile foundation of convertibility, as well as its devastating consequences on production and employment. At first, GDP growth was unstable – and jobless – and became definitively negative from mid-1998 onwards (Table 1). Unemployment stabilized at double-digit rates, with poverty levels rising from 19 per cent in 1994 to 35.4 per cent in 2001. The primary fiscal result did not improve due to the decline in revenues, a consequence of economic stagnation and the privatization of the pension system. Additionally, the growing bulk of interest payments deepened the negative fiscal result and increased pressure on the balance of payments. Fiscal austerity and the appreciation of the peso resulted in a decline of tradable sector activities, with the exception of the traditional primary low-value-added sector, as imported goods flooded the economy, deepening the structural current account deficit. With a few exceptions, Argentina's manufacturing sector was significantly reduced: its contribution to GDP decreased from 16.5 per cent in 1991 to 13.6 per cent in 2001.

The mid-decade crisis also made it apparent that the convertibility regime relied on unlimited flows of foreign currency to maintain an increasingly overvalued exchange rate. At the beginning of the decade, foreign currency was mostly provided by a massive privatization process – strategic state companies were undersold overnight – and foreign direct investment (FDI),

---

9 For an analysis of convertibility, see M. Damill, R. Frenkel, and R. Maurizio, 'Argentina: A decade of currency board. An analysis of growth, employment and income distribution' (2002) ILO Employment Paper 2002/42. On the privatization process in Argentina, see, among many, E. Basualdo et al., *El proceso de privatización en Argentina. La renegociación con las empresas privatizadas* (2002).

Table 1. Performance of selected macroeconomic variables, 1993–2002

	Real Economy			Fiscal Result			Balance of Payments		
	GDP growth rate	Industrial GDP growth rate	Unemploy-ment rate	Primary Fiscal Result (to GDP)	Fiscal Result including interest payments (to GDP)	Interest Payments to Public Tax Revenues	Capital Account ($ million)	Current Account ($ million)	Current Account (to GDP)
1993			9.6%	2.59%	1.25%	6.0%	14,180	−8,209	−3.77%
1994	5.79%	4.50%	11.5%	1.29%	−0.04%	6.9%	13,764	−10,981	−4.63%
1995	−2.66%	−7.16%	17.5%	1.14%	−0.58%	9.2%	7,687	−5,104	−2.14%
1996	5.16%	6.45%	17.2%	−0.36%	−2.20%	9.7%	12,198	−6,755	−2.69%
1997	7.69%	9.15%	14.9%	0.54%	−1.60%	10.9%	17,643	−12,116	−4.49%
1998	3.82%	1.85%	12.9%	0.94%	−1.48%	12.2%	18,281	−14,465	−5.25%
1999	−2.93%	−7.93%	14.3%	1.32%	−1.82%	15.9%	13,623	−11,910	−4.54%
2000	−0.72%	−3.82%	15.1%	1.09%	−2.58%	18.5%	8,826	−8,955	−3.40%
2001	−3.96%	−7.36%	17.4%	0.58%	−3.48%	23.4%	−5,442	−3,780	−1.51%
2002	−9.32%	−10.96%	19.7%	0.77%	−1.54%	13.3%	−11,339	8,702	2.95%

Source: Elaborated by the authors with data from Argentina's Ministry of Economy and National Statistics Agency (INDEC)

104

Table 2. Public Debt, 1992–2002

	Total Public Debt ($ million)	Total Public Debt (to GDP)
1992	63,250	
1993	71,112	33%
1994	81,820	34%
1995	88,711	37%
1996	99,046	39%
1997	103,718	38%
1998	114,134	41%
1999	123,366	47%
2000	129,750	49%
2001	144,222	57%
2002	152,974	166%

Source: elaborated by the authors with data from Argentina's Ministry of Economy and National Statistics Agency (INDEC)

but these sources slowed after the crisis. As a result, foreign borrowing became the main way of sustaining convertibility.[10] The debt path was explosive (Tables 2 and 3). Private sector debt increased sevenfold between 1991 and 2001.[11] But it fell to the public sector to cover convertibility's ever-increasing foreign currency needs. Foreign indebtedness became the main channel for financing the balance of payments, maintaining international reserves, and sustaining the nominal value of the domestic currency.

The economy fell into recession in the fourth quarter of 1998, and the debt burden began to escalate. Additionally, the successive crises in emerging markets in the second half of the 1990s (the 1997 Asian financial crisis, the Russian crisis in 1998, the Brazilian crisis and devaluation in 1999) had inevitable contagion effects on Argentina, as liquidity fled (back) to advanced economies. The country's risk premium rose, increasing the weight of interest debt payments (for both public and private debt) and making it harder (more expensive) to issue new international bonds to cover upcoming debt maturities.[12]

10 On the relation between capital flight, debt, and FDI, see C. Nahón, 'Financiamiento externo y desarrollo económico en la Argentina: la dinámica de *flujos cruzados* durante el régimen de Convertibilidad' in *Transformaciones recientes en la economía argentina: tendencias y perspectivas*, eds. V. Basualdo and K. Forcinito (2002) 279.

11 On private debt evolution, see E. Basualdo, C. Nahón, and H. Nochteff, 'La deuda externa privada en la Argentina (1991–2005). Trayectoria, naturaleza y protagonistas' (2007) 47 *Desarrollo Económico* 193.

12 Public debt interests over GDP expanded from 1.6 per cent in 1993 to 3.8 per cent in 2001. The average risk premium was 430 points in 1997, 675 in 1998, and 870 points in 1999: see Graph 1.

Table 3. International bonds issued by Argentina, 1991–2001

	Number of operations	Nominal Value ($ million)	Average maturity (years)
1991	2	500	2.0
1992	1	250	5.0
1993	6	2,121	6.9
1994	19	2,600	3.3
1995	18	6,370	4.0
1996	30	10,413	8.2
1997	18	10,214	14.9
1998	24	11,664	13.3
1999	40	11,869	7.6
2000	16	12,359	11.8
2001	11	32,519	16.8
1991–2001	**185**	**100,879**	**12.2**

Source: elaborated by the authors with data from Ministry of Economy, Argentina

Notwithstanding these challenges, the Argentine government, in tandem with the IMF and World Bank, determined to comply with the currency parity, kept the debt wheel going. New schemes were implemented to capture international liquidity, such as issuing debt securities in European markets (mostly in Germany and Italy) through second-tier local banks, or

Graph 1: EMBI+ Argentina (monthly average)

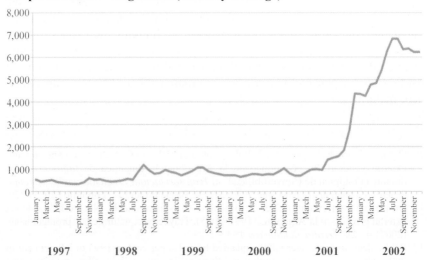

Source: elaborated by the authors, based on Bloomberg

offering instruments with odd structures that would become very expensive for the country in the end.

By the early 2000s, very few genuine sources of capital were available for the country. To cover debt maturities, the government put together a so-called '*blindaje*' (shield) involving $39.7 billion in loans from international institutions, Argentine institutional investors, and private bondholders. Disbursements of funds under these facilities were conditional upon the implementation of additional reforms and adjustment policies overseen by the IMF, including a 13 per cent nominal reduction of public employees' wages and pensions to reach a 'zero fiscal deficit'. But a few months later, the country needed new financing to pay the debt services, while the risk premium doubled again. A last, desperate attempt to avoid default and devaluation of the local currency took place in the second half of 2001: a mega debt swap (the so-called '*mega-canje*') for close to $30 billion in short-term debt in exchange for bonds with longer maturities but higher interest rates and face value. The IMF played a significant role in the design and implementation of these successive debt arrangements and supported Argentina's efforts to sustain convertibility through 2001.[13]

Lastly, in the midst of a depressed economy, convertibility collapsed in December 2001.[14] Almost immediately, Argentina's Congress formally declared a default on all of the country's public external debt. Soon after, in early 2002, the peso was sharply devalued and the debt-to-GDP ratio rocketed to 166 per cent, as most of the public debt was held by non-residents denominated in foreign currency. It was the biggest default in history: 152 different types of bonds in eight legislations and six currencies that represented $81 billion at face value and interest in arrears.

HOW ARGENTINA GOT TO THE 'TRIAL OF THE CENTURY' IN SOVEREIGN DEBT RESTRUCTURING (2003–2015)

1. *'The dead do not pay their debts'*

In 2001, after a decade of being the poster-child of neoliberalism, Argentina defaulted on its sovereign debt. It also defaulted on its people. Contrary to claims that 'the Argentine people essentially had a wild party and woke up with a hangover,'[15] Argentines were unquestionably the default's main

13 The role played by the IMF raised sharp criticism, even from its own Independent Evaluation Office (IEO): see IMF, *Report on the Evaluation of the Role of the IMF in Argentina, 1991–2001* (2004).
14 See M. Damill and R. Frenkel, 'Argentina: Macroeconomic Performance and Crisis' in *Stabilization Policies for Growth and Development*, eds. R. French-Davis, R.D. Nayyar, and J.E. Stiglitz (2003).
15 D. Bandow, 'Supreme Court Moves Us Closer To Holding Deadbeat Argentina Accountable' *Forbes*, 31 October 2013.

victims. With 53 per cent of the population living in poverty (May 2002), Argentina was at a critical juncture, with a paralysed economy and a dire political situation.

It took the country more than two years to hold new presidential elections and be able to face its sovereign debt default. The total amount of defaulted public external debt was close to $100 billion, including $81 billion of debt with private bondholders. In the absence of an international bankruptcy framework for sovereign nations, Argentina followed established international market practices to restructure its debt through a voluntary debt exchange. In 2005, Argentina launched a global bid to exchange defaulted bonds for new securities with modified terms. Contrary to the experience in the 1990s, the country chose not to resort to the IMF and World Bank for assistance in the restructuring, avoiding therefore any conditionality on economic policy.

Two main principles guided the restructuring. First, Argentina's offer was determined based on its real payment capacity, which required a significant 70 per cent haircut and a lengthening of maturity.[16] The so-called financial community around the world accused the government of imposing too big a haircut, triggering enormous pressure on the country to 'sweeten' the deal. However, the Kirchner administration argued that the debt restructuring would have to be deep enough to provide the conditions for sustainable economic growth with social inclusion, that would ultimately be convenient for investors too. The rationale was very simple but still ground-breaking at the time: Argentina needed to grow to be able to honour its debts. As President Kirchner famously stated at the United Nations General Assembly in New York in September 2005: 'The dead do not pay their debts.'

In order to increase acceptance among bondholders, the final exchange offer incorporated Gross Domestic Product (GDP)-linked securities, through which bondholders would receive extra payments if the economy grew at a higher than base-case threshold growth rate of around 3 per cent.[17] In fact, restructured bondholders benefited greatly from Argentina's high growth rates until 2011, because almost every year GDP growth surpassed the base-case threshold value.[18] However, the fact that these securities were valued at low levels at the time of the exchange raised questions about their effectiveness.

---

16 Estimates of the haircut applied in this case range between 65 per cent and 75 per cent, depending on the methodology used in the calculations: see Ministry of Economy of Argentina, 'Exchange Offering. Final Announcement', at <http://www.mecon.gob.ar/finanzas/sfinan/documentos/180305_anuncio_resultados.pdf>; Cruces and Trebesch, op. cit., n. 6.

17 See S. Kim Park and T. Samples, 'Towards Sovereign Equity' (2016) 21 *Stanford J. of Law, Business and Finance* 31.

18 See M. Guzman, 'An Analysis of Argentina's 2001 Default Resolution' (2016) CIGI paper no. 110, at <www.cigionline.org/publications/analysis-argentinas-2001-default-resolution>.

Table 4. Public debt, 2003–2014

	Total Public Debt ($ million)	Total Public Debt (to GDP)	External Debt (to GDP)	Debt with private sector in foreign currency (to GDP)
2002	152,974	166%	95%	NA
2003	178,821	139%	79%	79%
2004	191,296	106%	62%	60%
2005	128,630	60%	29%	16%
2006	136,725	52%	21%	15%
2007	144,729	44%	19%	13%
2008	145,975	39%	15%	10%
2009	147,119	39%	15%	9%
2010	164,330	36%	13%	10%
2011	178,963	33%	11%	8%
2012	197,464	35%	11%	8%
2013	202,630	39%	12%	8%
2014	221,748	43%	13%	9%

Source: Elaborated by the authors with data from the Ministry of Economy, Argentina

The second principle that guided the debt restructuring was inter-creditor equity, guaranteeing all similarly-situated private bondholders the same deal. This equal treatment commitment was critical to maximize the level of acceptance of the offer, stimulating bondholders to join the swap voluntarily, since no better exchange deal would be offered to bondholders in the future. Legally, this principle was introduced in the bonds' prospectus as a clause known as Rights Upon Future Offers (RUFO). According to the RUFO clause, if Argentina 'voluntarily' made a better offer to some creditors before the end of December 2014, the rest of the bondholders would be entitled to the same treatment.

Over three-quarters (76.1 per cent) of Argentina's bondholders adhered. A second debt exchange, under the same terms of the 2005 debt swap, followed in 2010 during President Cristina Fernández de Kirchner's first term, elevating the total restructured bonds to 92.4 per cent of the original defaulted nominal value. Participants received new performing debt instruments honoured ever since. The debt-to-GDP ratio rapidly reflected the impact of the restructuring: public debt declined from 106 per cent of GDP in 2004 to 52 per cent in 2006, and external public debt came down from 62 to 21 per cent in the same period. After the 2010 exchange, these ratios reached 36 per cent and 13 per cent, respectively (Table 4). Consistent with the strategic goal of reducing dependency on foreign flows and recovering policy sovereignty, in 2006 Argentina paid all of its IMF obligations ahead of schedule ($9.5 billion).

The two exchange transactions meant that the country issued more than $40 billion in face value of new bonds, and honoured from that moment on all its serviced maturities, including almost $10 billion in additional payments between 2005 and 2011 because the real GDP growth rate passed the base-case threshold of the GDP-linked securities.

2. *Heterodox economics on the move: a model of growth with social inclusion*

The process of debt reduction was a key element within the major goal of growth with social inclusion that Argentina implemented since 2003.[19] The devaluation in early 2002, in a strongly recessive environment with high levels of unemployment and idle capacity, had a moderate impact on prices (pass-through). Consequently, in the following years, the country was able to sustain a competitive real exchange rate. In addition, active policies to promote production and to reactivate the domestic market – through both consumption and investment demand – were put in place. In a favourable international context due to high commodity prices, Argentina also reintroduced taxes on its main primary export products. These taxes, together with the fiscal relief resulting from the default status, allowed the government to develop active inclusion policies and allocate resources to subsidize production – and consumption of certain basic services – without putting at risk the fiscal result (Table 5).

In the years following the exchange, the country did increase its payments to bondholders of the GDP-linked securities as a result of the high growth rates achieved (Table 6). The mechanism was virtuous: debt servicing did not prevent the country from growing at high levels and, in turn, economic growth allowed for increased debt payments. All in all, since 2007, public debt interest payments stabilized at around 2 per cent of GDP, nearly half the burden it represented at the end of the 1990s.

Between 2003 and 2008, within a context of favourable terms of trade for Latin America, domestic output grew by 7.7 per cent per year on average and unemployment dropped to 7.3 per cent over the same period, after reaching levels of around 20 per cent in 2002.[20] The recovery and later expansion of the manufacturing sector was critical for the creation of millions of jobs. As a result, income distribution improved considerably. According to the World

---

19 There is an intense on-going debate about the achievements and shortcomings of the economic policy over those years: see Centro de Investigación y Formación de la República Argentina (CIFRA), 'La naturaleza política y la trayectoria económica de los gobiernos kirchneristas' (2015) Working Paper no. 14, at <http://www.centrocifra.org.ar/docs/final.pdf>; M. Damill, R. Frenkel, and M. Rapetti, 'Macroeconomic Policy in Argentina during 2002–2013' (2015) 57 *Comparative Economic Studies* 369; M. Guzman and J. Stiglitz, 'Argentina shows Greece there may be Life after Default' *Huffington Post*, 5 March 2015.

20 Official 2003–2015 GDP growth estimates are currently being revised; we take available data as of August 2016.

Table 5. Selected macroeconomic indicators, 2003–2015

	Real Economy		Fiscal Result		Income Distribution
	GDP growth rate	Unemploy-ment rate (4th quarter of each year)	Primary Fiscal Result to GDP	Fiscal Result including interest payments to GDP	GINI index*
2003	8.84%	14.5%	2.31%	0.48%	53.54
2004	9.03%	12.1%	3.88%	2.60%	50.18
2005	9.20%	10.1%	3.70%	1.77%	49.27
2006	8.36%	8.7%	3.54%	1.78%	48.26
2007	8.00%	7.5%	3.17%	1.14%	47.37
2008	3.10%	7.3%	3.13%	1.41%	46.27
2009	0.05%	8.4%	1.51%	−0.62%	45.27
2010	9.14%	7.3%	1.74%	0.21%	44.50
2011	8.55%	6.7%	0.27%	−1.66%	43.57
2012	0.95%	6.9%	−0.20%	−2.57%	42.49
2013	2.93%	6.4%	−0.67%	−1.93%	42.28
2014	0.38%	6.9%	−0.87%	−2.48%	NA
2015	2.20%	5.9%	−2.06%	−4.44%	NA

* For the GINI index we used the World Bank Database; 2013 is the last available figure for Argentina.
Source: elaborated by the authors based on IMF, World Bank, and Argentina's Ministry of Economy and National Statistics Agency (INDEC) as of August 2016

Bank, the GINI index descended from 53.5 in 2003 to 46.3 in 2008 (Table 5) and the income share of the lowest 10 per cent almost doubled from 2003 to 2008. Despite persistent inflation – in two digits for most of the decade – wages and pensions experienced a positive evolution in real terms due to higher nominal increases that more than compensated for price rises.[21] This sustained improvement in purchasing power and income distribution was essential to increase aggregate demand and create a virtuous cycle of inclusive growth.[22] With a growing domestic market and a significant

21 Briefly, the inflationary process was a consequence of several domestic and international factors. The cycle of rising commodity prices pushed local food prices up. Also, the existence of rigidities and non-competitive market structures in certain productive sectors put extra pressure on prices. Moreover, the increase in the exchange rate also fuelled inflation over this period.
22 Due to the controversy raised about the reliability of the official inflation indicators in 2007, alternative estimates were developed with uneven degrees of accuracy. Despite the differences among them, all official and private sources agree that real wages and pensions increased every year between 2003 and 2015: see CIFRA, op. cit., n. 19.

expansion of public works, investment also boomed: gross capital formation recovered from 12 per cent of GDP before 2003 to more than 20 per cent in 2008, comprising domestic and foreign investment alike.[23]

The 2008 outbreak of the financial crisis at the heart of Wall Street shocked the global economy. In a context of volatility and flight-to-quality in international capital markets, Argentina's low debt levels and limited reliance on foreign flows served as a positive buffer. However, the global crisis did impact the domestic economy, mainly through the 'trade channel.' In 2009, output stagnated, but active counter-cyclical fiscal policies were put in place, which allowed the country to recover high growth rates in 2010 and 2011. During the following years, the global economy remained unstable and anaemic, hitting Argentina's main trading partners – notably Brazil and, to a much lesser extent, China. The collapse of commodity prices, which started after the peak of 2011, added to an already difficult international scenario, as Latin American countries faced a reversal of the favourable terms of trade they had benefited from in the previous decade.

As a result, the 2013–2015 period in Argentina was characterized by a heterodox economic policy in a highly adverse international and regional landscape.[24] Numerous speculative financial attacks against the Argentine peso were also registered during this phase, putting additional stress on the balance of payments and the Central Bank's international reserves. Macroeconomic policy was defensive in many aspects, but it proved effective in sustaining employment and economic activity thanks to capital controls, import barriers, and counter-cyclical fiscal and income policies as well as credit incentive measures (Table 5).

Even in this challenging context, Argentina managed to make all its debt payments without resorting to the austerity and adjustment policies widely 'recommended' by the IMF and World Bank. Indeed, in 2013, Argentina reached an agreement with the Paris Club creditor nations to repay its 2001 overdue debt ($9.7 billion). Argentina also settled outstanding investment treaty (ICSID) arbitration awards in 2013. As a result of this decade-long process of international financial normalization, public debt as a percentage of GDP declined from 166 per cent in 2002 to 43 per cent in 2014, with public debt in foreign currency with private creditors standing below 10 per cent (Table 4). However, the strength of the debt strategy would be seriously challenged in 2014 in the United States.

3. *From restructuring to litigation, from litigation to extortion*

Vulture funds filed a lawsuit against Argentina as early as 2002, and followed different litigation strategies throughout the decade until their

23 See World Bank data indicators, at <http://data.worldbank.org/indicator>.
24 As Menéndez explains in his contribution to this volume, the 2008 collapse is far from over.

decisive legal victory in 2014. This small minority of bondholders refused to join the 2005 and 2010 Argentine debt exchanges, converting themselves into 'holdouts.' They had never lent money to Argentina. Instead, they purchased already defaulted bonds for pennies on the dollar on the secondary market with the sole purpose of making windfall profits by suing the country for the original face value of the bonds plus interests and penalties.[25]

Vulture funds profit from the absence of an international sovereign bankruptcy regime and have preyed on stressed sovereign debt on all continents for more than three decades. During the debt crisis in the 1980s and the Brady restructurings, collective action was possible because debt was in the hands of a fairly small number of large creditors. However, the global shift since the 1990s from syndicated bank loans to bond markets has made sovereign debt restructurings much more difficult due to the increasing atomization of creditors, leading to the rise of debt serial litigators.[26] Furthermore, the partial elimination in 2004 by the New York state legislature of the so-called 'Champerty defense', a law that prohibited the purchase of debt with the intent of bringing a lawsuit, provided significant impetus to the sovereign debt litigation business in the United States.[27]

The Argentine case was the last link in a chain of events eroding sovereign immunity, tilting the playing field in favour of the most aggressive and speculative stakeholders of the financial system. In the case of *NML Capital Ltd.* v. *Argentina*, New York Federal Judge Griesa adopted a novel interpretation – contrary to established market understanding – of the *pari passu* boilerplate clause included in sovereign bonds and ruled that Argentina had breached it.[28] According to the most widely held inter-pretation, the *pari passu* clause typically provides that certain bond debt will rank *pari passu* with other debt, protecting creditors against legal sub-ordination to another debt issued (or to be issued) by the same borrower. However, Judge Griesa gave it a wider, odd, interpretation, ruling that a sovereign cannot pay any of its debts without a ratable payment of other (defaulted) debts within the scope of the *pari passu* clause.[29] By declining to

25 Guzman provides evidence of how the overwhelming majority of the bonds held by the main litigant against Argentina, Paul Singer, were purchased after the debt exchange of 2005: Guzman, op. cit., n. 18.

26 For an analysis of the process of debt atomization, see Schepel's article in this volume. See, also, J.I. Blackman and R. Mukhi, 'Evolution of Modern Sovereign Debt Litigation: Vultures, Alter Egos, and Other Legal Fauna' (2010) 73 *Law and Contemporary Problems* 47.

27 In 2004, the prohibition of the purchase of debt with the intent of bringing a lawsuit was eliminated in New York State for debt purchases above $500,000.

28 'Brief for the United States of America as Amicus Curiae in support of the Republic of Argentina's petition for panel rehearing and rehearing en banc', 28 December 2012.

29 Allen & Overy Global Law Intelligence Unit, 'The *pari passu* clause and the Argentine case' (2012).

review the case, the United States Supreme Court let Griesa's interpretation stand.[30]

Specifically, the ruling stated that Argentina was to refrain from making any payments on its exchange bonds until a ratable payment – of face value plus interests, and a compensatory interest rate – was made to the holdouts. The required payment amounted at the time to $1.6 billion, four times the bonds' face value of $0.44 billion. The ruling crafted an 'equitable remedy' that brought about the most inequitable result. The *Financial Times* chief economics commentator, Martin Wolf, put it bluntly: 'This is extortion backed by the US judiciary.'[31] In its brief filed before the New York Court of Appeals for the Second Circuit (4 April 2012), the United States government stated that:

> the district court's interpretation of the *pari passu* provision could enable a single creditor to thwart the implementation of an internationally supported restructuring plan, and thereby undermine the decades of effort the United States has expended to encourage a system of cooperative resolution of sovereign debt crises.

As the Brookings Institution said, this may be '[. . .] the first broadly replicable remedy against sovereign debtors since the days of gunboat diplomacy a century ago.'[32] It could be argued that the new *pari passu* interpretation by United States courts contradicts international law, violates third-party rights, and goes against well-established financial practices and common sense. Not surprisingly, the ruling also opened a Pandora's box of cross-litigation, because the courts overstepped their jurisdiction and also obstructed collection of payments of Argentine bonds denominated in euros, yens, and pesos issued under European, Japanese, and Argentine laws.

Faced with such a ruling, Argentina reaffirmed its committed to honour its obligations with 100 per cent of its bondholders under fair, equitable, legal, and sustainable conditions, refusing to accept the vulture funds' extortion. First, because in addition to paying the litigants $1.6 billion, Argentina would have had to make additional payments of more than $15 billion to the rest of the holdouts. Second, offering the vulture funds privileged treatment over the overwhelming majority of its creditors would have violated Argentine legislation and the RUFO clause, in force until the end of 2014. The exchange bondholders would have had the right to demand the same conditions as the vultures, which would have derailed Argentina's entire debt

---

30 For an in-depth analysis of the different interpretations of the *pari passu* clause, see L.C. Bucheit and J.S. Pam, 'The pari passu clause in sovereign debt instruments' (2004) 53 *Emory Law J.* 869; S. Chodos, 'From the *pari passu* discussion to the "Illegality" of making payments' in Guzman et al., op. cit., n. 8.

31 M. Wolf, 'Defend Argentina from the vultures' *Financial Times*, 24 June 2014.

32 Brookings Institution, 'Argentina and the Rebirth of the Holdout Problem' in *Revisiting Sovereign Bankruptcy* (2013) ch. 3.

restructuring and led to claims for more than $120 billion.[33] Simply put, Argentina could not pay all bondholders what the vulture funds were demanding for themselves.

In July 2014, after several meetings between Argentine authorities and the litigants, no agreement was reached. Once again, the holdouts refused to join the debt exchange under equitable conditions to those accepted by 92.4 per cent of the bondholders, a deal which would have given them an immediate profit of 300 per cent.[34] But they were litigating – and speculating – for a lot more. On April 2016, a newly elected Argentine government would make their wildest dreams come true.

HOW ARGENTINA GAVE IN TO THE VULTURE FUNDS (2016)

1. *Back to the old business of issuing debt to pay debt*

In December 2015, immediately after Mauricio Macri became President of Argentina, the economic policy of the country underwent a complete reversal, shifting back to a neoliberal economic model. A new package of austerity policies and structural reforms – detailed below – is being forcefully implemented.

The new government announced the removal of all existing restrictions on foreign capital flows, devaluating the domestic currency by around 40 per cent. In addition, the Central Bank increased the interest rates by more than a third. These joint decisions exposed the domestic economy overnight to highly volatile short-term speculative flows, providing for a lucrative financial business at the expense of productive investments.[35] Additionally, taxes relating to commodity exporters were lowered or eliminated, a measure which, along with the currency devaluation and the significant hikes in public utilities' prices, more than doubled the level of inflation to around 40 per cent.[36] An abrupt process of trade liberalization also had a negative impact on domestic production – especially manufacturing activities – and employment, contributing to a profound decline in GDP. According to the

---

33 This figure is a conservative estimate based on what the 2005 exchange bondholders would have received in 2014 if granted the same financial treatment that vulture funds obtained from Judge Griesa (net of the present value of the portfolio received in the 2005 exchange).

34 To estimate this, we consider the price MNL paid for the defaulted bonds as documented by Guzman, op. cit., n. 18, versus the present value of the 2005 exchange portfolio.

35 Between January and May 2016, US dollar speculative investors benefited from 38 per cent annual yields on the Central Bank peso bills.

36 The Buenos Aires City CPI Index reported a 43.5 per cent inter-annual increase in August 2016: see data in <https://www.estadisticaciudad.gob.ar/eyc/wp-content/uploads/2016/09/ir_2016_1045.pdf>.

IMF, the Argentine economy will fall by 1.5 per cent in 2016.[37] Supporters of the neoliberal policies being implemented argue that this drop is an inevitable consequence of the macroeconomic adjustments necessary to deal with the so-called 'heavy legacy' inherited. However, the clear-cut shift for the worst in most – if not all – economic indicators in the first months of the new government supports the perspective of a self-inflicted recession. These abrupt policy changes were justified in the name of promised future rewards, under the logic of trickle-down economics, of which there are no signs. In fact, in the first six months of the new government, average real wages fell by 12.1 per cent.[38]

The Macri administration was also eager to put a quick end to the debt litigation, and so they did. Two reasons stand out. The first was a political decision to send a strong signal to investors of the new, market-friendly Argentina. Second, there was a financial decision to clear the way for a new phase of indebtedness. At the beginning of 2016, the new authorities began a process of hurried 'negotiations' with the holdouts. Within less than two months, the country settled with the vulture funds and other smaller groups of holdouts for a payment very close to the terms that Judge Griesa had set. The Macri administration also agreed to pay tens of millions of dollars in legal fees for the litigants that had harassed the country around the globe for more than a decade.[39] On 31 March 2016, the Argentine Congress passed a law to comply with the signed agreements, authorizing payments of up to $12.5 billion to the holdouts.[40] Days later, Judge Griesa lifted the *pari passu* injunction, releasing the disbursements made to good-faith bondholders. On mid-April, Argentina issued New York jurisdiction bonds worth $16.5 billion in face value to raise the money required to pay the holdouts in cash.

The vulture's victory was as wide-ranging as was Argentina's capitulation. First, the dispute resolution was very expensive for Argentina which, in the end, paid the face value of the original defaulted bonds many times over, in some cases up to nine times (Table 6). Whereas in the 2005 and 2010 restructurings, new debt of $43 billion was issued in exchange for defaulted bonds with a face value of $75 billion, representing 92.4 per cent of bondholders, the 2016 deal implied that the country issued bonds worth $12.5 billion in exchange for about $6 billion in old debt in the hands of less of 7.6 per cent of bondholders. Basically, the country paid almost four times

---

37 See IMF, World Economic Outlook database, updated as of 19 July 2016. The impact on the industrial sector has been strongly reflected from March on, with the following performance of the INDEC industrial index: −3.8 per cent in March, −5.2 per cent in April, −4.5 per cent in May, −6.4 in June, and −7.9 per cent in July.

38 CIFRA, *Macroeconomic Report No. 20* (2016).

39 Argentina was forced to litigate in the courts of France, Japan, the United States, Belgium, Switzerland, and Ghana, among others, to prevent vulture funds from seizing diplomatic and military assets and bank accounts protected by international law.

40 See Law 27.249 of 'Public Debt Normalization and Credit Recovery'.

116

Table 6. Settlement with selected holdouts, 2016

	Original Face Value ($ million)	Amount of Settlement ($ million)	Amount of settlement as percentage of the defaulted bonds' principal value
Italian bondholders	900	1,350	150
NML Capital, Ltd	617	2,426	393
Blue Angel	177	410	232
Aurelius Group*	299	845	283
Bracebridge Capital, LLC**	120	987	823
EM Limited	595	849	143
Montreux Group***	42	308	733

* Aurelius Group includes four hedge funds: Aurelius Capital Master LTD, Aurelius Capital Partners LP, Aurelius Opportunities Fund II LLC, and ACP Master LTD.
** Bracebridge Capital is the owner of three hedge funds that litigated against Argentina: Olifant, FFI Fund, and FYI Fund.
*** Montreux Group includes four hedge funds: Montreux Partners LP, Los Angeles Capital, Wilton Capital LTD, and Cordoba Capital.
Source: elaborated by the authors based on Office of the Cabinet Chief (August 2016)

more for each dollar restructured in 2016 than in the two previous restructurings.

Second, the Macri Administration's deal enshrined inter-creditor inequity, not only in favour of holdouts vis-à-vis exchange bondholders but also among holdouts themselves.[41] Table 6 shows the cash amounts received by different groups of Argentine holdouts, illustrating the unequal yields steaming from the settlements with the different holdouts, which range from one and a half to nine times the face value.[42] However, a closer analysis

---

41 See A. Gelpern, 'Sovereign debt: now what?' (2016) 41 *Yale J. of International Law Online* Special Edition; M. Guzman and J. Stiglitz, 'How Hedge Funds Held Argentina for Ransom' *New York Times*, 1 April 2016; and Guzman, op. cit., n. 18.
42 Though Table 6 does not exhaustively list all the holdout deals, it includes the most relevant ones. For example, in the case of the Italian bondholders that litigated against Argentina at ICSID under the Italian Bilateral Investment Treaty, the settlement was less favourable since the case was not over: they received a payment of 150 per cent of the original face value. For the holdouts litigating in New York, the differences between the settlements relative to the original face value are mainly explained by: (i) the different structures and interest rates of the defaulted bonds (not all the holdouts had the same defaulted bonds) and (ii) the year in which each hedge fund obtained the favourable judgment from the Court. Until the moment of the judgment, the Courts recognized the full original face value plus the full interest, plus a 'compensatory' pre-judgement interest rate. In New York courts, this compensatory interest rate is fixed at a usurious 9 per cent level since 1981. However, the post-judgment interest rate follows the annual United States bond interest rate, considerable below 9 per cent. In this sense, a favourable judgment earlier in time was a disadvantage compared with those who received judgment more recently.

reveals that the disparities were much greater. Considering that the vulture funds purchased most of the Argentine bonds at huge discounts after the 2001 default, their return after the settlement was substantially higher. It is insightful to review the case of NML Capital, the most aggressive litigant: since they received three times the original face value of the defaulted bonds but they purchased them for only 28 per cent of face value on average, they received 14 times their original disbursement. NML's profitability was close to 1,300 per cent.[43] This exorbitant profit contrasts with the situation of the exchange bondholders – the 92.4 per cent – who accepted a haircut of around 70 per cent of face value. Even when considering the recovery in the market value of the new Argentine bonds and the additional payments of the GDP-linked securities, the current value of the 2005 exchange ranged between 0.99 and 1.33 dollars per dollar of the original face value in 2015, according to estimates by Cruces and Samples under different scenarios.[44] Hence, although restructured bondholders recovered the original face value thanks to the GDP growth rate, the profits gained by vulture funds produced a sizeably unequal distribution.[45] In a word, aggressive speculation and litigation paid off, as holdouts multiplied their profits compared with good-faith investors.

Issuing debt to pay off the vulture funds was the first step into a new tunnel of increased indebtedness. New additional debt has already been issued by the federal government and certain provinces to pay maturities, to finance current fiscal expenditure, and to provide foreign currency for incessant capital flight. Though the low debt ratios achieved by the Kirchner governments after 12 years of debt reduction provide room for a certain degree of new commitments without affecting sustainability, this space is being consumed all too rapidly, putting the Argentine economy on a risky path once again. Numbers speak for themselves: in less than a year, the debt to GDP ratio of total Argentine external debt increased by 12 percentage points and the public external debt grew by more than 10 percentage points (Table 7). Debt is growing again; the Argentine economy is contracting again.

1. Beyond Argentina: the systemic implications of the Argentine case

The vulture funds' litigation against Argentina was a game changer in sovereign debt markets. Multilateral and regional organizations, heads of state and members of congress across the globe, NGOs, world-renowned

---

43 See Guzman, op. cit., n. 18.
44 J.J. Cruces and T. Samples, 'Settling Sovereign Debt's "Trial of the Century"' (2016) *Emory International Law Rev.* (forthcoming). Available at <https://ssrn.com/abstract=2719282> or <http://dx.doi.org/10.2139/ssrn.271928>.
45 Gelpern acknowledged that creditors who participated in the restructurings netted a 20–25 per cent return on principal: Gelpern, op. cit., n. 41.

Table 7. External total and public debt, December 2014 to June 2016

	Total External Debt ($ million)	Public External Debt ($ million)	Total External Debt to GDP	Public External Debt to GDP
December 2014	144,801	80,731	29.40%	16.40%
September 2015	157,271	86,273	28.91%	15.86%
December 2015	152,631	83,876	36.78%	20.21%
March 2016	163,236	92,470	40.95%	23.20%
June 2016	188,266	121,299	40.30%	25.95%

Source: elaborated by the authors with data from Argentina's Ministry of Economy and National Statistics Agency (INDEC)

experts, and academics warned about the grave consequences of this case for the predictability and stability of the international financial system and for the rights of sovereign nations.

By blocking the flow of payments to creditors unrelated to the litigation, United States courts empowered holdouts to sabotage sovereign debt restructurings, rendering them virtually impossible in the future. Roubini argued: 'why would any future creditor who benefits from an orderly restructuring vote for it if its new claims can be blocked by even a single holdout creditor?'[46] The incentives to hold out have dramatically increased. Indeed, while there is a way out for a company that has gone bankrupt, sovereign nations have almost no sustainable way of restructuring their debts to recover growth.

In the aftermath of the ruling, coordinated international efforts to limit predatory behaviour and ensure orderly and predictable sovereign debt restructurings have gained ground. Two main approaches stand out. On the one hand, a 'contractual' or 'market-based' approach has been led by the IMF, the G20, and the International Capital Markets Association (ICMA) to promote the inclusion of so-called 'vulture-proof clauses' in sovereign debt contracts. An aggregated Collective Action Clause (CAC) and an updated *pari passu* clause will make it more difficult for holdouts to block debt restructurings. Despite its positive value, this approach does not address the vulnerabilities generated by the $900 billion stock of performing international sovereign bonds, with maturities ranging from short term to 15–20 years, without the enhanced clauses.[47] In addition, there can be no certainty that these provisions will not be circumvented – or wrongly interpreted by a court – in the future. There are no fully 'vulture-proof' clauses. In addition,

46 N. Roubini, 'Gouging the Gauchos' *Project Syndicate,* 1 July 2014.
47 IMF, *Progress report on inclusion of enhanced contractual provisions in international sovereign bond contracts* (2015).

this approach does not address the root causes of 'too little, too late' restructurings.

In a different approach, within the framework of the United Nations, sovereign nations took action to build a 'statutory' solution for sovereign debt restructuring processes. On 10 September 2015, the United Nations General Assembly (UNGA) adopted Resolution A/69/L.84 on 'Basic Principles on Sovereign Debt Restructuring Processes' with 136 states in favour. With this historic resolution, the UN stated that sovereign debt restructuring processes should be guided by customary law and by basic international principles of law, such as sovereignty, good faith, transparency, legitimacy, equitable treatment, and sustainability.[48] Despite the resolution's approval by the vast majority of countries, it faced *harsh opposition* from creditor nations: the United States, Germany, Japan, Canada, Israel, and the United Kingdom.

CONCLUSIONS

The *Great Recession* has brought sovereign debt sustainability back to the forefront. A recent McKinsey study concludes that, since 2007, global debt has grown by $57 trillion, raising the ratio of debt to GDP by 17 percentage points.[49] Global debt has grown in absolute and relative terms – outpacing GDP growth – and has expanded in advanced and developing countries alike.

Within this fragile global context, the review of Argentina's sovereign debt and growth process over the last 25 years delivers valuable lessons for domestic and international debt policies in the future. The following lessons stand out:

i.   The combination of a cyclical overabundance of market liquidity at the global level – endlessly seeking profits through a lavish supply of financial instruments – with a highly deregulated domestic balance of payments pushes countries all too often into the trap of accumulating more and more debt to deal with present and future challenges. Specifically, foreign indebtedness has played a relevant role in the short-term survival of neoliberal economic models, but with dreadful longer-term results when debt, most likely, becomes unsustainable. When output stagnates (and unemployment increases) as a consequence of recessive policies, tax revenues decline further, and public debt becomes the main source for financing fiscal expenditures and meeting debt maturities, without increasing either productivity or repayment capacity. As Argentina's vicious-cycle experiences of the 1980s and late 1990s

---

48 UNCTAD, 'United Nations General Assembly adopts basic principles on sovereign debt restructuring' (2015), at <http://unctad.org/en/pages/newsdetails.aspx?OriginalVersionID=1074>.
49 McKinsey Global Institute, 'Debt and (not much) deleveraging' (2015).

120

show, austerity policies combined with a lax approach toward indebtedness make for a dangerous cocktail. Indeed, current trends in Argentina are also an issue of concern, as debt/GDP ratios are rising all too fast.

ii. The pervasive incentives and pressure to continue increasing debt, which lie at the heart of the current international financial system, coexist with a highly unbalanced playing field in favour of creditors – investment funds, bondholders, banks, and their advanced 'home' nations – at the expense of debtor nations. This means that after being pushed to increase debt to sustain structural reforms and replace the downturn in tax revenues resulting from austerity policies, highly indebted countries tend to avoid restructurings as much as they can. Threats of the financial plagues stemming from recognizing debt stress, or the mere intention of restructuring, tend to lead countries to postpone a resolution as long as they can. They may end up cutting key public services in order to service the sacred debt. The Argentine case shows the failure of such attempts to overcome high debt levels through fiscal adjustment policies, because austerity ended up deepening the recession and, as a consequence, both the fiscal deficit and the debt-to-GDP ratio increased. Evidence shows that the only effective way of addressing a significant debt overhang is through debt restructuring with debtors accepting a significant haircut. As President Kirchner said: 'the dead do not pay their debts.'

iii. Argentina's case also exposes the obstacles and challenges over-indebted countries face – as was the case of Argentina in 2002 after a decade of austerity policies – in attempting to restructure their debts sustainably within the current international (non)system. The 2005/2010 deals show it is possible to undertake deep-enough debt restructurings, compatible with output growth and social inclusion. However, this precedent also revealed there are still too many loopholes in the international sovereign debt system, and amplified uncertainty regarding the legal framework and enforcement process, that make this outcome extremely complicated and vulnerable. Recently, Argentina paid the holdouts almost in full, and a new phase of austerity and increasing debt has started. Briefly, the 'trial of the century' raised bondholders' incentives to sabotage debt restructurings, making it even harder for countries to obtain the haircuts needed, when needed, to restore economic growth.

iv. Is debt a bad thing? Though acquiring debt can have a positive effect on growth, Argentina's case confirms that debt *levels* matter: sooner or later, high public debt levels, typical of neoliberal austerity phases, have had a negative impact on growth; conversely, lower levels of debt, achieved through a heterodox economic model, have been a necessary condition for sustainable growth. The use of such debt flows also matters: issuing debt to pay for debt maturities and finance capital flight gets countries into downward debt traps; conversely, longer-term debt

121

flows channelled to expand the real economy or conduct public works could be a positive intertemporal assignment of resources, if they are limited in volume and bring about repayment capacity.

In conclusion, despite Argentina's own shortcomings, its debt trajectory over the last 25 years reveals that we are faced with an international sovereign debt (non)system that disproportionally rewards speculation at the expense of the people, and in which financial institutions and creditor nations hardly ever pay their fair share or shoulder their responsibility. The overwhelming support for the 2015 United Nations sovereign debt resolution across developing nations exposed the profound need for stronger inter-national legal and financial reform to deal with sovereign debt in a way that is compatible with inclusive economic growth. We urgently need a new framework to ensure that the growth of debt does not impede our ability to honour the debt of growth.

© 2017 The Author. Journal of Law and Society © 2017 Cardiff University Law School

JOURNAL OF LAW AND SOCIETY
VOLUME 44, NUMBER 1, MARCH 2017
ISSN: 0263-323X, pp. 123–49

Social Rights Constitutionalism: An Antagonistic Endorsement

EMILIOS CHRISTODOULIDIS*

The article discusses how we might understand solidarity as the organizing concept behind the institutionalization of social rights. I argue that writing solidarity into social rights constitutionalism carries productive tension into constitutional thinking because it disturbs the smooth passage from civil to political and finally to social rights. Marshall's influential argument that social rights are continuous *to civil and political rights has become both the grounding assumption in constitutional theory and at the same time the most obvious lie in the constitutional practice of advanced capitalist democracies, clearly belied in EU constitutional practice under* austerity. *I explore the various attempts to* accommodate *the continuity of civil, political, and social rights in the face of the contradictory articulation of social democracy and capitalism before undertaking something of a defence of the* antinomic *significance of social rights constitutionalism, and probing what mileage might be left in 'exploiting' the contradiction between capitalist interests and social rights.*

> There is in capitalism a debt, and the creditor is the proletariat.
>
> J.-F. Lyotard[1]

* School of Law, University of Glasgow, 5–9 The Square, Glasgow G12 8QQ, Scotland
Emilios.Christodoulidis@glasgow.ac.uk

With thanks to Fernando Atria, Marija Bartl, Ruth Dukes, Marco Goldoni, Stephanie Jones, Markos Karavias, Martin Krygier, Pablo Marshall, George Pavlakos, Johan van der Walt, and Scott Veitch.

1 The original formulation by Lyotard, in the 'unpublished introduction to an unfinished book on the movement of March 22' runs like this: 'By calling it labor force Marx is perhaps only forcing bourgeois political economy to recognise that there is, in capitalism too, a debt, and that the creditor is the proletariat.' (J.-F. Lyotard, *Political Writings*, trans. B. Readings (1993) 64. I have removed the brackets, and the caveats, and pared it down.)

123

I. PROLEGOMENA TO ANY FUTURE SOCIAL RIGHTS CONSTITUTIONALISM

1. *Social rights in the era of austerity*

Lyotard's implicit reference to Marx in the above quote links politics to debt in a counter-intuitive reversal of the debtor/creditor relationship. It is a reversal that will be explored as an instance of the antinomic in the last part of this article. We begin our discussion with a reference to debt and will close with it, tracing in its suffocating embrace of politics, perhaps something of an opportunity. But we begin with a prior question. We ask: *what does it mean to raise today – under conditions of austerity – the question of social rights constitutionalism?* The usual answer is that it means little. Under the dominant rationalization, social rights are increasingly less affordable compensations for the social costs of the integration of markets on a global scale. Social rights are the more obvious casualties, however 'regrettable', of the seemingly inexorable process of globalization, a result of the economic freedom afforded to capital to circumvent the national systems of social protection by relocating to cheaper sites – whether it be the reality, or merely the threat, of relocation. Systems of social and labour protection have thereby been thrown into the vicious circle of competitive alignment, with the devaluation of labour as the principal adjustment factor. The effects of the 'race to the bottom' on social rights have been devastating. The *social constitution* entrusted with the redress of the worse effects of market integration can only be mobilized at the extreme end of the released social devastation, as the last refuge for guaranteeing the needs of biological existence, and remains otherwise toothless in regard of the majority of the effects of globalization.

Austerity comes to compound the devastation. For those economies that austerity has locked into the vicious circle of shrinkage, the spectre of sovereign debt has come to displace social constitutionalism as such. The transition of the southern European states from 'tax states' to 'debt states' – states, that is, that cover the larger part of their expenditure through borrowing rather than taxation and have to service that accumulating debt with an ever increasing share of their revenue[2] – introduces a faultline that cuts across the constitutional landscape and that only widens under the momentum of its own operation. The loss of budgetary sovereignty shrinks the political capacity of the state; state functions are transferred to markets; and the constitutive coincidence between addressors and addressees of law making is broken. The problem now is that with states beholden to markets through sovereign debt, the earlier notion that states can also serve as addressees of social rights claims – typically as demands to shelter certain

---

2 For a fuller analysis, see W. Streeck, *Buying Time* (2014).

fundamentals of existence from market allocations – becomes meaningless. In the gesture of underwriting the credit-worthiness of states, markets perform an inclusionary move that collapses the opposition that gave social rights leverage, and reconfigures them as debts.

Austerity politics in the era of sovereign debt are the desperate, rushed, and brutalizing attempts to contain the contradiction between democracy and capitalism,[3] and, in Wolfgang Streeck's eloquent title, characterize capitalism's attempt to *buy time*.[4] The defeat of the Syriza 'interlude'[5] in Greece in this context is variously instructive, offering lessons that we have only just begun to discern. The intensification of the contradiction, the rapid acceleration of the appropriation of surplus value out of the 'failed' experiment of monetary union *(failed for whom?)*, the generalization of market thinking at every turn, also stake the continuation of the system on an increasingly brutal implementation of austerity that walls itself up against alternatives. The development has a major effect on the question of legitimation, and what once might have been a reason to invoke a 'legitimation crisis'. The horizon of debt and the mutations and substitutions it effects relieves capitalism of the need to mobilize the customary legitimatory narratives of individual freedom, innovation, progress, rational choice, market veridiction. Instead, it instils compulsion at the point of the recovery of meaning. With that move it substitutes reflexivity for necessity. It is against the false generalizing of necessity[6] that, one might hope, politics might rediscover its opportunity; not in the apocalyptic terms of a global response to global capital, but in a more local, pragmatic democratic assertion of solidarity – and the social rights it underwrites – as the animating principle of social constitutionalism, of the kind that dignified European post-war democratic societies.

When the democratic description of 'peoplehood' and our sense of our position as subjects become problematic, constitutionalism begins to falter on its social axis. It falters in those situations when the question of the social dimension of constitutionalism is begged: as it is begged in the paradoxical 'sovereign' decision of a people to hand over sovereign determination.[7]

---

3 The organizing hypothesis of this contradiction has been developed by W. Streeck, 'The crisis of democratic capitalism' (2011) 71 *New Left Rev.* 5 (see, also, W. Streeck, 'Markets and Peoples' (2012) 73 *New Left Rev.* 63).

4 Streeck, op. cit., n. 2.

5 I am referring here to the period between January 2015, when the left-wing party was voted into power, and July 2015 when, after the referendum that in effect rejected the EU's austerity package and the conditionalities imposed, the government capitulated under the extreme pressure of the EU.

6 See, also, Clemens Kaupa's contribution in this volume.

7 The case of Greece in instructive. The Greek Court of Cassation had the opportunity to reflect on the constitutionality of the first memorandum and the 'conditionalities' it contained in its decision 668/2012 in a case brought before the Court by the Athens Bar, arguing that the MoU, as incorporated in the legislation, compromised budgetary sovereignty because it transferred national competences to international bodies.

125

These are shorthand formulations that cover over the more complex realities of the lived experience of constitutional practice coming undone at the seams, making it impossible for people to rationalize the political conditions under which they dwell, that shape their life chances and the ties of inter-generational solidarity. I will insist in what follows on this experiential dimension because it is this dimension onto which the antinomic grafts. Not because, as Husserl put it,[8] 'all reflection undertaken for existential reasons is naturally critical', because the problem as we will see involves the emergence in the first place of a problem, or stake, as open to question and therefore to reflection. Nor, as per Ulrich Beck, can we assume that 'a public emerg[es] not on the basis of consensus of decision but *out of dissent* about the consensus of decisions',[9] because what counts as 'dissent', and the scope of reflexivity, overstates the capacity of the constitutional subject to make sense of the constitutional situation that confronts it, the intelligibility, even, of the situation *as* constitutional. We will return to all this in the last section. Suffice it here to note that we may understand this reflexive dissent not in a key of imperfect or failed consensus but in a key of the antinomic, which makes it radically unproductive on a register of 'deliberation' aiming at rational consensus, but productive perhaps as a clear indicator of its con-stitutive limitation. A different tradition, of the *material* constitution, invites us to begin with the thought that those who produce value in a society also determine its disposal, and that *to act on the contradiction* – as will emerge here in the fraught articulation of social rights and capitalist interests – is to act against the usurpation of value and the denial of a speaking position to the producers of value. It may take the form of dissent against the integration of interests by the agents of capital as orchestrated through the EU. Or, in the constitutional key of this article, it may take the form of the stubborn assertion of social rights, of constitutional warrant, against their elimination through 'total' market activity.

At the point of entry let us state, as 'prolegomena', two fundamental premises that I assume near-axiomatic for any theorization of *social rights constitutionalism*. First, that as *social* rights they give institutional form to *solidarity*. Secondly, that this institutional form, as *constitutional*, involves constitutive assumptions about entrenchment, hierarchization, and rationali-zation. A commitment is constitutionally *entrenched* when it can only be modified through political decisions as mandated through constitutional amendment procedures; *hierarchy* elevates constitutional provisions above the ordinary institutional activity of the legal regulation of economic and social life; and '*rationalization*' means that the meaning of norms is informed by constitutional principle. As 'prolegomena', these constitutive

---

8 E. Husserl, *The Crisis of European Sciences and Transcendental Phenomenology: An Introduction to Phenomenological Philosophy* (1970) 60.
9 U. Beck, *Cosmopolitan Vision* (2006) 339.

conjunctures first, on the substantive level, with 'solidarity' and then, on the formal level, with the three aspects of the reflexivity it deploys, are conditions of the meaning of social rights constitutionalism.

The structure of the argument is as follows. In the remainder of this section we look at the 'social' of social constitutionalism, that is, its connection with solidarity as *dogmatic resource* and as *frame and interdiction*. The accommodations of the following part (section II) relate to the continuity between generations of rights, as famously stated by T.H. Marshall.[10] I will argue against these accommodations that they only 'reconcile' social rights to individual rights by subsuming the former to the latter. If Marshall's continuity thesis is to be pursued, then *with* him we must theorize social class as contradictory to citizenship and understand continuity in light of this antinomy, where citizenship, as realized through social rights and the value of solidarity, involves a qualitative, transcendent, step. This is the subject of the third part (section III), where the argument will take its antagonistic turn, as it seeks to push antinomy onto constitutional terrain and to reinstate its lost connection with the dogmatic resources and the particular form of constitutional reflexivity they sustain. To persist along this practical-theoretical trajectory, even where these recouplings have now come to be seen as improbable, is to tap the logic of immanent critique.[11] It is important, I argue, not to displace the antinomic significance of social rights constitutionalism. If the endorsement of social rights adopts a vocabulary of antagonism, it is to return *against* the dominant rationalizations to what is lost when market thinking eclipses solidarity, and to clear a space for strategic constitutional intervention.

2. Solidarity and constitutionality

Alain Supiot reminds us that in its original juridical sense – that dates from Roman law – *solidarity* was the term for what was effectively a technique of holding co-responsible all those who played a role in the generation of a certain risk.[12] 'The Roman legal concept *in solidium*', adds Hauke Brunkhorst, 'means an obligation for the whole: joint liability, common debt, solidary obligation.'[13] The original solidary 'asymmetrical' obligation is 'sublated' in the direction of *reciprocity*,[14] and this sense of reciprocity is generalized with the advent of the social state which introduced the pooling of the risks of existence and gave solidarity the organizational form of social security and public services, to which one contributed according to one's

---

10 T.H. Marshall, 'Citizenship and social class' in *Sociology at the Crossroads and Other Essays* (1963).
11 I refer here to Marx's notion, as developed in particular by Adorno.
12 A. Supiot, 'Grandeur and misery of the social state' (2013) 82 *New Left Rev.* 99.
13 H. Brunkhorst, *Solidarity* (2015) 2.
14 id., p. 60.

resources and benefited according to one's needs. That the crisis of social rights constitutionalism marks today the decline of solidarity as *organizational* form does not, for Supiot, mark also its decline as a dogmatic resource. After all, 'the social state is simply one moment in the long history of human solidarities which have taken multiple forms, none of them definitive nor guaranteed.'[15] This is because, for him, solidarity underpins and sustains juridical reason in a way that is never exhausted by any one of its (organizational) instantiations. He captures this with the concept of *dogma*. His *Homo Juridicus* is a restatement of *law as social hermeneutic*; the *hermeneia* referred to is unique to juridical reason and sustains the dignity and autonomy of *ratio juris*. Its achievement is to provide the shared symbolic medium that *binds* by 'interposing shared meaning between people.'[16] In its hermeneutic function, dogma furnishes the conditions of intelligibility and at the same time marks the limit beyond which *hermeneia* is undone. This notion of limit point is, I think, important; one might think of dogma as that which prevents passage to a different register to measure the adequacy of law's solutions. In this gesture of self-reference, law turns its reflexivity back on itself as dogma and thereby resists the 'truths' of market veridiction.

As *constitutional value*, solidarity orientates teleological and systematic interpretation; it furnishes its particular instantiations in legal practice with meaning that will indeed be open to reinterpretation, but also marks the point beyond which no such (re)interpretation can go without becoming a lie. In terms of its institutional realization, it underwrites social and labour protection and the obligation of social security, legally buttressing them with forms of objective liability. The forms that the institutional support may take is negotiable, but the value the institutional forms support is not; it affords constitutional protection to collective forms of representation and action and collective procedures. We need go no deeper into the function of institutional instantiation, protection, and warrant than to look at the sources of vulnerability that form solidarity's specific vis-à-vis. To understand solidarity as the foundation of the social state, and the founding commitment to mutualize the risks of existence through the provision of social protection, is to appreciate the gesture that understands societal valorization as irreducibly collective, where even those less exposed to risks bear a duty of responsibility, given that they partake as beneficiaries of the totality of social production.

If *social rights* give institutional form to solidarity, the fact that they receive sanction as constitutional rights involves, as we said earlier, a commitment to entrenchment, hierarchization, and rationalization. Against the vagaries of market activity, Supiot gives us a way to hold on to solidarity under the framing conditions of the 'dogmatic' which installs at the root of

15 Supiot, op cit. n. 12, p. 99.
16 A. Supiot, *Homo Juridicus* (2007) xxiv.

128

the properly juridical a certain unquestionability: to constitutionalize solidarity in the forms of social rights, of social protection and social insurance, means, at minimum, to introduce it as axiomatic and non-negotiable interdiction. 'Collective self-determination' sanctions collective capacity for action in the forms of freedom to associate, to bargain, and to strike. The institutions of social insurance, and public services offer a collective defence against the risks of existence: together they offer the institutional realization of solidarity, historical and therefore contingent, and subtended by legal dogma.

And while it would exaggerate the function of social constitutionalism to suggest it has ever *resolved* the contradiction between democracy and capitalism, it has had demonstrable capacity to shelter democracy from capitalist excess, imbuing democratic institutions *within* the economy with force, and enabling the recognition of the constituent role of *virtue* in the economy.[17] It is but a symptom of the pathological expansion of total market thinking that to understand and theorize the economy by means of demo-cratic and moral categories is either seen as some kind of category mistake, or folds into the a priori 'truths' of rational action thinking. We will return to this too. Let us simply say that when George Herbert Mead spoke of 'the working hypothesis in social reform' as the application of intelligence to the control of social conditions,[18] he was talking about the economy as an expression of *democratic* life, and social policy in terms of the reciprocal recognition of vulnerability and dependency, and was certainly not invoking the banalities of rational action thinking.

II. ACCOMMODATING CONTINUITIES

The accommodations explored here relate to the *continuity* between generations of rights.[19] Keen to remain with Marshall's normative argument about citizenship, current 'resolutions' to the contradiction between democracy and capitalism have variously invoked, rationalized, and deployed social rights *as continuous* to civil and political rights. As we

---

17 See M. Glasman, *Unnecessary Suffering: Managing Market Utopia* (1994) ch. 1: 'The Virtue economy'.
18 As Mead says:

> In social reform, or the application of intelligence to the control of social conditions, we must make a like assumption, and this assumption takes the form of belief in the essentially social character of human impulse and endeavor. We cannot make persons social by legislative enactment, but we can allow the essentially social nature of their actions to come to expression under conditions which favor this.

G.H. Mead, 'The working hypothesis in social reform' (1899) 5 *Am. J. of Sociology* 367, at 370.
19 Marshall, op. cit., n. 10.

explore these 'accommodating' syntheses they are gradually exposed as forms of the reconciliation-cum-subsumption of democracy to capitalism, and all too often captive forms of thought.

1. *Budgetary continuity*

In his seminal 1949 lecture, Thomas Marshall argued that successive waves of rights – civil, political and social – should be conceived along a continuous trajectory as markers of society's struggle to contain and *overcome* the constitutive significance of class. Social rights in the continuity argument are tied to the efforts of:

> political power to supersede, supplement or modify operations of the economic system in order to achieve results which the economic system would not achieve on its own, ... guided by values other than those determined by market forces.

His theory engaged a 'secondary system of industrial citizenship', where syndicalist activity assumes 'the guise of an action modifying the whole pattern of social inequality.'[20]

The 'continuity argument' appears to stumble early on the objection that the successive categories of rights involve different bases of justification. To argue for their continuity presupposes therefore some prior alignment at the deeper level of justification. For theorists of *discontinuity*, to place the categories on a continuum misses the fundamental opposition between the rationales of entitlement and liberty, underlying civic rights; participation, underlying political rights; and need satisfaction, underlying social rights. For them, where not actually zero-sum, the rights might align in a relationship of mutual limitation, or, at best, mutual correction. Continuity arguments, their objection goes, miss this.

Take the varieties of the argument popularized under the rubric of 'tragedy of the commons'. With its connotations of overstepping and inexorability, it stands as a warning against hubris. The lesson conveyed is that rational action – taken unquestionably by the theorists of tragedy as coincident with the maximization of individual returns – cannot guarantee the sustainability of the commons. Although presented as an argument that individual motivations, typically greed, stand in the way of sustainable use, it is only a small step to the argument that the satisfaction of need, inexhaustible and unchecked, will invite a raiding of the common pool of resources through overfarming, overfishing, and so on, where that pool as freely available is bereft of the sanction of the exclusionary device of individual property. Property and civil rights typically come to the rescue as framing conditions to what the requirements of ordering the commons might require. Discontinuities abound: property rights are pitted against the

20 id., p. 28.

130

potentially excessive demands carried by social rights, and pitted also against political rights, the apparent risk here being that the motivation of politicians to promise too much to electorates, in order to secure re-election, makes democracy an inappropriate register and means to achieve any kind of equilibrium, let alone the delivery of efficient outcomes. The rational response in the face of the tragedy is to understand the individual (negative) rights as corrective of social (positive) rights. Against the hubris of organizing a society solely on the principle of need satisfaction, the threatened raiding of the common pool of societal resources is controlled through individual negative rights and property title.

In their much quoted and admired book, *The Cost of Rights*,[21] Stephen Holmes and Cass Sunstein took issue with Garrett Hardin's influential rendering of the 'tragedy' thesis[22] and argued against the naïve separation of negative and positive rights that marks out the discontinuity thesis, and in favour of the *budgetary* continuity between categories of rights. The 'negative rights/positive rights distinction' turns out to 'be based on fundamental confusions', they argued, for 'all legally enforced rights are necessarily positive rights, as the legal maxim "where there is a right, there is a remedy" highlights.'[23] Every first-generation civil/political right is exercised in the shadow of public enforcement: the right to vote requires a publicly-funded polling station; the right to property must be protected by firefighters and the police; contracts would be useless if creditors could not instigate a public judicial procedure against a defaulting debtor.[24] Importantly the normative separation of the private and the state realms is unsustainable, as even 'rights in contract law and tort law are not only enforced but also created, interpreted, and revised by public agencies.'[25] In short, the 'opposition between "government" and "free markets" turns out to be largely spurious.'[26] Finally, a budgetary perspective of rights undermines the notion that some rights are non-derogable, or 'absolutes', for if rights imply budgetary costs, then their enforcement engenders opportunity costs, and in a world of scarce resources a 'no-compromise attitude will therefore produce confusion and arbitrariness and may, on balance, disserve the very rights it intends to promote.'[27] In short, the 'cost of rights' approach undermines a plethora of conventional binary oppositions (negative rights versus positive rights, private law versus public law, government versus free markets, and so on) which may obfuscate more than they clarify.

21 S. Holmes and C. Sunstein, *The Cost of Rights: Why Liberty Depends on Taxes* (1999).
22 G. Hardin, 'The Tragedy of the Commons' (1968) 162 *Science* 1243.
23 Holmes and Sunstein, op. cit., n. 21, p. 43.
24 id., pp. 53, 13, 48.
25 id., p. 49.
26 id., p. 64.
27 id., p. 125.

In an eloquent acclamatory comment on the Holmes/Sunstein thesis, David Garland also invites us to 'question the distinction between social rights and individual rights' and to see instead that 'individual rights are themselves thoroughly social'. He says:

> All rights, including those we conventionally call 'individual' rights, are *positive* (they imply remedies, provide benefits and entitlements, trigger state action and the resources needed to make it effective); all rights have *costs* (they entail the transfer of resources, typically from general taxation); and all rights are *social* (they mobilize social resources and social authority to remedy rights violations or facilitate the exercise of political and civil rights). And all rights are fundamentally *public*, involving social resources, state authority, and the supportive conduct of state officials.[28]

For Garland, 'rights, properly so-called, are legally actionable claims that the rights-holder may make against others.' Rights are thus power resources – allocated to, and at the disposal of, rights-holders. In this 'social rights' are certainly not 'anomalous' with respect to 'bourgeois law'. In both directions a relatively smooth continuity holds across the continuum, both as an empirical matter ('social rights ... have been established in the legal systems of many capitalist nations for more than half a century, without noticeably disruptive or revolutionary effects') and in terms of theoretical construction, 'if we look more closely at supposedly "non-social" individual rights, setting aside the ideological terms in which these are usually discussed', and acknowledge that 'they too have these same redistributive, co-operative, economic characteristics.'[29]

At one level Garland is right of course.[30] But why, we ask, such relentless moderation? What theoretical-political leverage is this form of ('non-ideological') continuity argument to offer social rights, especially as smothered under austerity's budgetary stringency? That is not to say that the professed 'accommodation' suggested by the budgetary continuity argument is not problematic on its own terms, even before we get to the brutality of austerity politics. Why assume that the fact that the defence of all categories of rights is overlaid by their administration by the state effecting transfers and making public provision is salient or *decisive* to continuity? Or the fact that they all involve costs, collapse any qualitative definitional feature, and place civil and social rights on a continuum, the latter distinct from the former as a question of 'degree rather than kind' in being 'more

---

28 D. Garland, 'On the Concept of "Social Rights"' (2015) 24 *Social and Legal Studies* 622, at 626.

29 id., p. 625.

30 Especially if one insists on his suggestion to 'use [social rights] to rethink what that standard conception ought to be', although it is not clear how radically he takes the argument: 'Our jurisprudence too often embraces a liberal individualist conception of rights when in fact *all rights are social*' (id.). Much depends on how far one is prepared to take the suggestion – see my last section, 'Constitutionalizing contradiction'.

expensive and more redistributive'?[31] Why would the fact that 'all rights depend on the availability of economic resources and political will' establish any kind of common denominator that might accommodate continuity other than in its most surface manifestation, given that the political question and the fight are over the justification of the allocations? The political question thus reinvokes a deep *dis*continuity, under which the tenuous accommodations across the faultline of democracy and capitalism are potentially torn asunder.

The budgetary argument that establishes continuity by stringing together the shared *surface* characteristics of rights offers an argument for continuity-cum-elision. Where the difference of kind (of social rights vis-à-vis individual rights) is transfigured into a difference of degree, their *differentia specifica* – their eidetic specificity – collapsed, they are forced to blend seamlessly into the long postscript of the political, then social, accommodations of capitalism. And with this blending-in the very thing they name, *solidarity*, is supercoded to capitalist determinations and thereby cancelled out. To argue that both social and property rights are 'positive', institutional', 'costly', and 'social' is hardly controversial but certainly inattentive to the redistributive demand at the heart of the clash of their respective essential justifications. Unless an argument is offered that writes redistributive demands into property relations, in the way, say, of deviationist doctrine or 'the commons', the 'social' nature of the property rights regime remains comfortably immune to the demands of solidarity.

And this is all *before* we get to the governance of austerity and its field of fierce appropriations. Because if the 'budgetary continuity' argument already falters on its own gathering principle, it certainly collapses with the transition from the tax state to the debt state, that gives the lie to the proffered accommodation of liberty – negative, positive, collective, what have you – under conditions of sovereign debt and the partial or wholesale hollowing out of budgetary sovereignty, the first to lose any credible line of defence to the 'Matthew effect' of globalization.[32] The separation of economic from social constitutionalism creates the conditions of a staggering asymmetry between the power to damage that labour markets wield and the remedies available in terms of social rights jurisprudence, and 'budgetary continuity' simply seals over this damage.

Take the example of the European Union and the unleashing of its very

---

31 id., p. 627
32 Alain Supiot refers to the bizarre effect where the very commitment of national economies to political redress of the social costs of globalization becomes self-defeating because it weakens the state's ability to deliver it. Accordingly those most in need of protection are those most bereft of it, due to the labour market's flexibility at circumventing the costs of social protection by relocating to cheaper sites. See A. Supiot, *L'esprit de la Philadelphie: la justice social face au marché total* (2010).

133

particular brand of austerity.[33] The Maastricht Treaty had already introduced the key requirement that in the absence of a lender of last resort, member states' self-imposed frugality would ensure the smooth function of the currency against potential turbulence from financial speculation; frugality that (already enshrined in the accession criteria) involved the reduction of the state deficit and of public debt vis-à-vis the national GDP, forcing states into the contraction of public expenditure which, in turn, would supposedly attract investors to buy their national bonds. When the 2008 crisis transformed public debts into sovereign debts, the only solution envisaged for near-defaulting states, now constitutionally unable to self-finance and with their budgetary sovereignty handed over to EU bodies, would be to regain the confidence of markets by slashing their welfare budgets.[34] A series of ersatz laws imposed through emergency procedures and without democratic scrutiny ensured that the monetary area is actually governed through strict criteria of budgetary austerity. These included the large-scale privatization of public services, cuts to pensions, salary moderation, attacks on trade unionism, and the wholesale flexibilization of labour. There can be little doubt that in all this we witness a transformation of the role of the state in protecting social rights, where it has to resort to financial markets in order to fund social services. The whole 'philosophy' of Euro governance is in effect geared toward the entrenchment of austerity policies in such a way that the decoupling of social rights from European citizenship is fully realized in the name of competitiveness and 'total market' thinking.

A short aside: a powerful illustration of how citizenship has been transfigured and class reinvigorated in these processes is provided by Maurizio Lazzarato.[35] Lazzarato argues that whereas the 'real' economy impoverishes wage earners through wage freezes and a variety of forms of flexibilization of employment, and while it impoverishes social rights claimants through rolling back social spending, it ostensibly offers *finance* as a means to 'enrich' them through credit and stock market investment. The 'entrepreneurs of self' under the new dispensation are in debt, poor, and precarious; their 'entrepreneurship' consists in managing their employability, debt repayments, and a drop in wages. Their 'stake-holding' is a holding of debt. This form of political participation – their 'partaking of the

---

33 Marco Goldoni and I have developed this argument in our paper, 'The Political Economy of European Social Rights' in *Social Rights in Europe in an Age of Austerity*, eds. S. Civitarese and S. Halliday (2017).

34 In the most recent case, the French National Assembly approved the labour-undercutting 'El Khomri' Law, drafted without any prior consultation with trade unions and rushed through the emergency procedure of Article 49.3 of the French Constitution, which stipulates the emergency procedure that allows the government to pass a Bill into law *without a vote*, unless a majority of deputies pass a motion of non-confidence, thus forcing the prime minister to resign.

35 M. Lazzarato, *The Making of the Indebted Man: An essay on the neoliberal condition* (2012).

sensible', as Rancière would put it – involves what they take upon themselves as a matter of responsibility and, deeper, of self-discipline and constitution, their self-valorization in the mirror of financial capital: an indebtedness that instils unprecedented levels of existential precariousness through the risks and costs that capital externalizes onto society. What is achieved in the process is a comprehensive shift in the experience of the right-holder as debtor, bent on maximizing his or her employability, self-equipping in preparedness, availability, flexibility. This is what Marx in his *Comment on James Mill* called 'the lie of moral recognition' and 'the immoral baseness of this morality' where 'the moral recognition of man ... takes the form of credit.'

2. *Justiciability*

A second, highly popular, statement of the continuity thesis explains it in terms of a justiciable constitutional guarantee to individuals of all rights across the three categories. In his important book, *Law and Irresponsibility*, in the process of discussing the complex ways in which the *legal form* both organizes and dissipates responsibility, Scott Veitch revisits the 'legalisation of politics' thesis and the generalization of the language of rights.[36] Significantly, the demand that society provide solutions to its political conflicts (and as far as social constitutionalism is concerned the demands of distributive justice and the meeting of needs) drives this 'legalisation of politics', the instrumental deployment of law that carries justiciability as the answer, and with it, as Veitch puts it, a certain reversal is effected where 'the demand *of* law, can be seen as providing the demands *for* law': the delivery of authoritative verdicts. Justiciability becomes the legal reduction of politics, and this 'reduction achievement', to use Niklas Luhmann's term, conditions the claims of social constitutionalism and its authentication. 'The shift in expectations and presentation that comes with the presence of legal rights and third-party decidability', says Veitch, 'affects how the original normative practice or conflicts arising from it are understood.' Here 'other forms of normative claim that seek authentication, recognition or approval' must be made to conform to the specific modes of legal cognition, reasoning, and decision making.'[37]

The important point to take from this is that the recognition of social rights as individual actionable entitlements and as '*authentication*' of individual demands are at the same time forms of *blockage* of collective claims of

36 S. Veitch, *Law and Irresponsibility: On the legitimation of human suffering* (2007). By 'justiciability', he understands the 'insertion into the realm of political conflict [of] a mode of dealing with that conflict, which now comes to be understood in justiciable terms' (p. 83). The introduction of the legal form allows for a resolvability of political conflict on the back of law's introduction of commensurability into politics.
37 id.

135

distributive equality and societal needs satisfaction as a political-democratic question. Simply stated, social rights are *not* individual entitlements to societal resources, actionable in courts. The social right to solidarity and dignity, as informing the protection of health, housing, work, education, and so on are not, and should not, be cashed out as the state obligation to provide a diabetes sufferer with treatment (*Soobramoney*[38] in 1997), a homeless person with a home (*Grootboom*[39] in 2000) or the inhabitants of the Soweto with free water (*Mazibuko*[40] in 2009). I refer to South African cases here for a reason;[41] 'activist'/transformative constitutionalism has rarely been as insightfully developed as it was in the post-apartheid constitutional juris-prudence, that had to face up courageously to such dilemmas.[42] The Court struggled with what was the unworkable and unjust constitutional practice of allocating limited societal resources on a 'first-come, first-serve' basis that would make a mockery of the political responsibility of government to all its citizens. While the argument about the proper limits of the reasonableness of judicial review raged for over a decade in both the courts and the academy, the constitutional consensus gradually emerged that 'it is impossible to give everyone access even to a "core" service immediately. All that is possible, and all that can be expected from the state, is that it act reasonably to provide access to socio-economic rights',[43] and within the available resources 'to achieve a progressive realisation'[44] of social rights. The question of judicial oversight of governmental action in the direction of meeting urgent social needs has been recommended, rightly, as a further constitutional commit-ment to the protection of social rights. That such political responsibility be directed to distributive justice and conform to the ideal of solidarity is what

---

38 *Soobramoney* v. *Minister of Health (Kwazulu-Natal)* (CCT32/97) [1997] ZACC 17; 1998 (1) SA 765 (CC); 1997 (12) BCLR 1696 (27 November 1997).

39 *Government of the Republic of South Africa and Others* v. *Grootboom and Others* (CCT11/00) [2000] ZACC 19; 2001 (1) SA 46; 2000 (11) BCLR 1169 (4 October 2000).

40 *Mazibuko and Others* v. *City of Johannesburg and Others* (CCT 39/09) [2009] ZACC 28; 2010 (3) BCLR 239 (CC) ; 2010 (4) SA 1 (CC) (8 October 2009).

41 It is not just the South Africans who have struggled with these dilemmas. There has also been a debate in the North American academy over the actionability and justiciability of social rights. Frank Michelman has been a leading figure in this debate, and the shift in his position from advocating a justiciable constitutional guarantee of basic welfare benefits in 1969 (F. Michelman, 'On protecting the poor through the 14th amendment' (1969) 83 *Harvard Law Rev.* 7) to treating them as constitutional aspirations to which governments can be held accountable (F. Michelman, 'Socio-economic rights in Constitutional Law: explaining America away' (2008) 6 *International J. of Constitutional Law* 663 is worthy of note). For an illuminating account of the shift, and Michelman's work more generally, see J. van der Walt, 'Delegitimation by Constitution?' in (2015) 98 *KritV/CritQ/RCrit* 303.

42 See Karl Klare's influential statement to this effect: K. Klare, 'Legal Culture and Transformative Constitutionalism' (1998) 14 *South African J. on Human Rights* 146.

43 *Minister of Health* v. *Treatment Action campaign*, 2002 (5) SA 721 (CC) para. 35.

44 D.M. Davis, 'Socioeconomic rights: Do they deliver the goods?' (2008) 6 *I·CON* 687.

136

social rights constitutionalism demands, and of course there is an important place for justiciability in this; but that actionable individual rights is its proper *modus operandi* misconceives it as an *individual* entitlement, and miscasts continuity on the back of that misconception.

3. *Capability*

A third line that the restoration of continuity takes involves the highly influential thesis of enhancing market participation. According to the theory of 'capabilities', uncontrolled – or 'disembedded' – markets deplete human resources, and thus threaten the very conditions on which markets depend for their operation. The answer comes in the form of a participation-enhancing *social market*.

The argument runs along the following lines: while the market, as harnessed to capitalist production, grants societies a significant increase in productivity and innovation, it also effects a significant increase in social inequality and social exclusion, with the very real threat of generating vicious circles that cause the depletion of the human resources. For capabilities theories, social rights are conceived as an answer to the inequality and the depletion. If capitalism privatizes the gains and socializes the costs of running the economy, social rights orchestrate (at least in part) the attempt to meet those costs of the operation of markets and guarantee the conditions of participation and meaningful citizenship. If 'negative rights' underpin and sustain liberty in the sense of a demand that the state does not encroach on private spheres of activity, in a complementary gesture social rights sustain 'positive duties', demands on the state to meet the population's needs for education, healthcare, sustenance, housing, and so on, *without* which personal autonomy or meaningful participation in society would remain fundamentally unrealized, and *with* which, growth and macro-economic performance can be achieved on the back of such 'fiscal multipliers'.

In the last few decades, Amartya Sen's work has been at the centre of the general attempt to invest in the capabilities of the poor to engage in economic activity in order to address the problem that there are actors who do not possess the practical capability to pursue their interest – or to take action – within the market system as it stands.[45] While the market is unwaveringly held up by the 'capabilities' theorists as the mechanism that best distributes social resources amongst possible uses, once it is acknowledged that the conditions of general competition will never obtain empirically, the efficiency of 'actually existing' markets becomes question-able. The capabilities approach is an attempt to consolidate, not substitute, the range of *information* that is available through the price mechanism. And

---

45 A. Sen, *The Idea of Justice* (2009) 7–8.

the enhancement has to do with addressing the opportunities that economic actors actually have of revealing their preferences through their choices. With an eye on opportunity-structure, equality – understood as equal basic capability – measures itself against the promise of equal participation. For Sen and the capabilities theorists, a market order must *complement* its distribution of formal bargaining positions (that secure equal formal participatory positions in the market economy) with the just distribution of 'conversion factors' that allow economic actors to pursue their advantage within the framework of the exchange, to furnish them, in other words, with the *capabilities* necessary to undertake autonomous action in the context of market exchange. As Simon Deakin, one of the theory's most eloquent and fervent defenders transfers the insight across to his own thinking about 'capacitas',[46] what is new are:

> the elements of a concept that goes beyond purely formal guarantees of market access, to encompass the conditions needed for effective participation in the complex economic orders which characterise our time.[47]

'Capacitas', he says:

> should be thought of as the juridical concept through which the legal system defines the conditions of access to the market by human persons ... In a narrow conception, capacity is defined as the ability to engage in rational economic action ... In a wider conception it is the sum total of the preconditions of effective participation in market relations.[48]

Against paradigms where 'resources, endowments and preferences are taken as given' and so 'exogenous to the operation of the market mechanism',[49] the *capacitas* argument asks whether the economic actor is self-sufficiently capable of revealing his or her preferences through his or her choices – and reorients our attention to 'the process by which preferences and endowments are formed'[50] and thus to the conditions needed for effective participation in the economic order.

For a position that balances finely between market-enhancing and market-correcting logics, its privileging of market over political allocations in the final instance leaves it tainted for the Left, while the fact that its prescriptions *must* involve some welfarist leverage in order to materialize opportunity-structure for the powerless and therefore cannot avoid regulatory 'coercive transfers' leaves it tainted for the Right. Theorists on the Right will go further; Luhmann argued that under conditions of the separation of the political and the economic systems, it becomes nonsensical to attempt to redress deficits on the supply side of the economy with political devices like social rights.[51]

---

46 S. Deakin and A. Supiot (eds.), *Capacitas* (2009).
47 id., p. 1.
48 id., p. 28.
49 id.
50 id., p. 19.
51 N. Luhmann, *Law as a Social System* (2004) ch. 12.

138

Given the attacks from both Left and Right, given the difficulties of sustaining capability-enhancing programmes under conditions of the global organization of production, and given the vulnerability of the continuity argument to the antinomies that must be tamed to establish complementarities of sorts, it is perhaps no wonder that social rights have receded to such an extent, only 'to blunt the harsh edge of market forces on the fabric of social life':[52] 'blunting' devices for the redress of the more extreme pathologies, results, and costs of economic systems. With the public/private law divide replicating that between politics and the economy, social rights are left to hover on the borderline, toothless in the face of property title and 'discredited' as policy or regulation interference by the champions of market thinking. Attractive as the notion of a *social* market is in theory, it has been shown in practice that the market does not entertain predicates lightly. Instead, the market has the unnerving power to enfold and define for itself what is 'social' about it, reflexively, so that any *political* attempt to vary market allocations *must* take a form of external limitation, buttress, and containment.

4. *Proportionality*

To understand proportionality as a language of accommodation, we need to apprehend how it came to cast continuity as commensuration between rights and as 'optimization'. An older constitutional problematic defined the test of proportionality exercised by constitutional courts as a corrective *within* the democratic framework and not *of* it, as its more recent, expansive, restatement does. In that older, more modest understanding, the court would make sure that legislative and executive action complied with the requirements of appropriateness (is the action compatible with democratic law making?), rationality (do means correlate to ends?), and necessity (is the action, amongst functional equivalents, the least intrusive available?). There is nothing incompatible with democracy about proportionality in this classical form; in Johan van der Walt's insightful formulation, it stipulates 'the scope of judicial scrutiny [as] limited to the way parliamentary majorities have *decided* – through a simple procedure of voting that testifies to its own groundlessness – *exactly that which cannot be balanced.*'[53]

But it was difficult for this self-restriction to sustain itself in the force field of the contradiction between democratic organization and capitalist accumulation. Already with the German Federal court's 1958 decision in *Lüth*[54] and its reference to the balancing of competing values, the test of

---

52 K. Rittich, 'Social Rights and Social Policy' in *Exploring Social Rights: Between Theory and Practice*, eds. D. Barak-Erez and A.M. Gross (2008) 110.

53 In van der Walt, op. cit., n. 41, p. 329; and for a more extensive treatment, see his excellent *The Horizontal Effect Revolution and the Question of Sovereignty* (2014) 361–99.

54 *Lüth*, BVerfGE 7, 198; 1 BvR 400/51, 15 January 1958.

proportionality becomes unhinged from its classical, limited, conception[55] to be released in a self-propelling move as substitute for democratic decision-making. By the time we reach the European Constitutional Court's decisions in *Laval* and *Viking*,[56] and the flurry of the subsequent jurisprudence entrenching the economic freedoms of capital against labour protection, the test of proportionality has been magnified out of all proportion to a travesty of its former self, as involving a comprehensive pooling of stakes, values, and interests, to be calibrated on the vague metric of 'optimization'. Proportionality in this form mobilizes a measure of 'proportion' that answers the 'tragedy of the commons'-related fear of democratic excess and of the irrationality of the moment of decision, in order to rein in the 'disproportion' of industrial action and protect the economic freedom of employers.

For the workers of the Nordic states, little more needs to be said about how injurious the removal of key questions of the organization of labour and social protection from democratic fora has proven. But the jurisprudence of EU law remains strangely inattentive to this catastrophe, and under the loud proclamations of the 'new' members, a paralysing dissensus appears to be emerging over what precisely is at stake. A certain unease can be detected amongst academic commentators too, once the argument is repackaged, from a clash between economic freedoms and social rights, as, instead, a clash between the social rights of different constituencies of workers in terms organized by the logic of 'market access' with its very particular recasting of inclusion. How remarkable, in this context, that the dominant position in legal thinking has shifted enough to lend credence to this abdication from democracy and the transferral of key political decisions to the courts. And is this failure to understand social rights as devices that *stem* rather than *facilitate* social dumping not an indicator of how the critical nerve of constitutional thinking has been dulled?

Let us ask, instead, the question that critical theory invites: with the help of what distinctions are we able to resist the surrender of democracy and the subsumption of solidarity to market thinking? Against the market's move to flood the field with functional equivalents, let us fasten onto the non-negotiability of solidarity as a constitutional *value* and as an *achievement* of political constitutionalism. As such, it is non-negotiable as a matter of the self-determination of political society. This does not of course mean that the interpretive questions over what solidarity requires in any one practical context will go away, or that the question over relative thresholds will become uncontroversial. As a question of *determinatio*, such questions remain central to how we understand and operationalize constitutional reason.[57] But what it

---

55 van der Walt, op. cit. (2014), n. 53.
56 *Laval* and *Viking* decisions of the CJEU: C-341/05, *Laval un Partneri Ltd*, ECR 2007, I-11767 and C-438/05, *International Transport Workers' Federation and Finnish Seamen's Union* v. *Viking Line ABP and OÜ Viking Line Eesti*, ECR 2007, I-10779.
57 See J. Finnis, *Natural Law and Natural Rights* (1980).

does mean is that a significant distinction emerges between the (contextual) determination of constitutional value and the optimization of constitutional goods,[58] and that, further, decisions over relative thresholds are not subject to the pricing of their relative weights. In the lexicon famously introduced into jurisprudence by Lon Fuller, solidarity (as constitutional value) remains the aspiration on which any instantiation in any particular case is measured, enjoining, as a matter of definition collective categories, and forging relationality on its own, particular register. And while any instantiation remains an interpretive matter, one that is forced to drop below a certain threshold (Fuller called it the 'morality of duty') surrenders the value altogether and (however 'optimal' on some free-floating register) can no longer count as an instantiation of *that* value.

There is of course a great deal more that can be said about all four of these accommodations but suffice it for present purposes to see how uneasily they connect capitalism and democracy, individual and social rights, how unsustainable the professed continuity: first, as strung alongside the more robust property- and civil-rights counterparts in an argument about budgetary continuity, in the face of the obvious realization that such sovereignty has been handed over to creditors and markets; secondly, in the inflationary invocation of social rights as individual rights in the shrill tones of an unrealistic justiciability across the board; thirdly, as harnessed to capabilities to facilitate 'market access' and enhance market participation in an attempt to initiate a potentially *virtuous* cycle in the global race to increase the rates of return for capitals; fourthly, as flattened out in the relentless weightings and calibrations of 'proportional' balancings. Against the various problematic syntheses of rights, we ask what it might mean to allow *their contradictory articulation* to be played out in constitutional practice.

Before that, two caveats. First, the argument that follows is not an abandonment of Marshall's argument about continuity but its (improbable) restatement in the framework of fundamental antinomy. To hold on to continuity in the face of the contradictory articulation of categories of rights gives antinomy its epistemological significance. Secondly, the insistence on the question of continuity addresses it not (only or principally) as a matter of political philosophy, but of institutional practice. Perfectionist forms of liberal thinking have long advocated a liberalism that constitutively implicates the embeddedness of individual life, identity, and capacity in their social context, arguing that the well-being of the individual is dependent on the social environment. My concern is not with that, which I accept, but with the difficult 'constitutional' juncture. Because it is one thing to say that individual goods and the exercise of negative freedoms must be conceptualized *in tandem* with positive freedoms. It is quite another to establish

---

58 I have offered a short elaboration of the value/good distinction in E. Christodoulidis, 'The European Court of Justice and "Total Market" Thinking' (2013) 14 *German Law J.* 2005.

on that basis a smooth passage between individual and social rights where, under conditions of liberal economic arrangements, capitalist control over social resources trumps the redistributive demands of social justice. The 'accommodationist' positions did indeed address the question of continuity *institutionally;* and it was the institutional junctures of selective coupling and decoupling that invited us to probe the dynamics of alignment on which so much of their casting of continuity in fact hangs *and falters.* The continuity-as-commensurability of the 'budgetary continuity' argument, the toothless corrective of the *social* market, the insidious attribution of proportionate weightings, cast continuity on a register where market allocations always-already skew distribution, where *re*-distribution comes too late, where the recuperation of what is owed to the producers of value – Lyotard's injunction – is obscured and undercut.[59]

III. THE ANTINOMIC SIGNIFICANCE OF THE SOCIAL CONSTITUTION

1. *'Anomalous grafting'*

In an intriguing contribution to the debate on social rights,[60] Fernando Atria prompts us to look at how the demands that solidarity places on the constitution forces *a competition* within the rights category itself. If Atria's is an argument about *dis*continuity, it is emphatically not because individual rights are not social or sensitive to social context. On the contrary, for him, '[s]ocial rights arise as a way of affirming – in terms of justice – the importance of understanding human self-realization as reciprocal rather than individual'. For him, individual rights (negative freedom rights) and social rights (positive freedom rights) cannot be conceived or thematized on a continuum except at the cost of hollowing out social rights or collapsing them in a way that 'de-socialises' them. Individual rights depend on a paradigm of 'contractualism' that as a 'way [of] bridg[ing] the gap between interest and duty [. . .] implies that what is politically relevant is not equality but poverty (more or less extreme).' But social rights – we have already insisted on this – properly understood realize the principle of reciprocity, not charity. In the context of the contractual paradigm, Atria will insist, 'the ideal of citizenship cannot play but a secondary role, because what is politically fundamental is the protection of interests.' For Atria, successes in securing the justiciability of social rights are nothing but toothless victories at best, at worst a sign of how their political leverage has been wasted; in his

---

59 Thanks to Scott Veitch for suggesting the link back to Lyotard's opening: 'There is in capitalism a debt', and 'it is this – their – debt that is being called in.'
60 F. Atria, 'Social Rights, Social Contract, and Socialism' (2015) 24 *Social and Legal Studies* 598.

terms, 'of how the political meaning of social rights properly so-called has been defeated.' The contradiction that besets the category of rights replicates the contradiction between two competing logics of resource allocation: on the one hand, on the basis of what is revealed as merit in the free play of market forces and on the other, on the basis of social need or entitlement as conferred through democratic choices. This is a real contradiction between individual rights and social rights that cannot be sealed over or harmonized, but instead sustains their political potential. That is why for Atria, 'it is central to the very idea of social rights to preserve the distinction between them and individual rights, because the point of social rights is to subvert the idea of individual rights, to turn it against itself.'[61] And why 'social rights can only be understood as anomalous grafts in bourgeois law; the foundation for the latter is the idea of individual rights.'[62]

Further on the metaphor of 'grafting':

> Grafting creates an unstable situation, that is, a situation which has an immanent tendency towards its resolution. This resolution can, in principle, adopt one of two forms: the transformation of the host or the normalization of the graft.[63]

The metaphor of 'anomalous grafting' is wonderfully apt. It might be objected that grafting is already too high a demand and too 'thick' an assumption in the following sense: that if, with Atria, we take the argument about the 'deep grammar' of rights seriously, the operation may be lacking a host altogether, its meaning deprived of a register. We must confront this as a real danger, that the language of social rights becomes merely an attempt that achieves no traction in a system rationalized in a way that already, constitutively, undercuts any notion of *the public* or collective as an *irreducible* category. The assumption that a *more fundamental* notion of the public is available as grounding for social rights is axiomatic here: it is 'dogmatic'. Otherwise, for Atria, the inflationary use of social rights becomes merely ideological.

Atria runs the argument about institutional innovation (grafting) alongside one about 'slow pedagogy', the relation between the two arguments consistently intriguing. The argument turns on the potential release of learning processes that dovetail with the embeddedness, and re-embedding, of practices. Ultimately what is fashioned in the context of *slow* pedagogy, and against the form of *abrupt* market adaptation, is the unfolding of processes of recognition and solidarity, such as are harboured in the notion of social rights. Atria's is not an argument against the market as such. The tenor that remains unwavering in Atria's defence of social rights is the resistance to their (full) internalization by the market and their measurement

---

61 id., p. 605.
62 id., p. 603.
63 id.

on *its* solutions, and the insistence, instead, that the solutions that we need to find for the demands that social rights articulate remains political, on the register of political justice, engaging collective categories and decided as a matter of and for democracy.

We began from the fundamental, if controversial, premise that social rights are incongruous to capitalism and its particular structures of opportunity and reward.[64] Where the market does *all* the work of allocating value to resources amongst possible uses, the distribution of resources with the explicit aim of meeting needs is, from the point of view of market thinking, *irrational*. This incongruity make the 'accommodations' problematic, incapable of managing the faultline between democracy and capitalism except by subsuming the former to the latter. What does it mean to insist on the incongruity, and to act on this assumed 'irrationality'? In essence, I suggest that if social rights are beset by the contradiction between capitalism and democracy, that we explore the significance of their constitutional iteration, as enunciated, that is, with constitutional force, and as unyielding to the various accommodations we explored above. With the urgent appeal not to displace the antinomic significance of social constitutionalism, we might begin to conceptualize how the insistent strategic use of social rights may import a real contradiction, the Hegelian/Marxist moment of the *Dasein der Widersprach*, from which the system cannot retract. Let us look a little more gradually about what this means, and why antinomy matters.

2. *Constitutionalizing contradiction*

To focus on antinomy is to pick up from Hegel, with Marx, not the drive to culmination and synthesis, but the self-undermining moment of contradiction, of thought hitting upon its limit *given* the categories available it. While in Marx contradictions are indices of concrete historical situations, contrary to the cruder materialisms (of Engels and others), they [contradictions] are not to be understood as merely the reflections in thought of real material antagonisms. They point instead to a shortfall of the categories available to us to make sense of the processes of value production and social reproduction, the mismatch between the categories of thought and the modes of social being. Their emergence as contradictions marks the crisis points of articulation, of expressibility, and of intelligibility: of *meaninglessness* that is experienced as such. It is important to emphasize this experiential dimension, the lived incomprehensibility (the '*Dasein*' of the contradiction,

---

64 A Foucauldian reading of incongruity in the theory of rights is suggested by Ben Golder: '[Foucault's] invocations of rights are strategic in this *incongruous* sense as they are situated within the spaces of political formation but are intended to resist and go beyond that formation, to transcend it': B. Golder, 'Foucault's critical (yet ambivalent) affirmation: Three figures of rights' (2011) 20 *Social & Legal Studies* 283, at 295.

as it were) that emerges in particular experiential contexts and that carries its potential energies. It is the lived dimension that is the potential site of disruption of the economy of representation that would otherwise organize meaning, seal it over and, in this state of self-immunization, place it out of reach. For Frederic Jameson who has given us one of the most thoughtful restatements of the concept, it is the *dialectic* that disrupts such finitude, that refuses the sealing-over, that, to use his formulation, 'translates the experience of finitude back into upsurges of transcendence.'[65] Whether, as in Marx, this movement receives a historical guarantee, is a separate issue. The complexities that attend both Marx's and Jameson's positions need not concern us here. Let us focus instead on what forces through as contradiction against the structural conditions that make such an appearance, one might put it, *improbable*. The reference to structural conditions here are those under which people dwell and experience meaninglessness.

This discussion points us in a direction that we cannot possibly take here, and I retain only the elements that return it to our concern with social rights. And the key point is this: social rights as markers of society's commitment to sustain lives of dignity for all its members, extend a vocabulary on which meaninglessness may achieve what we might call *hermeneutic traction* as *injustice*. To retrieve the hermeneutic link to injustice, let alone to act on it, is improbable precisely because the register of justice that would authenticate such a link has been disarticulated under the compulsion of market thinking. Under these conditions, that the injunction 'this is unjust' may still invoke the aspiration of solidarity contained in social constitutionalism is at once the mark of the antinomic and of constitutional 'traction'.

Let us be clearer through the use of a few examples. The following are instances of meaninglessness felt and lived as an experiential deficit. In each case (political) reflexivity, that is, the notion that things could be otherwise, has collapsed into a semblance of necessity. The critical task is to disrupt this semblance and to level against that which carries the mark and seal of necessity an injunction against injustice: to confront it as *unnecessary suffering*.[66] In each case, then, the critical task is to discern in the situation the antinomy that might acquire hermeneutic traction, be signified as injustice, and acted on as such. It is here that the constitutional contradictory iteration of social rights constitutionalism against market thinking, and the former's unwavering insistence on solidarity, may provide the leverage.

Where it *is made to appear* that there is no other rational way to organize the economy than through markets, political-democratic alternatives are

---

65 F. Jameson, *Valences of the Dialectic* (2009) 34.
66 The term 'unnecessary suffering' is borrowed from Maurice Glasman who, in his important book of the same title (Glasman, op. cit., n. 17), used this formulation to capture the threshold of political rationality. Unnecessary suffering is what we, as a society, can attempt to redress, and this possibility is what constitutively invokes the political.

© 2017 The Author. Journal of Law and Society © 2017 Cardiff University Law School

eclipsed as a matter of reason. Necessity takes the form of the 'unaffordability' of social protection, antinomic because it occurs in the midst of a general increase in resources that derives from expanded capitalist reproduction. The antinomy *appears* in the life of those who toil to generate value for the market, is experienced as the injury of massive job insecurity and stagnant wages, and can emerge as the injustice of the withdrawal of recognition. Where it *is made to appear* that there is no other rational way to organize social labour than through the deregulation of the labour market, the injury is expressed as the sacrifice of a generation, where with unemployment raging at over 50 per cent amongst the young (I am referring here to the cases of Greece and Spain) only one in two are likely to be able to *ever work at all*. Meaninglessness inheres in the situation of a sacrifice exacted and not acknowledged. The antinomic is experienced as a crisis of intelligibility and expressibility: an injunction of injustice that cannot achieve inscription on a register of market justice, but only as a claim against the withdrawal of (intergenerational) solidarity. Where it *is made to appear* that there is no other rational way to organize social production than through the profit motive and through market-driven innovation, it appears as the meaninglessness of the destruction of work, where labour-intensive forms of production radically yield to capital-intensive forms, rendering labour superfluous and turning working people into redundant populations: the meaninglessness lies in the experience of redundancy, and, as above, the withdrawal of recognition. Where it *is made to appear* that there is no other rational way to organize the workplace than through the maximization of individual utility, it appears in the assumption of *individual* responsibility for one's occupational degradation, the necessary surrender to the dictates of management. The meaninglessness is felt as the privatization of discontent and sense of occupational failure. The 'antinomic' here points to the withdrawal of *collective* speaking positions and *collective* action opportunities to reverse the degradation, as underwritten and guaranteed by the social right to work, properly understood as enjoining collective and democratic categories.

At none of the junctures on which the withdrawal of meaning occurs is a communicative-'agonistic' stance capable of redressing the usurpation of value or the withdrawal of speaking position; the collapse, in other words, of democratic defence to capitalist expropriation. Recognition, dignity, solidarity can only be interpreted as *antagonistic* to the given economies of representation, the recognition orders, the given distributions of contingency and necessity, what Rancière with such insight called the '*partage du sensible*' (the distribution of the sensible). The antinomic here, expressed by Rancière as 'dissensus', elevates contradiction as condition of the staging of political subjectivities, where the collective is not thought of in terms of identification but of enactment.

We can transfer this insight of Rancière's to radicalize Marshall's, in the only way that does justice to his argument about continuity, one that could not have foreseen at the time the paradigm change brought about by the totalizing ideology of the market. If Marshall argued for the continuity of generations of rights as a means to overcome the injuries of class, it is because the form of continuity that culminates in social rights can be read back across the preceding generations to disturb received distributions and class positions as sanctioned by property rights, *by means* of political rights. To the dialectic unfolding of rights, each successive generation promises a moment of transcendence. There is a clear message in Marshall against the priority of market allocations and a synthesis that projects back along the path of its culmination a different logic of distribution: at this point the sequential dialectic turns *transversal*. For the radicalized Marshall, then, continuity is understood as antinomic or not at all.

A useful practical example refers us back to the right to strike. In *Laval* and *Viking*, the social right of Scandinavian workers to act to protect the significant achievements of decades of social and labour protection was deemed disproportionate vis-à-vis the economic rights of entrepreneurs to move their capital and hired labour around in a classic case of the race to the bottom. Emboldened, perhaps, by the new constitutional mindset of Europe's Constitutional Court, the employers' group at the ILO, in a move that has created a protracted deadlock particularly conducive to the interests of capital, challenged the settled interpretation of Convention 87 and decades-long jurisprudence of the ILO that the constitutional protection of the Freedom of Association extends to the right to strike.[67] Note how clearly the collectivist and individualist paradigms diverge here to fall on either side of this dispute. Understood as a *social* right, freedom of association enjoins democratic and collective categories and is therefore inseparable from the right to strike as the collective-democratic expression of its exercise. As an *individual* right, freedom of association attaches to the individual's right to (or not to) associate, and is in fact inimical to collective democratic expression and ultimately, to the extent that it may undercut collective agreements and syndicalism, a clear move to 'de-socialize' freedom of association. Pooling the rights and their interpretations here achieves nothing except an insidious commensuration, and the right, as a social right, needs to be understood and exercised, against market-driven harmonious and proportionate realignments, in its *contradictory* articulation to individualism.

A series of political, and therefore reversible, decisions[68] have constructed, buttressed, and underwritten the collapse of the constitutional imaginary into its market form. There has been nothing necessary about this construction or its protection; in fact it marks the increasingly desperate

---

67 See T. Novitz, *International and European Protection of the Right to Strike* (2003); C. La Hovary, 'Showdown at the ILO? A Historical Perspective on the Employers' Group's 2012 Challenge to the Right to Strike' (2013) 42 *Industrial Law J.* 338.

68 See Supiot, op. cit., n. 12.

attempts of Europe's commissars to protect the market from itself.[69] The result has been an insidious constitutionalization of soft instruments, a creeping, rushed, and unsystematic campaign to shore up monetary union under the aegis of the constitutional, backed by the noxious exercise of proportionality as optimization according to market metrics. The modest suggestion of this article is to insist on the constitutionality of the political decisions of societies to protect solidarity; it is that we insert 'social rights' in the gap between normative language and social experience, to enable the hermeneutic traction I suggested earlier, to provide a measure against which suffering is experienced not as necessary, but as a wrong. The suggestion is, in other words, to import constitutional contradiction and to act on it.

As ever there are important limits to this political-phenomenological endeavour to be conceded. We cannot suggest that the constitutional iteration will provide anything like full expression: whatever the dividends of the recourse to social rights, they will be 'disciplined' to the Constitution's semantic reach and the relative inertia of its imagination.[70] Whatever the constitutional register provides as means to harbour resistance to market allocations will be over-determined by the particular selectivity of the medium, in terms of what limits are placed on content, its self-referential reach, its immunization against a range of alternatives, its constitutive reductions. There is a second, more pervasive, danger, to be discerned. In time there emerges a mis-alignment between the constitutional semantic of social rights protection and the structures of market expansion. For Luhmann, 'if the level of complexity changes, the semantics that orients experience and action must adapt to that change, otherwise it loses its connection to reality.'[71] In other words, when the embeddedness of the (constitutional) semantics in the social structures that they give expression to, is troubled, the ensuing *strain* between semantics and structures calls forth a realignment of the former to the latter, an adaptation of semantics to the new configuration of structure. Against this evolutionism, with its threat of a comprehensive shift of the constitutional terrain, the question of holding on to the semantics of solidarity and dignity becomes key to a *critical* project of constitutionalism. The elevation of solidarity – as *dogmatic* resource – to

---

69 What, one might ask, from the market perspective, allows one to draw the line, à la Draghi, between usual and unusual market turbulence that licenses the ECB's highly selective and arbitrary decisions over the grant of liquidity?

70 I have written about this in E. Christodoulidis, 'The inertia of institutional imagination: a reply to Roberto Unger' (1996) 59 *Modern Law Rev.* 377.

71 See N. Luhmann, *Gesellschaftstruktur und Semantik, Vol. 1* (1980) 22. For Luhmann's problem-oriented functional analysis, the disruption of the fit between the meaning of the constitution as attached to nation-state structures and the post-sovereign structural formation to which it is transferred, is emphatically not an abandonment to 'floating' signification; it is, instead, a productive misalignment that accompanies and enables a definitive shift, a shift that will reorient a constitutional semantics-in-crisis to emerging structural patterns.

constitutional value at the substantive level, and the constitutional entrenchment of its non-negotiability at formal level, expresses the political achievement of social rights constitutionalism, the *decision* to hold on to the aspiration of solidarity in the face of all that the market presents under the sign of necessity.

How interesting to rethink the notion of a 'constitutional *placeholder*' on the cusp of antinomy of the critical project: hostage to no functionality – because what is functional about contradiction? – but with an emphasis now on what is being *held*, and held *to,* the constitutional marks the limit point beyond which there can be no yielding to market determinations without collapsing the constitutional achievement itself.

149

JOURNAL OF LAW AND SOCIETY
VOLUME 44, NUMBER 1, MARCH 2017
ISSN: 0263-323X, pp. 150–68

Contesting Austerity: On the Limits of EU Knowledge Governance

MARIJA BARTL*

Lacking robust democratic foundations, EU authority is founded on output legitimacy – delivery of (economic) prosperity through rational governance. Yet current austerity policies are the epitome of irrational governance. While this volume highlights the EU's limited ability to deliver rational output through law and legal rationality, I argue that, without democracy, the EU cannot deliver the desired output through knowledge and technical rationality either. In fact, embedding expert institutions in democratic institutional settings plays a crucial epistemic role, contributing to the production of more reflective, socially inclusive knowledge. Lack of such democratic input in the EU's knowledge production is one of the root causes of its crumbling output legitimacy and the creation of many disenfranchised (internal) peripheries. Three recent challenges of Brexit, TTIP, and austerity may be seen as attempts to reclaim the democratic responsiveness of EU technocratic rule. However, the strategies of exit and voice have not been available in all these cases: in the Greek tragedy, contesting austerity ended in subjugation: a mirror image of 'rational' governance if unaided by inclusive democratic process.

* University of Amsterdam, Oudemanhuispoort 4–6, 1012 CN, Amsterdam, The Netherlands
M.Bartl@uva.nl

I would like to thank Candida Leone, Ronan O'Condon, Daniela Caruso, Martijn Hesselink, Harm Schepel, Markos Karavias, Ingo Venzke, Cristina Eckes, Mirthe Jiwa, and Maria Weimer, as well as the participants of the 'EU Law Conference 2016' at Boston College. Any remaining errors are mine.

I. RATIONALIZING AUSTERITY

1. *Austerity and legal rationality*

In this volume, the contributors understand austerity as a political rationality, or as Mattei puts it, 'a rationality that is intrinsically theory and practice, policy and pedagogy'. They are, however, very much aware that austerity is a *messy* rationality. The purity of theory behind austerity is not a goal in itself; instead, hybrid practices emerge in order to bend EU reality to theory, and theory to EU reality, ultimately allowing for an unchecked exercise of power in the EU.

European law has played an important role in mediating austerity. Menéndez's intervention shows that EU law has certainly not been a backstop if one were intent on controlling the powers of various EU institutions or selected member states. If anything, it has been used as a tool facilitiating the practices of austerity, while often undermining our basic intuitions about the rule of law. Schepel's contribution demonstrates that the Court of Justice of the European Union (CJEU) is, ironically, naturalizing the market at the very moment when we see it failing. In its case law, the CJEU uses positive law to read rationality and regularity into market 'laws' in order to turn those into instruments regulating the conduct of EU member states. In his intervention, Kaupa deconstructs the alleged links between EU law and any particular economic theory. The Treaty mandates no particular economic theory. We *choose* to read such economic theory into the Treaty as a matter of political choice.

While the contributors to this volume expose current practices of austerity in the EU as the poster-example of the naked exercise of power, rather than an attempt at rational governance, EU law has largely been used to enable and rationalize these practices. Failing to protect the constitutional rule of law (Menéndez), or legally constructing market rationalities in order to attribute them regulative power (Schepel), the contributions add further support to Kaupa's argument regarding the indeterminate character of the EU constitution, which on its own cannot save us from sliding into collective irrationality.

2. *Austerity and technical rationality*

If legal rationality does not shield us from governance turning into a pure exercise of power, does technical knowledge perhaps perform better in steering EU governance toward rational outcomes? Mattei, an economic historian, offers a much needed historical perspective – how did the theory and practice of austerity 'work' in the past? Her account is unequivocal: whether measured by economic performance or distributive impacts, austerity has never served us well. López and Nahón, both economists, give us a more contemporary account from outside Europe. They discuss

Argentina's 'sovereign debt crisis' that – contrary to the EU – focused on sustainable debt levels and expansionary policies, and succeeded, both in terms of repaying debt and obligations to creditors as well as putting the country's economy back on its feet.

Given the historical and empirical knowledge available, why did Europe not rely on this knowledge? In fact, the Argentinian case has had remarkably limited influence on EU public debate. In response, one could perhaps point to differences in Europe's case. The times are different now, while the Argentinian experience has little relevance for the EU because of various constrains in the EU's legal-institutional design. Europe had to adopt 'downturn' austerity (Kaupa) since it needed to preserve the euro while, at the same time, avoiding too much solidarity.

Yet how do European institutions actually 'know' this? How do they produce such knowledge and interpretations? The final contribution to this volume focuses on the technical rationality of EU governance. If legal rationality has not been able to prevent us from sliding into collective irrationality, to what extent has scientific/technical rationality – the other stronghold of EU legitimacy – shielded EU governance, despite its limited democratic legitimacy, from becoming an exercise in naked power?

I will argue that technical rationality, and the EU's administrative legitimacy,[1] can go only so far, because EU institutions engaged in knowledge production processes have been largely dissociated from inclusive democratic process.[2] Because of this, EU governing knowledge will often suffer from (unintentional) bias and/or irrelevance for a growing number of peripheries, not only failing to create output legitimacy, but also becoming easy prey to the pursuit of authoritarian projects.

The article proceeds as follows. I start by analysing institutional conditions for the production of knowledge in liberal democracies, as compared to the EU (part II). I then compare the three recent challenges to EU knowledge governance – Brexit, TTIP, and austerity – which may be seen as attempts to reclaim the democratic responsiveness of EU technocratic rule (part III). The strategies of *exit* and *voice* utilized by various actors in these contestations have, however, not been available across all three examined cases: in the Greek tragedy, the contestation of austerity has ended up in a state of subjugation. (part IV). I conclude, however, on a moderately optimistic note.

1 P.L. Lindseth, 'Democratic Legitimacy and the Administrative Character of Supranationalism: The Example of the European Community' (1999) 99 *Columbia Law Rev.* 628–738.
2 By governing knowledge I mean knowledge produced by the governing institutions in order to make sense of the outer world, to articulate the problems and possible solutions. Sheila Jasanoff, for instance, talks in her work about 'regulatory knowledge', which is knowledge produced in a regulatory process as a basis for regulatory choices: S. Jasanoff, *Science and Public Reason* (2012).

II. *TAKING KNOWLEDGE SERIOUSLY:*[3] ON THE EPISTEMIC ROLE OF DEMOCRACY

In this part I argue that governance through knowledge – technocratic or administrative modes of governance – cannot on their own deliver what they promise: objectively best knowledge and 'rational' governance. While a significant consensus may be built around the premise that *knowledge contestation* is a precondition of democratic politics in modernity, I show why equally the *democratic* contestation of governing knowledge is a precondition for the epistemic validity, or 'true-ness', of such governing knowledge.

1. *Knowledge in politics*

In the liberal democratic state, disagreements about knowledge represent a crucial element of ideological struggles. To gain political support for their programmes, political parties summon not only alternative scales of value, but also alternative bodies of knowledge. For instance, to substantiate claims regarding the desirability of progressive taxation, privatization of public services or free trade, political parties need to mobilize different bodies, or even paradigms, of knowledge. Thus, politics is as much about production and contestation of knowledge as it is about values and principles.

2. *Politics in knowledge*

The reason why *democratic* contestation of governing knowledge is crucially important relates to the nature of knowledge. Knowledge always has a certain discretionary political or normative dimension.[4] Expert judgement, however well meant, can never be entirely objective and neutral. Rather, experts form various expectations and assumptions dependent on their

---

3 Report commissioned by the Directorate-General for Research: U. Felt et al., *Taking European Knowledge Society Seriously* (2007) DG for Research, EUR 22, at <http://ec.europa.eu/research/science-society/document_library/pdf_06/european-knowledge-society_en.pdf>.

4 M. Foucault, *Security, Territory, Population* (2007); S. Jasanoff (ed.), *States of Knowledge: The co-production of science and social order* (2004). In legal scholarship, any challenge to the modernist views of knowledge as objective and neutral has only very slowly reached the mainstream. Quite to the contrary, faced with the 'real politics' of globalizing governance, with its discourses of truth, knowledge, objectivity, and expertise, the modernist belief in expertise seems to have only gained more traction in the past decades. Several arguments justified this approach. Our more complex worlds and lives demanded increased deference to experts in various areas. The same concern for complexity has driven the institutional formation of public governance, the proliferation of standardization bodies, scientific/evidence-based governance, the juridification of politics, and the shift to market forms of governmentality further supported the expertization of governance.

personal situatedness (the expectations that relate to their belonging to social networks, social classes, their educational level, and so on), their institutional affiliation (with a particular institution, a broader institutional framework, or a state of origin) or disciplinary belonging (discourses, frames, assumptions).[5] These expectations and assumptions will also have their normative and distributive (interests) dimension – as scholars in critical (legal) theory of gender, race or sexuality have abundantly shown.[6]

If we accept that values and interests map onto such expert-produced governing knowledge, then it follows that limiting the contestation of knowledge will become *epistemically* problematic.[7] Such knowledge can accumulate various sorts of biases that relate to experts' belonging to various social groups, various institutions in which they are embedded, or broader ideologies.

The significance of democratic contestation of knowledge goes beyond the concern with bias only. The contestation of knowledge also has an important steering function: it steers the governing bodies toward certain questions and concerns that experts may not otherwise entertain – either because they are differently situated or because they are embedded in particular epistemic communities and discourses. Thus, democracy has a checking function but also – just as crucially – a steering dimension.

An excellent example of the steering role of democratic institutions, and the importance of the embeddedness of expert institutions in a broader socio-politico-economic context, may be found in a recent speech by the Chief Economist of the Bank of England, Andrew G. Haldane.[8] Haldane tries to reconcile post-crisis data, suggesting an exemplary economic recovery in the United Kingdom, with the much more negative picture shared with him by people and organizations during his visits to peripheral regions of the country. Disaggregating the statistics regarding the changes in income, wealth, region, age, and housing situation after the crisis, he shows that the data behind the recovery story miss important distributive implications: the improved economic performance of the United Kingdom has not 'lifted all boats', and certainly not in the same way.[9] Beyond the academic merits of

---

5 Support for this claim can be found in organizational sociology, sociology of knowledge, theories of power, but also in the studies of risk regulation and administrative governance.

6 For instance, C.A. MacKinnon, *Toward a Feminist Theory of the State* (1989); R. Delgado and J. Stefancic, *Critical Race Theory: An Introduction* (2012).

7 Support comes from the sociology of knowledge, science and technology studies, and organizational sociology. Liberal philosophy of science, most notably the work of Karl Popper, would also underline the role of contestation for the *quality* of knowledge. The project of 'open society', however, does not acknowledge the political element of all knowledge – instead, this is equated with politicization of knowledge, in turn, associated with totalitarianism.

8 A.G. Haldane, 'Whose Recovery?', speech delivered on 30 June 2016, at <http://www.bankofengland.co.uk/publications/Documents/speeches/2016/speech916.pdf>.

9 id.

that contribution, the question as to what has prompted this high official to reconsider his epistemic framework in reaction to the inconsistent picture presented by peripheral constituencies, is of crucial importance for understanding the constraining and steering role of embedded expert institutions.

3. Institutions of knowledge contestation

The most important institution for contesting governing knowledge in liberal democratic states is 'political opposition'.[10] Opposition serves not only to politicize a particular articulation of the common good, but also to problematize knowledge produced to support the majority's conception of the common good, and to produce conflicting knowledge. To challenge the policies of progressive taxation, privatization of public services or free trade, the opposition will always mobilize different bodies of knowledge alongside (and often more importantly than) different scales of value.

The contestation of governing knowledge does not end however with opposition and parliamentary politics. The institutional structures of knowledge contestation extend to the media, the public sphere, bureaucracy, various agencies, and social and political movements. Ultimately, these institutions include the 'street': protests are a crucial element of democratic politics, and as the TTIP case shows, an important means to channel popular sentiment into knowledge production and policy making.

Now, the openness of governing knowledge to democratic contestation is ultimately related to the embeddedness of expert institutions in the political, economic, and social contexts of the governed polities. This embeddedness gives experts and expert institutions cultural material to determine meaning, but it also constrains them in deciding what kind of meaning is *socially acceptable*.[11] For instance, a claim that monetarism is 'true' knowledge makes far more sense in Frankfurt than in Athens.

Political exchange, the public sphere, the media, protests, the street, or just 'seeing' the material reality of the people,[12] will have an impact on how experts exercise the discretionary or value-based element of knowledge production. Democratic contestation provides both a popular check on governing knowledge and a sense of direction, raising concerns and issues

---

10 I. Ley, *Opposition Im Völkerrecht: Ein Beitrag zur Legitimation internationaler Rechtserzeugung* (2015).

11 The contribution of Sheila Jasanoff on 'civil epistemologies' is very instructive in this regard. She discusses how the general public provides an important steering function when it comes to the direction of technological development and the desirability of certain scientific knoweldge: S. Jasanoff, *Designs on Nature: Science and Democracy in Europe and the United States* (2005) ch. 10 ('Civic Epistemology').

12 Disembedded expert institutions are to democratic governance what gated communities are to the city. See R. Atkinson and J. Flint, 'Fortress UK? Gated communities, the spatial revolt of the elites and time-space trajectories of segregation' (2004) 19 *Housing Studies* 875.

possibly crossing disciplinary and institutional boundaries. The production of governing knowledge, therefore, cannot be dissociated from the democratic process without losing both its legitimacy *and* its validity.

4. *European institutional deficit in knowledge production*

Europe's democratic deficit is a problem for its democratic legitimacy but also for the epistemic validity of the knowledge through which it governs. The *input* and *output* perspectives merge in this case. Dissociated from democratic institutions, the EU's governing knowledge is prone to bias on the level of articulating both goals and means.[13]

The contestation of knowledge in EU governing institutions is constrained in several different ways. A large-scale juridification of EU objectives and purposes in the EU Treaties legitimizes the depoliticization of EU operations (see, also, Menéndez in this volume), while the EU's expert governing bodies further mask the contentious, political character of the (usually economic) knowledge that is necessary in order to interpret the EU's legal commitments.

The exchange in 'political institutions', such as the European Parliament, is also at a certain level depoliticized. The discussion in the Parliament often remains deeply embedded in the legislative frame proposed by the Commission, focusing on details and small gains instead of problematizing goals.[14] Any more fundamental contestation is often limited on the level of *Yes–No* Europe, with little space for fundamental contestation from within.[15] The glaring institutional deficiency in this regard is the lack of political opposition. The depoliticization of the European Parliament is amplified by secretive negotiations in the Council which, as the recent sovereign debt discussions have shown, give free rein to bargaining in the shadow of (economic) power.[16]

Ultimately, the failure to democratize the EU has been a failure to re-embed the EU in a democratically more inclusive manner. Years ago, when discussing the two grand pre-crisis projects – the EU Constitution and EU Civil Code – Hans Micklitz argued that both projects failed because they did not respond to the challenge that the EU has so far favoured organic solidarity,[17] and mobile, active, educated, and young market citizens, while

---

13 M. Bartl, 'Internal Market Rationality, Private Law and the Direction of the Union: Resuscitating the Market as the Object of the Political' *European Law J.* (forthcoming, doi/10.1111/eulj.12122).

14 M. Bartl, 'The Way We Do Europe: Subsidiarity and the Substantive Democratic Deficit (2015) 21 *European Law J.* 23 (doi:10.1111/eulj.12115).

15 C. Green-Pedersen, 'A Giant Fast Asleep? Party Incentives and the Politicisation of European Integration' (2012) 60 *Political Studies* 115.

16 U. Puetter, *The European Council and the Council: New Intergovernmentalism and Institutional Change* (2014).

17 As introduced by Emile Durkheim.

leaving too many others behind.[18] The 'Brussels Bubble' is the expression commonly used to represent the EU as selectively re-embedding through elite circles of post-national institutions and big businesses, while failing to provide voice to many peripheries (be it the European periphery, or peripheries within the core states).

My hypothesis is that this disembeddedness is detrimental not only to the EU's democratic legitimacy (input) but also to the quality (output) of its governing knowledge. On this account, EU 'output legitimacy' is a chimera, which cannot be achieved in an institutional design that does not allow for the democratic contestation of governing knowledge.

III. THE INSTITUTIONAL CONDITIONS OF KNOWLEDGE CONTESTATION IN EUROPE *WRIT LARGE:* THE UNFOLDING OF THREE CASES

Brexit, the breakdown of TTIP negotiations, and the attempts at resisting austerity have often been portrayed as the responses to the negative consequences of economic globalization. Disenchanted internal peripheries in the United Kingdom, or the disappointed citizens of peripheral EU member states such as Hungary or Poland have struck back by means of national politics. The contestation of mega-regional trade agreements, such as the TTIP and CETA, builds on previous anti-globalization movements. Economic crisis and austerity seem to be the outright consequences of economic integration beyond the state, built upon market mechanisms rather than solidarity (see, also, Christodoulides in this volume).

In the following, however, I lay out these three challenges as also, importantly, *epistemic struggles.* These struggles over the content of EU governing knowledge have a particular importance in a polity which draws much of its legitimacy from governing through knowledge while, as argued above, hardly *taking knowledge seriously.*[19] I analyse the possibilities for the contestation of EU governing knowledge both *within* its institutions as well

---

18 'Leaving behind' in legal scholarship has often encapsulated the concerns about selective citizenship (see D. Kochenov, 'Neo-Mediaeval Permutations of Personhood in the European Union' in *Constructing the Person in EU Law: Rights, Roles, Identities*, eds. L. Azoulai, S. Barbou Des Places, and E. Pataut (2016); reverse discrimination (the undermining of the provision of public services through the CJEU's fundamental freedoms case law, see M. Dougan, 'Fees, Grants, Loans and Dole Cheques: Who Covers the Costs of Migrant Education within the EU?' (2005) 42 *Common Market Law Rev.* 943); or access to justice (A. Somek, 'From Workers to Migrants, from Distributive Justice to Inclusion: Exploring the Changing Social Democratic Imagination' (2012) 18 *European Law J.* 711).

19 The Commission has itself commissioned interesting reports on the nature of knowledge and knowledge society. These reports seem to have had limited, if any, impact on the way EU sees governing knowledge: see Felt, op. cit., n. 3.

as from *without*: from non-institutionalized corners (for instance, street protests) to more anti-systemic forces (for example, exit from the EU).

1. *Case I: Brexit*

Possibly one of the most famous Brexit phrases, 'British people are tired of listening to experts', was uttered by Michael Gove in response to Faisal Islam (Sky News), who had warned about the negative economic impacts of Brexit. The Leave voters – if we are to judge by the outcome of the referendum – did not take 'expert' warnings seriously. Why?

Expert bodies – this global knowledge elite – emerged as the harbingers of the negative changes associated with economic globalization.[20] The British public disregarded the (possibly well-founded) economic warnings of institutions such as the City of London, the British Treasury, the European Commission, the OECD, PricewaterhouseCoopers, and so on. Their predictions were considered unreliable both because this very elite had contributed to the current malaise and because these actors would profit from the perpetuation of the status quo.[21] While slogans such as 'taking back control' have been interpreted as a concern for sovereignty, one may also see them as the resistance to elite articulations of futures which leave too many behind.

Brexit epitomizes a strategy contemplated by many challengers from the far right. Currently, different parties on the right of the political spectrum in Europe call for *exits*, for instance, Geert Wilders for *Nexit*, or Le Pen for *Frexit*. Hungary and Poland have both also opted out in a certain way – albeit by distancing themselves from the EU mode of thinking rather than the EU itself. Viktor Orbán openly characterizes the form of democracy in Hungary as an 'illiberal democracy'.[22]

The causes and response to the shift to right-wing populism is perhaps one of the major contemporary 'knowledge' disputes. Is the shift a consequence of economic malaise, which politically eventually calls for a more egalitarian Europe and greater redistribution? Or has it been caused by lack of education, which renders masses prone to populism – so that Europe simply needs

---

20 S. Watkins, Editorial, 'Casting Off' *New Left Review*, July/August 2016, at <https://newleftreview.org/II/100/susan-watkins-casting-off>.

21 The British public seems to have been more willing to buy into bogus claims by the domestic Leave campaigners than the knowledge produced by the elite governing bodies. One of the reasons may be that the elite institutions have professed the miraculous recovery of the United Kingdom post-crisis, which many of the Leave voters have not seen: see Haldane, op. cit., n. 8.

22 For a translation of one of Orbán's speeches, see <http://budapestbeacon.com/public-policy/full-text-of-viktor-orbans-speech-at-baile-tusnad-tusnadfurdo-of-26-july-2014/10592>. See, also, M. Bánkuti, G. Halmai, and K.L. Scheppele, 'Hungary's Illiberal Turn: Disabling the Constitution' in *The Hungarian Patient: Social Opposition to an Illiberal Democracy*, eds. P. Krasztev and J. van Til (2015) 37.

© 2017 The Author. Journal of Law and Society © 2017 Cardiff University Law School

to explain better what it does? Or is the shift caused by a justified concern with immigration, which endangers economic security, personal safety, and cultural integration, and thus Europe should reconsider the disruptive effects of its economic and immigration policies?

Whatever the outcome of this discussion, it will likely not take place within the EU's institutional framework.[23] None of these concerns (and the knowledge that supports them) are easily brought up in the EU's political spaces. Equally, the solutions for these broader challenges are not offered as part of the toolbox of 'the possible' in the EU. Yet, ironically, the EU remains a major force shaping the very same (economic) conditions that are not considered changeable within its own institutional framework.

2. *Case II: TTIP*

The epistemic challenge is readily observable in the movement against the Transatlantic Trade and Investment Partnership (TTIP) and, to a lesser extent, against the Canada Europe Trade Agreement (CETA). The renewed post-crisis EU trade policy, with stress on bilateral trade agreements, was seen as one of the major instruments to respond to the economic malaise.[24] Powered by the representatives of the Directorate General for Trade (DG Trade), who saw exports as the best way of ensuring EU economic growth, the European Commission embarked on the negotiation of several bilateral trade treaties, including the two mega-regional agreements: the CETA, and the TTIP.[25]

The growing social movement did not accept the framings offered by the Commission's trade experts, or their consultancies, as to the benefits of these agreements or their democratic implications. Large-scale mobilizations have incorporated everything, from challenging the numbers that are deployed to justifying the alleged economic benefits of the TTIP to questioning the possible impacts on environmental and social regulation.[26] The quarter of a

---

23 Concerns regarding the deficiency of EU institutional structures in dealing with the causes of Brexit were also expressed in many academic contributions: see, for instance, the Special Issue of the *German Law J.* on Brexit, at <http://www.germanlawjournal.com/brexit-supplement/>. See, also, A. Menéndez, 'Can Brexit be turned into a Democratic Shock? Five Points' (2016) ARENA Working Paper 4/2016.

24 P. Defraigne, 'Departing from TTIP and Going Plurilateral' (2014) Madariaga Paper 3/2014, at <http://www.madariaga.be/images/madariagapapers/october%202014%20-%20defraigne%20-%20departing%20from%20ttip%20and%20going%20plurilateral.pdf>.

25 F. De Ville and G. Siles-Brügge, *TTIP: The Truth about the Transatlantic Trade and Investment Partnership* (2015).

26 Some of the most vocal critiques of the treaties have come from NGO alliances such as STOP TTIP, NGOs such as Corporate European Observatory or BEUC, but also parliamentary groups (such as GUE/NGL or Verts/Ale), all of which have produced or commissioned reports on the trade agreements, from the estimation of economic

159

million protesting in Berlin made it clear: no, there is no good knowledge that supports the Commission's position that the world would be better off because of the TTIP; that each family will be 540 euros per year richer; and that regulations coming out of the TTIP bodies are going to respect the environment. These claims were both political and epistemic, for, as discussed in the previous chapter, in modernity politics is staged against the backdrop of knowledge; political claims are often (also) knowledge claims.[27]

Now, in order to understand the available space for the contestation of knowledge from within the EU institutional structures, we need to consider how the European Commission operates. The logical place to create the EU trade vision and policy was 'obviously' the DG Trade. Trade officials, coupled with the so called 'regulatory affairs officials',[28] framed the TTIP debate – including goals, benefits, and the structure of the agreement. These two groups of officials positioned themselves at the centre of any future regulatory cooperation between the two blocks.[29]

Discussion within the EU institutions was limited in several ways. The 'consultations' before the start of the negotiation process (the *Report of the High Working Group*)[30] overwhelmingly featured (big) business.[31] The successful 'citizen's initiative' challenging the TTIP has been sidelined on formal grounds.[32] The Commission's officials have been largely con-

---

benefits and harms (see, for instance, <http://www.guengl.eu/news/article/ttip-myths-shattered-by-new-gue-ngl-backed-report>) to substantive issues such as trade agreements and the EU data privacy regime (at <https://edri.org/files/dp_and_trade_web.pdf>).

27 This is indeed to collapse the construction that knowledge provides information for politics: claims that progressive taxation is going to bring more or less economic growth, or that monetary policy has to be prudent in order to improve economic performance, are drawing their power from the knowledge on which they rely rather than from values and principles.

28 By regulatory affairs officials I mean those government members who are responsible for what the European Commission calls 'regulatory analytics'. This includes the administration of impact assessments and reviewing regulations. In the United States, these are the representatives of the Office of Information and Regulatory Affairs (OIRA) and in Europe, the members of the Secretariat General of the European Commission. Cooperation among those officials has been taking place for years. See, for instance, F.G. Nicola, 'The Politicization of Legal Expertise in the TTIP Negotiation' (2015) 78 *Law and Contemporary Problems* 175.

29 M. Bartl, 'Regulatory Convergence through the Back Door: TTIP's Regulatory Cooperation and the Future of Precaution in Europe' (2017) *German Law J.* (forthcoming).

30 See <http://trade.ec.europa.eu/doclib/docs/2013/february/tradoc_150519.pdf>.

31 For the empirical analysis of the participants in consultation, see M. Bartl and E. Fahey, 'A Postnational Marketplace: Negotiating the Transatlantic Trade and Investment Partnership (TTIP)' in *A Transatlantic Community of Law: Legal Perspectives on the Relationship between the EU and US legal orders*, eds. E. Fahey and D. Curtin (2014) 210.

32 See <http://www.euractiv.com/section/trade-society/news/commission-opposes-european-citizens-initiative-against-ttip/>.

descending to the public response in various public meetings and confer-ences.[33] European Commissioner Malstrom has even called the democratic opposition practically Luddite.[34] To the extent that MEPs want to exercise oversight, access to documents was first limited to a certain number of MEPs, broadened to all MEPs in December 2015.[35] Furthermore, the MEPs can only access these documents in a high-security setting, while the documents themselves were often said to be incomplete.[36]

Unable to use institutional channels to challenge EU trade policy, public watchdogs have orchestrated an enormous social mobilization. Anti-TTIP protests numbered tens of thousands of participants. Reified, and often rather questionable justifications facilitated such social mobilization. Concern over investor-state dispute settlement (ISDS), never fully justified by the EC, was later followed by concerns about regulatory cooperation and the over-representation of businesses in negotiations and regulatory cooperation. Public media offered relatively comprehensive coverage of the challenges, and not necessarily in a manner hostile to the protesters.

The TTIP mobilization has created a space for contestation, and opposition to trade knowledge, qua this social mobilization. This movement can claim several achievements. First, in response to significant criticism regarding the lack of transparency, the Commission has slowly but gradually made its position papers available, initially as a response to 'leaks', whereas from circa 2015 in a pre-emptive mode.[37] Second, due to increasing con-testation, the Commission, also in 2015, opted for a public consultation on the ISDS. The result was that the Commission received more than 150,000 mostly negative answers.[38] This amounted to a historically unprecedented reaction that could not be disregarded. Soon after, the Commission came up with a – rather notorious – proposal for an Investment Court,[39] which sought to address some of the deficiencies of the previous system.[40] Lastly, perhaps

---

33 I have been personally present at many occasions where the Commission's officials have condescendingly addressed the social movement against the TTIP, implying that these people were not getting it.
34 See Commissionaire Malstrom's Opinion Piece, ('Don't believe the anti-TTIP hype – increasing trade is a no-brainer' *Guardian*, 16 February 2015, at <https://www.the guardian.com/commentisfree/2015/feb/16/ttip-transatlantic-trade-deal-businesses>.
35 See <http://www.europarl.europa.eu/news/en/news-room/20151202IPR05759/all-meps-to-have-access-to-all-confidential-ttip-documents>.
36 See <https://www.theguardian.com/commentisfree/2015/aug/31/transparency-ttip-documents-big-business>.
37 Position papers are different from negotiation documents, to which only a limited number of MEPs have access, under strict security conditions.
38 The Commission's analysis of responses to public consultation is available at <http://trade.ec.europa.eu/doclib/press/index.cfm?id=1234>.
39 The TTIP Chapter on Investment contains this proposal in sub-section 4: see <http://trade.ec.europa.eu/doclib/docs/2015/september/tradoc_153807.pdf>.
40 How far the proposal removes the deficiencies is, of course, the object of fierce controversy. Be that as it may, the proposal has been an important element in securing the signing of CETA.

161

the most important achievement from the perspective of this social movement was to delay the prospect of completing TTIP negotiations before the end of President Obama's term. The recent election of Donald Trump seems to have sealed the dismal fate of TTIP.[41]

The TTIP contestation may be seen as a successful democratic challenge to foreclosed EU knowledge production processes: an example of healthy, liberal democratic institutionalism. However, two questions remain open. First, street protests are an emancipatory, but rather costly, form of democratic governance. How big does the social mobilization have to be in order to bring about some reflexivity in the way the EU does business? Secondly, if this is to become a more prominent way of generating contestation of EU governing knowledge and practices, how far is the TTIP experience replicable? I return to these questions in the following part.

3. *Case III: Austerity*

The challenge to austerity in the EU, most vocally made by Syriza in 2015, was an epistemic challenge at its core. The Greek Minister of Finance and former academic, Yanis Varoufakis, challenged the intellectual premises of EU conditionality and austerity politics, and of EU debt management.[42] With regard to the latter, Greeks have made a case for what López and Nahón in this volume call 'sustainable debt' while, with regard to the former, they have fought for more fiscal space to support economic growth. The epistemic challenge to austerity in Greece has not only come from the so-called 'radical left' politicians. Renowned academics[43] as well as world economic institutions such as the International Monetary Fund (IMF) have amplified this challenge to the EU position.[44]

41 The challenge to CETA was less successful, and the agreement was recently signed and placed into provisional application (before ratification). The decision of the Council can be found at <http://www.consilium.europa.eu/en/press/press-releases/2016/10/28-eu-canada-trade-agreement/>.

42 The Greek position can be reconstructed on the basis of articles by Yanis Varoufakis, see <https://yanisvaroufakis.eu/>. His reflections on the conflict with German Finance Minister Schäuble are also interesting, see <https://www.project-syndicate.org/commentary/germany-versus-france-italy-by-yanis-varoufakis-2015-10?barrier=true>; also <https://yanisvaroufakis.eu/2015/08/31/varoufakis-on-schauble-extract-from-stephan-lambys-swr-adr-documentary/>.

43 Here one may count people such as Krugman, Stiglitz, Lance Taylor, groups of economists such as Euromemorandum Group, and so on. For an interesting review of the work by Varoufakis, Galbraith, and Stiglitz on the future of Europe, see A. Moravcsik, 'Europe's Ugly Future: Muddling Through Austerity' *Foreign Affairs*, November/December 2016, at <https://www.foreignaffairs.com/reviews/review-essay/2016-10-17/europe-s-ugly-future>.

44 In a recent article, (J.D. Ostry, P. Loungani, and D. Furceri, 'Neoliberalism: Oversold?' *Finance & Development*, June 2016, at <http://www.imf.org/external/pubs/ft/fandd/2016/06/ostry.htm>), IMF fellows Ostry, Lungani, and Furceri highlight the fact that 'austerity policies not only generate substantial welfare costs

© 2017 The Author. Journal of Law and Society © 2017 Cardiff University Law School

Qua output, if we are to trust Mark Blyth, saving Greece (and the Eurozone) in 2009 would have cost 50 billion euros.[45] Due to the compound effect of policy decisions taken thereafter, these cost have grown exponentially, leaving Greece with a sovereign debt of such proportions that it will never be able to repay it (see, also, the introduction to this volume). Under EU-imposed austerity and structural reforms, the Greek economy has contracted to an unprecedented degree, while everyone is losing, creditors included. This rather simple fact has been stressed by Nobel laureates in economics,[46] by the Syriza government,[47] by the IMF,[48] and by the United States administration, which has consistently urged Europe to reconsider its economic policies.[49]

If austerity policies have aggravated the performance of Greece on each and every economic performance criterion, why has the power engine of EU knowledge governance – the European Commission – continually supported rather than contested the austerity frenzy in recent years? Why does it still go with the Schäuble-led coalition – despite the economic failure of such an approach?

A quick response to this question goes as follows: 'political realities' – or Schäuble – *forced* the Commission to act in this way. But that barely makes for a sufficient response. As any institution, the Commission is subject to various forms of internal and external accountability, constitutional purposes, and legal constraints, which did not entirely cease to operate in the context of the economic crisis. Ultimately, we can hardly imagine that the Commission has ceased to see itself as a guardian of EU interest instead of, for instance, the interests of Germany.

So why did the Commission neglect the growing evidence regarding the economic problems of austerity policies vis-à-vis Greece? A part of the response to this question may be found in the institutional design of the EU,

---

  due to supply-side channels, they also hurt demand – and thus worsen employment
  and unemployment.'

45 See M. Blyth, *Austerity: The History of a Dangerous Idea* (2013).

46 For instance Joseph Stiglitz: see J. Stiglitz, 'Austerity has been an utter disaster for
  the eurozone' *Guardian*, 1 October 2014, at <https://www.theguardian.com/business/
  2014/oct/01/austerity-eurozone-disaster-joseph-stiglitz>; J. Stiglitz, *The Euro and its
  threat to the future of Europe* (2016). Or Paul Krugman, see P. Krugman, 'The case
  for cuts was a lie. Why does Britain still believe it? The austerity delusion' *Guardian*,
  29 April 2015, at <https://www.theguardian.com/business/ng-interactive/2015/apr/29/
  the-austerity-delusion>.

47 See, for instance, <https://www.theguardian.com/world/2015/jan/28/greek-people-
  wrote-history-how-syriza-rose-to-power>.

48 See Ostry et al., op. cit., n. 44 and the commentary at <https://www.theguardian.com/
  business/2016/may/27/austerity-policies-do-more-harm-than-good-imf-study-
  concludes>.

49 President Barack Obama has been one of the vocal critiques of the EU policies: see
  <http://www.repubblica.it/esteri/2016/10/18/news/obama_austerity_measures_
  contributed_to_slower_growth_in_europe-150019546/>.

discussed in section II.4. Furthermore, we need to consider (see (a)–(c) below) the institutional characteristics of the European Commission itself, (d) the role played by EU law and institutional design, (e) the problem of reification of knowledge production and path dependencies, and, finally, (f) the 'democratic' argument against the Greek contestation of austerity.

(a) The contestation of knowledge in the European Commission is limited, thanks to its institutional character. The Commission is a *bureaucracy* with an internal hierarchical structure and correspondingly limited spaces for *internal* contestation of knowledge. In such an institution, the voices contesting the course of action from within could likely be neutralized in the bureaucratic hierarchy.

(b) At the same time, the Commission may be seen as an expert institution *disembedded* from many of the spaces that it governs. This means that Commission officials are exposed to the lived reality of the European peoples only to a limited extent. This makes it easier to stick to whatever knowledge the Commission has adopted, and ignore any resulting hardships.

(c) Now, we have seen the introduction of various institutionalized forms of '*public consultation*' as an attempt to respond to the problem of knowledge.[50] However, this was a far from successful experiment. To the extent that consultation is about knowledge input and contestation, the pre-framed issues allowed only marginal contestations to be voiced.[51] To the extent that the consultations are the response to disembeddedness, the dominance of entities with concentrated interests and large resources[52] will tend to exacerbate the disembeddedness (as it has been seen in the context of the TTIP).

(d) The contestation of knowledge within EU structures also hinges on the placement of the Commission within a broader EU institutional design. For instance, the deference to the European Central Bank (ECB), in combination with seemingly strict rules on fiscal and monetary discipline (see Kaupa in this volume), may have shut off certain avenues of contestation. The ECB itself, on the other hand, located in Frankfurt and embedded in German economic discourse and political context, has all too often relied on legal argumentation concerning its mandate, exclusively

---

50 Especially once re-termed as 'participatory democracy'. See B. Kohler-Koch and C. Quittkat, *De-Mystification of Participatory Democracy: EU-Governance and Civil Society* (2013); J. Mendes, 'Participation and the role of law after Lisbon: A legal view on Article 11 TEU' (2011) 48 *Common Market Law Rev.* 1849.

51 id.

52 See, for instance, D. Carpenter and D.A. Moss, *Preventing Regulatory Capture: Special Interest Influence and How to Limit It* (2013); also, M.G. Cowles, 'The Transatlantic Business Dialogue and Domestic Business-Government Relations' in *Transforming Europe: Europeanization and Domestic Change*, eds. M.G. Cowles, J. Caporaso, and T. Risse (2001) 159.

related to price stability, in order to fend off any challenges to its governing knowledge – unless such a challenge is mediated through the markets.

(e) The contestation of knowledge is constrained due to a certain ideological path-dependency: the European Commission has for a long time and rather eagerly implemented neoliberal economic prescriptions, insofar as these have resulted in the expansion of the Internal Market, and consequently, of the Commission's own powers.[53] Austerity's affinity with (neo-)liberal political rationality (see Mattei in this volume), including a belief in 'market logic', evidenced also in the case law of the Commission's long-term co-traveller, the CJEU (see Schepel in this volume), may have rendered the shift away from the default neoclassical position more difficult.

(f) In the wake of a democratic challenge to the governing knowledge mounted by Syriza, certain prominent scholars have argued that respecting the outcomes of Greek elections and the referendum – the outcomes of Greek democracy – would in fact undermine pan-European democracy, insofar as the majority of EU citizens wanted Greek profligacy punished.[54] On this argument, the Commission's indifference to evidence may have been a populist democratic move.

Still, on what concept of democracy do we rely in such an account? If Europeans had a 'pan-European' public debate on Greece, it was limited to elites. In national public spheres, Greece and other PIIGS were presented as the profligate 'other' – rather than members of a polity, to whom we owed something like respect or solidarity. Since these 'others' were irresponsible childish peoples, they surely did not deserve voice, and instead deserved punishment, discipline, and control. Without respect or solidarity, however, we can hardly speak of liberal democracy.

IV. THE THIRD TRANSFORMATION OF EUROPE

In 1991, Joseph Weiler's landmark article 'The Transformation of Europe' used the binary of *exit* and *voice* to describe the dynamics of EU integration.[55] In the first period of EU integration, the less *exit* (non-compliance) was an option, the more *voice* (unanimity) became vital. During the second transformation of Europe, with the introduction of qualified majority voting, the member states' voice was reduced. The institutional hope may have been, however, that a strengthening of the EU democratic institutions would

---

53 N. Jabko, *Playing the Market: A Political Strategy for Uniting Europe, 1985–2005* (2006); Bartl, op. cit., n. 13.
54 See the interview with Brigitte Laffan, Director of the Robert Schuman Centre, European University Institute, at <https://www.youtube.com/watch?v=rDuQ4hGAKfA>.
55 J.H.H. Weiler, 'The Transformation of Europe' (1991) 100 *Yale Law J.* 2403.

compensate for such loss – shifting *voice* thus from the EU member states to the peoples of Europe. In that heyday of institutional enthusiasm for democracy and market capitalism,[56] no one could have envisaged that the voice of some in Europe could wither altogether – heralding a third transformation of Europe.[57]

The three cases presented above may be seen as different responses to the failure of the EU to give voice to the peoples of Europe. An important point that I have attempted to make is that failing to give voice, to institute channels for democratic input into knowledge governance, will not only likely result in frustration – but also in the creation of numerous peripheries and dwindling output legitimacy. The democratic and epistemic deficits in the EU are in this sense interrelated: the lack of democratic checks on the EU governing knowledge renders it vulnerable to various biases – with likely distributive consequences.

Now, a first strategy for the EU's failing input and output legitimacy has been *exit*. Brexit presents an example of how the creation of peripheries, even if certainly not attributable only to the EU, may result in their turning to national institutions in order to, however illusorily, 'take back control'. Countries such as Hungary and Poland may also be seen as adopting an exit strategy – even if their exit is more factual than *de jure*.[58]

The case of the TTIP shows us a more optimistic picture – a way to *create voice through large-scale transnational mobilization* (input), which has successfully challenged trade knowledge and policy (output). The TTIP may be, however, quite an exceptional case in this regard, making it a shaky precedent in the battle for the democratization of Europe. First of all, the common interest (for example, eating healthy food) converged across EU member states, and also across groups within these states, irrespective of class-belonging. More significantly, however, the common interest demanded relatively little economic solidarity among EU countries and citizens. There were no real 'costs' implied insofar as the purpose here was to stop certain action. Any successful transnational social mobilization in the near future could draw inspiration from the TTIP story on how to create a public issue for such mobilization.

---

56 F. Fukuyama, 'The End of History?' *The National Interest*, Summer 1989, 3.
57 M.A. Wilkinson, 'Authoritarian Liberalism in the European Constitutional Imagination: Second Time as Farce?' (2015) 21 *European Law J.* 313.
58 Much can be said for the disappointment of eastern member states who have eagerly implemented all the 'shock therapies' presecribed by the Washington institutions after the fall of communism, as well as implementing *acquis communitaire* at later stages, without, however, ever even coming close to catching up with their western counterparts. It is interesting to see that public support for Viktor Orbán in Hungary rises considerably whenever he takes measures that aim to constrain financial capitalism – rather than when promoting some xenophobic policies. The latest referendum failure is an interesting example thereof.

The case of austerity and Greece does not fall within either of the aforementioned strategies. Exit was hardly an option for Greece. First, the Syriza government had a Europeanist orientation, which made exit seem regressive. At the same time, exit was also economically impossible: the threat of state bankruptcy meant that Grexit was hardly an attractive option.

If exit was not an option, the Greeks should have had some voice. But the question is whether they did. The choice of Yanis Varoufakis as a Finance Minister, though controversial or even frowned upon, does not in itself justify the disregard for the economic arguments he presented in his official capacity. On the contrary, such disregard is, if anything, worrisome. On several occasions, this Minister of Finance was excluded from the Eurogroup meetings, on no grounds but power, while the Greek arguments regarding austerity ('austerity does not work') were not answered on their merits, but by moralistic claims regarding the irresponsibility or laziness of Greeks, or their profligacy.

Viewed from the perspective of democracy, the *democratic* choices of the Greek people in their national elections regarding their economic destiny have not been respected. What is more, Greeks were gradually excluded from the European and national public spheres. Instead of commanding a measure of respect and solidarity from their fellow-European citizens, they were depicted as the disturbing 'other', that needs to be controlled, disciplined, and punished.

Besides, the case of austerity in Greece failed to give rise to a pan-European transnational mobilization, capable of contesting austerity politics. This may be due to the sharply different interests of labour unions in many EU core states. Supposing that labour unions do still wield power, they did not exercise it in a manner that could credibly lend support to the Greek cause.[59] The same goes for the liberal and left-leaning middle classes. This does not mean to say that no support whatsoever was expressed, yet it was not enough to challenge the governing knowledge.

With the withering of the Greek voice altogether, we have ended up with *domination* within Europe: peoples who cannot exit, but whose voices can not be heard. Whatever term we use for such a condition – internal colonialism, authoritarianism, subjugation, domination – it presents a cataclysm for European values and principles.

This collection offers an account of why law, or EU governing bodies, have performed so disappointingly in safeguarding EU constitutional principles and values even though effectiveness, democracy, justice, and the EU Treaties require them to do this.

Law, similarly to governing knowledge, rather than imposing constraints on this abdication of European values, has been used to rationalize austerity,

---

59 This has been one of the explanations why, for instance, relatively strong German Labour Unions did not engage in expressions of solidarity with their Greek counterparts, when their labour and collective bargaining rights were being infringed.

to present it as *necessity*. What is more, as we have seen throughout this volume, the creation of such necessities was hard work, requiring many resources.

At the same time, the collection has unwrapped numerous ways of thinking about the contestation of EU governance *within the EU*: it shows the openness of EU Treaty norms, the amount of political choice heralded in both law and knowledge, and, ultimately, popular avenues to challenging governing discourses. TTIP offers an important model for such popular challenge by means of transnational social mobilization, leaving us thus with some hope in the face of despair.